RATHLIN
~disputed
ISLAND

WALLACE CLARK

"*The Common Receipt and Harbour of such Scots as do infest that realm of Ireland.*"

ELIZABETH I,
DUDLEY CASTLE, 12th AUGUST, 1575.

DATES

c. 6000 B.C.	First men in Ireland.
c. 2500-200 B.C.	Massive export trade in Rathlin stone axes.
c. 2000-1800 B.C.	Introduction of copper axes.
c. 1000 B.C.	Possible date for building of Dunmore fortress.
c. 400 B.C.	Arrival of Iron Age Celts.
c. 200 B.C.	King of Norway attempts to carry off Princess Taise of Rathlin.
432 A.D.	Arrival of St. Patrick in Ireland.
c. 400	Fifty Curraghs lost in Brecain's Cauldron.
470	Founding of Kingdom of Dalriada.
580	First Churchmen on Rathlin.
	Period of visits by St. Columba.
795	First Viking Raid.
1037	Imar the Viking defeats Randal Eochada on Rathlin and drives out the Churchmen.
1180	Rathlin becomes Norman fief.
c. 1200	De Courcy Earl of Ulster lays foundation of "Bruce's" castle.
1210–1216	Earls of Galloway rule Rathlin.
1242	John Bysset flees from Scotland and becomes Lord of Rathlin.
1274	Massacre by Sir Richard de Burgo.
1306	Robert the Bruce takes refuge in Rathlin.
1401	John Mor McDonnell Lord of the Isles marries Margery Bysset, heiress to Rathlin.
1551	James McDonnell of the Isles defeats Cuffe in the first English assault on Rathlin.
1557	Massacre by Sir Henry Sydney.
	Sorley Boy McDonnell appointed Captain of the Route.
1559	Sorley Boy defeats McQuillans at Battle of Aura.
1568	James and Sorley Boy McDonnell taken prisoner by Shane O'Neill.
1569	Wedding of Agnes Campbell, Countess of Argyll, to Tirlough Luineach O'Neill on Rathlin.
1575	Massacre carried out on orders of Earl of Essex by John Norris and Francis Drake.
1585	Perrot's forces raid Rathlin.
	Queen Elizabeth makes a treaty with Angus McDonnell and cedes Rathlin to him.
1588	Spanish Armada.
1617	Sir Randal McDonnell wins lawsuit before James I by proving island is Irish, not Scottish.
1642	Massacre on order of Archibald Campbell, 8th Earl of Argyll.
1722	First Parish Church built.
1746	Rev. John Gage buys Rathlin from 5th Earl of Antrim.
1798	Frustrated plans for rebellion on island.
1824	Coastguards established on island.
	South pier in Church Bay built.
1856	East light completed. First lighthouse on island.
1865	Roman Catholic Church built.
1898	Marconi establishes radio link to Rathlin.
1916	West Light first lit.
1917	H.M.S. Drake torpedoed. Rue Point light erected.
1930	Tenants buy out their farms under Land Act.
1950	Radio telephone link to mainland.
1955	First car on Rathlin.

FOREWORD

by

Brigadier R. F. O'D. GAGE, C.B.E., M.C.

Rathlin, the only sizeable island in Northern Ireland has been my family home for the last 200 years. It is visited every summer by several hundreds of the more adventurous tourists, many of whom have a desire to learn something of its history and its people; but there is little to satisfy their curiosity because published records are scanty and, in some cases, unreliable. The only comprehensive history of Rathlin was written 120 years ago by my great grandmother, but never published.

Rathlin lacks many of the amenities regarded as essential in cities and urban areas but, on the other hand, it evades some of the more disagreeable manifestations of modern society. There is no violence or vandalism, and there are no demonstrations, hippies or layabouts. Even if a policeman were stationed on Rathlin there would be little for him to do because serious crime is unknown. No one is better fitted to write a book on Rathlin than Wallace Clark. He has spent years of research on eliciting the facts of history and, though not himself a Rathlin man, he lives almost within sight of the island, visits it frequently and knows it and its people intimately.

In writing this book he has performed a valuable service which will be appreciated by many people, whether their interest is centred on the story of Rathlin's turbulent history or on the narrative of events in more recent times.

REX GAGE

THE MANOR HOUSE,
RATHLIN.

July, 1971.

Published by

VOLTURNA PRESS
PORTLAW
Co. WATERFORD
Also in Scotland, N. Ireland, Spain and California.
1971

Printed by CENTURY SERVICES LTD., Belfast

For

JUNE

who has sailed with me
to many
islands

LINE DRAWINGS
by
RICHARD McCULLAGH

275594

VIGNETTES
by
R. J. A. CARSON

APPENDIX ON MEANING OF THE NAME RATHLIN
by
DR. ALEX. B. TAYLOR, C.B.E., F.R.S.E.

FRONT COVER: *From Chart by Captain J. Huddart, 1794—*

Copyright—BRITISH MUSEUM

ACKNOWLEDGMENTS

To Captain Harry Barton are due my greatest thanks for reading all the typescript and making many suggestions. Brigadier Rex Gage, C.B.E., M.C., Commander Peter Campbell, M.V.O., Mr. Johnny McQuilkin, Mr. Jimmy McCurdy, Mr. Dougal Cecil, Mr. Tony McQuaig and Mr. Alex Morrison of Rathlin have all helped with information. Mr. Gracey of the Linen Hall Library in Belfast and the staff of the Londonderry County Library, and the Central Public Library, Belfast, have been of considerable assistance, also the staff of the British Museum in London, and Mr. Brian Hutton of the Public Record Office in Belfast. The Very Rev. Stephen Cave, Dean of Raphoe, and the Rev. Canon John Barry assisted with the chapters dealing with the Celtic Church, the Rev. Harry Woodhead with gaelic words and references. Mrs. Campbell, aged 95 and still as interested in Rathlin as ever, has kindly allowed me to quote from her "Sea Wrack". Dr. A. B. Taylor, C.B.E., of Edinburgh assisted with the history of the Viking period and wrote the appendix on the background of the name "Rathlin". Mr. Flanagan, Keeper of Antiquities of the Ulster Museum, also Mr. Nicholas Canny and Professor Waterman helped with information.

Mr. Richard McCullagh made the line drawings, several of them on his knee seated in a curragh in which we rowed round the island in 1971. Captain George Harvey kindly lent the picture of Church Bay painted by Mrs. Gage in the last century.

Mr. Hugh Boyd of Ballycastle read the typescript and made some useful suggestions. I am grateful to Mercier Press for permission to quote from "The Course of Irish History," Nelson & Co. for similar facilities from Adomnan, Life of St. Columba and Messrs. Dent for their permission to quote from "The Story of Burnt Njal" and to Professor Jope for his map showing distribution of Rathlin axes, to the Hydrographic Department, Ministry of Defence, Captain George Naish of The National Maritime Museum, The Irish Sword, The Irish Cruising Club, University of Cambridge Committee for Aerial Photography, Ulster Journal of Archaeology, The Viking Society for Northern Research and the Coleraine Chronicle for use of various material. Transcript of Crown-copyright records in the Public Record Office and extracts from Irish Coast Pilot appear by permission of the Controller of H.M. Stationery Office. The Northern Ireland Tourist Board helped with photography and information. My son, Bruce, helped with historical background. Finally, I owe a great deal to Elizabeth Gocher and Margaret Kirkpatrick for their patience and skill in completing the typing, including the many re-drafts which were necessary, and to Tom McKinley for his efforts with my photographs.

CONTENTS

Page

Acknowledgements 9

Island in the Straits 13

The Stronghold. c. B.C. 6000—A.D. 440 28

Shipwreck in the Sound. c. 440 A.D. 39

Dalriada and the Isle of Monks. 440—795 A.D. 45

The Vikings. 795—1189 A.D. 55

The Earldom of Ulster. 1180—1242 A.D. 62

The Byssets and The Bruce. 1242—1401 A.D. 67

Clan Donnell pushes South. 1401—1551 A.D. 71

The Tudors versus the Scots. 1551—1573 A.D. 74

Essex, Drake and a Massacre. 1573—1575 A.D. . . . 85

The McDonnells win Rathlin at last. 1575—1605 A.D. . 100

Irish or Scottish? The Legal Case. 1605—1642 A.D. . . 108

The Campbell Massacre and Recovery. 1642—1746 A.D. 116

Rathlin under the Gages. 1746—1820 A.D. 122

A Century of Island Peace. 1820—1914 A.D. 132

Two World Wars. 1914—1945 A.D. 149

Wanted a Harbour. Rathlin today 160

APPENDICES

Page

A Raid on Rathlin in about 200 B.C. 169
The Place Name Rathlin 174
Other Rathlin Place Names 175
Report by Essex to the Queen on Raid of July, 1575 . . 176
Sailing Directions 178
Populations 180
How To Get There 181
Bibliography 182

ILLUSTRATIONS

Full Page

Western Cliffs at Couraghy 24
Bruce's Castle 92
A Curragh from the Manor House Garden 121
The Manor House, 1840 138
The West Light 147
A Lough near Altacarry 158
Cattle for the Mainland (top) 159
The Mail Boat waiting for the Tide (bottom) 159
Island boatmen 161
North Cliffs and Doonigiall 168

Vignettes

Bruce's Sword, Viking, Elizabethan, Islesman 3
Rathlin from Fair Head 13
Detail of a Curragh 39
Handbell and Crozier 55
Kittiwakes 73
Scots Galley 74
Sloak na Calliagh 116
Swell and Solitude 122
Puffin 132
H.M.S. Drake 149

Maps

Church Bay . . . . Inside Front Cover
Locations of finds of Rathlin axes in various parts of
    British Isles 30
Rathlin chart: 1776 124
Rathlin: General
    Inset showing neighbouring islands . . Inside Back Cover

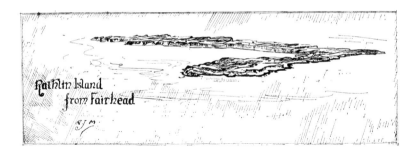

Rathlin Island
from Fairhead

CHAPTER I

ISLAND IN THE STRAITS

"An Irish stockin, the toe of which pointeth to the mainland."
—William Petty, 1660.

The seaway which divides Ireland from England is two hundred and thirty miles long and up to one hundred and thirty wide. Its sudden changes of weather, rough seas and strong tides have protected Ireland from Continental invasion and influence over the centuries. Mare Hibernicum, or the Irish Sea, stopped the Romans and Saxons. The Normans, having crossed at the south end with some difficulty, were so isolated by it from their kith in England that they fell before Ireland's second line of defence, her climate, and most of them became more Irish than the Irish themselves.

Only at the northern end does the Irish Sea narrow to the sort of distance which a boat under sail might cross in the course of an afternoon. Between the mountains of Kintyre in Scotland and the cliffs of Antrim in Ireland the seaway is only eleven miles wide. Across the waters which are now known as the North Channel came the first Irishmen to inhabit the country. In later years they recrossed to conquer most of Scotland. The Ulster Scots continued to use the North Channel as a highway for many centuries, and for three hundred years formed the kingdom of Dalriada which bridged it. They still preserve to a considerable extent their individual identity.

Almost exactly at the narrowest point lies the island of Rathlin.

The island is a stepping stone between the two countries, three miles from Ireland, thirteen from Scotland, so it is not surprising that throughout much of its history its ownership has been in dispute between the warlike inhabitants of its larger neighbours.

Not only was it a springboard for invasion or raid but also in the days of sail and oar the key to the narrows—an essential base for anyone who wanted to prey on or protect the concentrated stream of shipping passing through. Lack of a good harbour has limited its use for this purpose but as late as the eighteenth century it was employed by French privateers, and in Napoleonic times an appraisal of naval strategy named it as one of the four essential fleet anchorages for the defence of the realm of Ireland.

Most of us who live in the north of Ireland have seen Rathlin many times from the mainland. From Ballycastle its white cliffs gleam across the turbulent waters of the Sound, marking the edge of a mysterious and attractive land standing boldly out in the ocean guarded by its seven tides. Seen from Portrush its blunt point projects past the great red and black headland of Bengore which guards the Giants Causeway. By night the red light of the Bull winks confidentially across the dark seas every five seconds. From the corniche of the Antrim coast road running along the cliff tops you can look down on the channel between island and mainland and see where the eddies meet and the tide rips roar. The glimmering sea and across it the grass-topped cliffs of the island make a mixture of amethyst, emerald and ivory.

An island on the horizon is a challenge and an invitation. When we were children, grown-ups organised expeditions to Rathlin several times but on each occasion "the shore was up" and the trip had to be cancelled, so for us the island acquired the additional attraction of inaccessibility. It was not until just after the war that we first got there and then it was in our own boat. For a couple of seasons I had had a share in a twenty-foot half-decker. We sailed her to Scotland and along much of the Donegal coast but kept clear of Rathlin for of all places on the coast it is the one for beginners to avoid, with its sudden fogs and strong tides. In 1950 I bought the Fugitive, a fifty-year-old three-ton racing yacht of low freeboard and doubtful seaworthiness. The attraction was that she had a cabin that you could crawl into, even sleep in, which greatly extended the cruising possibilities. On a calm June morning my brother and I set out on the eighteen mile run east from Portrush, the wind behind us, a great green spinnaker billowing above our heads.

From this direction, to someone low in the water, Rathlin appears first, or in nautical language "makes," as the two separate islands into which it was anciently divided. As the cliffs of the west end grew gradually closer, the high ground towards Rue Point rose slowly out of the water in a separate mass to the south. Half an hour later the low neck of the island east of Church Bay had risen to join them. Suddenly a few hundred yards ahead of us a great mushroom of white water rose out of calm sea, hung for a moment and slowly subsided. I swung Fugitive's bow quickly to seaward and watched. A couple of minutes later there it was again and closer.

The Irish Coast Pilot is the sailor's bible. In those days I used to voyage clutching it in one hand and the tiller in the other. Published by the Admiralty it is sober, often lugubrious. For the hundredth time I turned up Rathlin Sound. *"CARRICKAVAAN, a small but dangerous rock, which dries one foot, lies one-third of a mile off Kenbane Head. CAUTION—Both tidal streams through Rathlin Sound run past Carrickavaan at a great rate, creating an eddy under its lee, which sets strongly back towards the rock, so much so that all objects drawn into this eddy, even boats, are liable to be set back on to the rock; great care is therefore necessary when in its vicinity."* The wind was light, and the tide sweeping us directly towards the rock but there was just enough wind to enable us to keep clear by altering course sharply to seaward. It is a dangerous rock but the only offlying one in the sound.

"A reef extends from Kenbane Head one third of the distance across to the rock and no vessel should ever attempt to pass between," went on the Pilot. Even as we watched, a coaster dodging the flood tide passed along the cliffs and inside the rock. A confident skipper was breaking the rules to get the Carrick ebb in his favour and save fuel.

As we headed north-west across the Sound, I re-read what the woe-book said about the island.

RATHLIN ISLAND—(Lat. 55°18′ N., Long. 6°11′ W.), the south extreme of which is about two miles north-west-ward of Benmore, is composed of high tablelands about 450 feet high, surrounded by precipitous cliffs of trap and white limestone, analogous in appearance and geological structure to the mainland southward. The southern portion, extending about 2½ miles in a southerly direction, is broken into hummocks, gradually declining in elevation towards Rue Point, a low, rocky point 2½ miles from Benmore on the mainland. In 1926 the population of the island numbered 299."

It is not a bad description apart from the Admiralty's retention, for Fair Head, of the obsolete name Benmore.

We sailed across the Sound, past the projecting reef of the Clachen Bo and white half moon of Cooraghy Bay, and under the piebald cliffs of Killeany towards the black nobs of the Clockadoos. Every niche and gully of the cliffs was filled with wild flowers. Primroses splashed and trickled in a yellow flood down dry runnel and green slope. They flower later here than on the mainland and now in June contrasted with vast round clumps of sea pinks. Milkweed, bedstraw, silverweed, and on some of the rock stacks, treemallow, added their delicate shades to the brighter colours.

Now we could see the pale semi-circle of Church Bay and just short of it the church itself nestling under high grassy banks so close to the water that in a southerly blow the spray wets the walls, giving the ground around it its reputation as the healthiest graveyard in Ireland. Just beyond this appeared the low Georgian Manor House which has been the Gage family home for two hundred years. We ghosted slowly on through the clear calm water and within two hundred yards of the pier began to get warps and fenders ready for the end of the voyage. Suddenly there was a thump and we rolled until the side decks were under water. Long blades of seaweed waved menacingly around our keel. The swell which was not apparent when we were sailing now showed its power; it raised us up a foot with every wave and banged down our iron keel on something which felt as hard as rock. As we ground and wallowed the movement seemed to be getting worse. Our first efforts to shove her off with a spinnaker pole were useless. There is not much rise and fall of tide at Rathlin, only a couple of feet at neaps which we had carefully picked for this first adventure, so there would be no help from rising water in getting her off. Thump . . . Splash . . . Crrack. My back teeth felt as if they were being shaken out; no yacht, particularly a fifty year old one, could stand up to this for long. I had begun to assemble the collapsible dinghy to try and get out an anchor when a boat full of people shot out from behind the pier. They rowed towards us and with quiet efficiency passed over a thick rope. In a few minutes we were off. "Ye were on the Bo," they said in soft voices with a Scottish lilt, "Hae ye no heard o' it?" I had to admit that I had not. "Well, next time come in on the line of the road down past the Rocket House there beyond the bay and ye'll be all right." They pointed out that this leading mark will bring a boat through the only gap in the Bo, a semi-circular reef about three feet under water, which encloses the two inner piers.

I subscribe to the theory that the only two things in the world you can trust for certain are a friend and a British Admiralty chart. But the Bo wasn't on ours, No. 2798, the biggest scale one of Rathlin published. The survey, like that of most of the Irish coast, was done in 1850, just a hundred years earlier. Even so they should have had the Bo on by now.

Half an hour later, steadying our nerves in the only pub on the island, I began to wonder whether Tony McCuaig, the owner, had been eyeing out a place on his walls for our smart brass nameplate when he saw us rolling on the reef. If things had worked out that way Fugitive would have had a permanent place beside relics which Tony has collected of a century of island wrecks.

The plan was to spend the night in Church Bay and we asked our rescuers where would be the safest spot. Johnny McQuilkin, with red hair and twinkling eyes, placed us carefully between the two piers anchored in six feet of water over clean sand, and told us about "the shores." This is the island name for a sudden swell which often comes up without warning during a flood tide and breaks with tremendous strength all round the western shores. "It'll break on the Bo ahead of you, and on the beach behind you, but you'll be all right in the middle," was his not particularly comforting advice. I pictured us precariously isolated in the trough of great crested seas and thought of our wee yacht anchor which weighed all of 15 lbs. But we told ourselves that sailors did not fret about trifles, and turned in fully dressed. In fact we hardly rolled during the short hours of darkness and when I looked out of the hatch in the morning all the charm of the island was instantly around us. In the stir and swing of the sealit air, a pair of seals on their backs out on the end of the Bo itself cocked a head over bulging tummy to look at us; dunlin picked their way like ladies along the tide line; oyster catchers, pompous as military policemen, watched us without moving. We could smell the heather, and peat smoke from a nearby cottage. Tangles of seaweed reflected dappled patterns along our white topsides.

Later as we finished a leisurely breakfast in the cockpit a window shot up in the Manor House and someone called out a welcome. We rowed over in the dinghy, landed on the steps of the rough stone pier, and sat for an hour in the sun on the lawn in front of the house talking of this and that to Brigadier Gage and his wife as we looked across the waters of the Sound, tranquillity itself on a calm day, towards the cliffs of Ballycastle and the mountains beyond.

Since that first visit in 1950 I have been to Rathlin almost every summer, usually in one of the various boats I have owned since the Fugitive, occasionally in the safe hands of one of the island boatmen.

Gradually I got to know more and more of the friendly straightforward people who live there and of the antiquities and history of the island. Each visit is different and there is always something new to do. I have been over the four-hundred-foot cliffs at Fargan Lack on the end of a rope to collect seabirds' eggs, been to a ceilidhe to dance the "Waves of Tory" and the "Siege of Ennis" in the village hall, watched islanders sailing model yachts on one of the freshwater loughs with as much interest as mainlanders might watch a cup final, flown over the island in a helicopter and patrolled off it in a submarine; and I've been entertained by the fireside of many a cottage and by the lightkeepers at the west end and at Altacarry Head.

Sometimes there has been a touch of drama like the October weekend when we set off from Portrush and sailed round the island looking into the numerous caves to see if there was a chance of bagging a rock pigeon for supper. There was too much swell however to get near the rocks for a shot from the dinghy, so with our gun barrels undirtied we anchored in the early dusk of autumn in Illan Carrig Bay on the east side. There was a west wind, about Force 5 and rising, but we turned in knowing that while the wind remained "in that airt," we were secure. Wild Goose rolled a good deal during the night but that was only to be expected. When I put my head out of the hatch in the morning it was to find that a south-east gale had blown up, almost direct on shore. I can still vividly remember the sight of our stern leaping up and down half a length from the foam-covered rocks. If the anchors had dragged twenty feet Wild Goose would have been smashed to pieces in a few minutes. We turned out in a flash and the small brown triangle of the reefed mainsail went up at record speed as we prepared to get out. We had three anchors down, and now there was to be a "mad minute" getting them all up at the same time. One of us took the tiller while the other two heaved at fathom after fathom of rope and tended alternately the two chains, as the jib flogged wildly round our ears. Any foul-up or delay would have let us drift back to destruction on the rocks. Then calmly Wild Goose took over. As the three anchors came up to near the bow, she cast her head to starboard, the mainsail filled and we sailed swiftly clear of Doon Point. Many and many a sailing boat or ship must have been caught in similar circumstances round the island, not all of them managing to claw off.

Another evening with another crew I sailed up from Larne and anchored on the east side in Arkill Bay unobserved, just as it was getting dark. We landed, and arrived on foot out of the November dusk at the door of the pub, to be greeted with looks as if we had been men from Mars. The company's stunned surprise at meeting strangers unannounced on the island was followed by the warmest of welcomes, and a hilarious party. Raghery men take a pride in not missing the passing or stopping of a vessel.

Rathlin from the Mainland

Rathlin lies just five sea miles from the town of Ballycastle, nowadays a busy seaside resort. Remarkably the island has preserved its individuality and isolation in spite of this proximity. The passage across the Sound is sheltered by the mainland from the prevailing south-westerly wind but the strength of the tides and lack of good harbours at either end have always deterred any bulk of traffic across it.

On a sunny day Rathlin from Ballycastle resembles a huge layer cake, for the white cliffs on its southern flanks are topped with a scalloped edge of black basalt, and steeply sloping above is the green grass. On a dull day it looks like the mysterious pirate fortress which it has so often been through the ages, hidden at times in the druidical mists which its early inhabitants used to be able to summon to hide their stronghold.

The best place on the mainland from which to see the island is the top of the clean cut cliffs of Fair Head. From there six hundred feet up you get the feeling of the breezy invigorating place that Rathlin is. You can see what is not at all apparent from Ballycastle, that it is shaped like a boomerang or a great letter "L," and how it is placed in the fairway between Scotland and Ireland. One leg is four miles long, the other three and most of the sixteen mile coastline of the island is cliffs. The top surface is uneven, very like the top of Fair Head itself, consisting of rocky outcrops and heathery hills, with fields and cottages in the hollows between, and near the south end thirty acres of freshwater lough. Two of the three light-houses which mark the extremities can be seen. Before the first was built only 120 years ago there were innumerable wrecks on the island, for it lies right in the path of all the shipping going round the north of Ireland bound to or from the Clyde, Liverpool or Belfast and the seabed around holds the smashed debris of a thousand tragedies.

Thirteen miles to the east across the waters of the North Channel lie the steep sided mountains of the Mull of Kintyre, with the white speck of its lighthouse like an eagle's eyrie halfway up the western slopes. To the north twenty miles away is the island of Islay, "Queen of the Hebrides," and beyond it on a clear day show the conical peaks of the Paps of Jura. Away to the west the cliffs and mountains of Antrim and Donegal stretch in a great arc. Behind lies the flattened hemisphere of Knocklayd, a landmark for forty miles around. The surroundings are dramatic, often beautiful.

In ancient days this seaway between Scotland and Ireland was called the Waters of Moyle after the "maol" or bare hills of Kintyre. Sailing across on a calm day, as I have done dozens of times, almost surrounded by overlapping headlands and islands, it is hard to see where Ireland ends and Scotland begins, and the waters seem more like a great lake joining the two lands than a sea dividing them. So they much have appeared to the early Irish and Scots who travelled freely across these waters and had ties of kin and landholding on both sides.

In summer the sea is calm far more often than it is rough. Up until the arrival of the railway, little over a hundred years ago, water united places rather than divided them. Sea travel was much easier than land and Ballycastle for instance was effectively much nearer the Scottish islands than to places a few miles inland. From this fact stems a good deal of the troubles which have beset Ulster throughout the last two thousand years. It seemed perfectly natural to the inhabitants of the west of Scotland that the isles and the adjacent coast of Ireland should be part of their rightful territory. The mainlanders of Ireland further south could scarcely be expected to agree but in early days accepted it. As land communications improved the rulers of Dublin have become more and more indignant at this apparent aggression and injustice, which has behind it the most natural causes.

Rathlin Fables

It was in these waters, Sruth na Maol, that in an old Irish fairy tale the four children of Lir, transformed into swans by Eva, their jealous stepmother, had to spend three hundred years in exile. Their story rates as one of the three Great Sorrows of Ireland, but I sometimes think, when having to rush home from a weekend's sailing, that it would not be such an unpleasant fate to spend a few years in the form of a swan in these beautiful waters. At times the swan-children were separated by gales and the eldest sister, Fiona of the White Shoulder, arranged that Carricknarone, a rock in Altachuile Bay on the north side of Rathlin, would be their rendezvous. There they often met until at last at the end of their sentence they flew to Inishglora off County Mayo and were returned to human form by St. Kemoc.

One of the other Great Sorrows of Ireland, the story of Deirdre the beautiful and the sons of Uisneach, also has Rathlin for a backdrop, for on the rocky projection of Carrig Uisneach, just east of Ballycastle, Deirdre landed on her return from Kintyre with her lover Naise in the Iubrach, the war galley of Fergus. Truth to tell Deirdre was more of a bad girl than a sorrowful one. She was the daughter of Feidlimid, storyteller to the Knights of the Red Branch and their leader, King Conor. One day when the king was holding court, the unborn Deirdre cried aloud in her mother's womb. Cathub, the court Druid, promptly foretold that she would be of great beauty but would cause endless misfortune. Perhaps she typifies the mysterious power of the female for which the Celts had a healthy respect. Conor confident of his own luck and the value of long term investment, refused to let her be killed at birth as many recommended, and had her reared apart, to become when she grew up, a member of the royal harem. One day she saw a calf slaughtered in the snow and a raven alight to drink its blood. "I could do with a man," she said, "with those three colours— raven black hair, blood on his cheeks and a snow bright body." Leborcham her nurse who had many shortcomings as a chaperone promptly suggested that Naise, one of Conor's bodyguard, would fill the bill. Deirdre vamped him so successfully that much against his better judgment he had to run off with her to Kintyre where they lived for some time in blissful happiness, subject only to occasional lecherous approaches from the local Scottish king. Naise's brothers, Ainli and Ardan, loyally accompanied him in his exile.

After a year or two Conor sent one of his heroes, Fergus, to offer safe conduct home and forgiveness. Fergus was a knight of the highest honour and the brothers decided to trust his word and accompany him. A few days later Naise, in the glory of his raven locks, high-coloured cheeks and white skin, wearing a crimson cloak trimmed with gold and armed with a silver bossed shield and sword of polished bronze, stepped ashore with his brothers on the long projecting reef of rock which still bears his father's name today. Beside him walked blonde Deirdre, fairest woman in the world with flashing green eyes, clad in saffron with much jewellery and painted fingernails. They soon found that Fergus, who was under a vow or "geasa" never to refuse hospitality, had to leave them to dine with a local chieftain, an invitation deliberately arranged by Conor. Deirdre, foreseeing trouble, advised the brothers to go to Rathlin which lies "between Eirin and Albainn," but they boldly refused. On their arrival at Conor's court at Armagh the trio were set on and after a heroic defence fell side by side. Fergus, in fury at being forced to break his pledge word, fought on their side; he burned Emhain Macha, King Conor's fortress and the fellowship of the Knights of the Red Branch was destroyed for ever. While Fergus went off to live in Connaught, Deirdre, after spending a year as the unwilling wife of Conor, ignored the advice nowadays given to railway passengers. She leaned out of a chariot while it was in motion and was killed when her head struck a stone.

Five miles to the west of Fair Head, off Kenbane, "The White Head," surf can usually be seen breaking about a quarter of a mile off the rock which is now called Carrick-a-vaan, the one which gave us a shock on our first passage to the island. The name comes from Carrick Manannan after Manannan MacLir, the King of the Sea. He was a mighty warrior and his horse, Enbarr of the Flowing Mane, was "as swift as the clear cold wind of spring." She travelled with equal ease on land and on sea and no one was ever killed on her back. The Answerer was his sword, and no one ever recovered from its wounds. Altogether Manannan was a useful man to have on your side in a battle, but he is dead now, and buried on the Tonns Sandbank, off the mouth of the Foyle, twenty five miles west of Rathlin. I am told that he only gets up very occasionally now to scowl at a Russian nuclear submarine or chat up a mermaid.

Rathlin Tides

To the north of Fair Head a great scimitar of broken water extends east of Altacarry, the north-east point of the island, where the sapphire of the ebb meets the darker blue of the flood. Taam McDonnell it is called, the tide rip where two McDonnells were drowned on their way to Scotland, so long ago that everyone has forgotten when it happened. Another and more deadly tide rip, Slough-na-More,[1] the "Swallow of the Sea," erupts in the narrows between the island and Ireland.

When the ebb tide running out of the Irish Sea thrusts west at full strength in the second hour it is pushed south by a counter stream or eddy running back along the south side of the island to Rue Point, and so out over the edge of a deep gully. Where the two tides meet great hollow troughs and pyramid waves are formed, deadly to open boats. At the "jabble of the ebb" Slough-na-more is an awe-inspiring sight, and its roar can be heard a mile away or more, but after two hours it subsides suddenly to a ripple, so he who knows his tides can avoid it. Slough-na-more and half a dozen other complex tidal intersections like the Bush tide, the Carrick ebb, the Ruddin, the Spoot and Tragh na vo, which only a boatman who has spent all his days in those waters can understand, make up the seven tides of Rathlin Sound, a great part of the protection and mystique of the island. The Irish Coast Pilot puts it prosaically:

"The streams in the Sound are frequently setting in opposite directions at the same moment with little diminution of force and at the line separating one stream from the other there are ripplings or overfalls of a more or less pronounced character which are dangerous to boats and small vessels".

Even now with all modern navigational aids there is a wreck on or near the island once every two or three years. Most of the disasters have been caused by the strength of the tidal streams and the complication which the jagged shape of Rathlin makes in them, although bad weather and fog has often played a part, for the Sound is the foggiest part of the whole coast of Ireland.

Through the narrow gap between Fair Head and Kintyre, only eleven sea miles wide and about four hundred fet deep, all the northern half of the Irish fills and empties to a depth of fifteen feet every twelve hours. A billion tons of water pour through this gap four times a day; half the power that goes to waste there would drive all the factories in Ireland.

---

[1] Also, and perhaps more correctly, called Slough-na-Morra. I have adopted the version used on Admiralty charts.

The rate of the stream at spring tides (which occur just after every full and new moon) is four knots north of the island but in the Sound six, a good deal faster than most open boats can be rowed. In the old days of sail and oar, the port of Ushet near Rue Point was used, as it cut the distance to the mainland down by nearly half, but nowadays Church Bay in the nick of the "L" is the port, and with motor-boats in the hands of such men as Jimmy McCurdy of the island and Jack Coyles of Ballycastle, Rathlin is rarely cut off. Ushet, since it has no road, has fallen out of use but there are still plenty of times particularly in west winds when the port could be useful if it were deepened and a quay built.

The other good place from which to see Rathlin is the road which runs through the forestry plantation above Glenshesk on the slopes of the Knocklayd. From here, a little further west than Fair Head, the arms of the island seem to stretch out yearningly towards Ireland. There is no doubt about which country it wants to belong to.

From afar Rathlin is a tiny island, on the map of the British Isles, an ink spot, from a high-flying aeroplane a flurry in the tide, but from Ballycastle it is a big island. It occupies more than half of the horizon, and its dark southern cliffs are an iron curtain hiding the secrets of its interior from the eyes of an observer. It has none of the rounded-off contours, none of the limpet-shaped profile of lesser isles but is a high rectangle with square ends, and plane surfaces at curious angles, like an impoverished ironclad.

Charles Kingsley was near the mark in another way when he called Rathlin "a half-drowned magpie," referring to the three points on its southern face where the white chalk glances out from under the black basalt.

The North Side of Rathlin

The north side of Rathlin is like the dark face of the moon. Hardly anyone ever sees it. Only a few lobster fishermen visit it regularly and they are so concerned with shallows and sunken rocks, swirls and counters of tide, creeks, coves and crannies, that they have not much time to admire the cliffs. To the sailor passing by at a distance in his great ship bound across the Atlantic the back of Rathlin is part of an iron bound coast usually fringed with heavy surf, something to keep well away from. Here there are few of the wild flowers so profuse on the warm southern cliffs. Only an occasional sprig of frustrated juniper and patches of salt-scorched grass decorate the cliff faces; the brightest colour is the vivid green of enteromorpha seaweed, which thrives in the splash zone above high water and tells by its height the power of the winter waves, but for people who enjoy bold scenery

The Western Cliffs
Rathlin Island
sketched from
Curragh

in remote places, the cold north cliffs are worth viewing from the water at close quarters in calm weather.

A voyage round Rathlin is a pleasant half-day's expedition. Do it under sail if you can, and go sunwise either to placate the old sun gods whom many generations of islanders worshipped, or for the more practical reason that by leaving at first flood from Church Bay you get a fair tide most of the way round.

Ghosting close to the dark cliffs on the side which faces Scotland you can hear the sea sounds, the sighing of the swell in the solitary caves, the wind whispering through the bent grass and the drip of water off moss-covered rocks. You can hear, too, the more cheerful sounds of Rathlin, the streamlets tinkling as they fall in successive cascades over the terraced precipices, the laughing cry of the kittiwakes echoing off the cliffs and back to them from the water, the impudent "chilloop" of the choughs as they flaunt their red bills round the headlands. In a lower key is the fully-fed and fizzy susurrus of the sea along the rocks at high water, quite different from the urgent hungry lapping of wavelets at the beginning of the flood.

At the west end is the most dramatic sight of all, the castellated rock stacks, like wedding cakes two hundred feet high, on which in June, fifteen or twenty thousand seabirds nest. Their community is a great strident city, so intent on the urgent business of raising its young that it is completely and refreshingly unconcerned with man and his affairs. Guillemots and razor-bills, singly or in parties, speed seaward to their fishing grounds with the direct purposefulness of a missile. Parrot-like puffins stare over their parti-coloured bills in condescension as they sit preening themselves beside their best burrows. Fulmars glide on motionless wings past the cliffs or sit caressing each other on their nest ledges. Cormorants soar clumsily around a high cliff. Shearwaters, black crosses gliding low over the water, show an economy of effort and a clean cut efficiency of line which leaves our greatest aeroplane designers a thousands years behind.

As you sail past the Stacks in calm weather you can see their bases stretching thirty feet down through the clear water to the slowly beckoning forest of seaweed which clothes the bottom. Past them many feet down float slowly by the great red Rhizostoma jellyfish which laze up here in a fine summer. Below lie the corroded bolts of ships and the polished bones of sailors.

Halfway up the cliffs sits the Bull lighthouse with the slightly comical air of a man whose hat has fallen off in the street, for the light and its dome stand at the bottom instead of in the usual way at the top of its tower.

In the amphitheatre of Derginan a white movement high up in the cliffs leads the eye to a family of wild goats grazing on a tiny patch of green grass; suddenly, when they see your interest turned on them, they leap away. They never fall, unless sometimes a kid gets too daring in trying to follow its parents, or an islander, furious at a raided garden, picks one off with a rifle.

At dusk sights and sounds become more evocative. Distant thunder is the breaking of ships' timbers on the rocks, and the clatter of farmyard machinery the shock of a Scottish claymore on an English buckler; the whistle of wings of a wild duck passing low overhead becomes an arrow flight. Shouts from inland and a fire in a hollow at Illancarragh are a carousal of Vikings after victory. The mighty rough and tumble of Slough-na-more are the waves closing over the head of Brecain.

Finally the anfractuous rocks of Rue Point, the last corner on the voyage, are menaces which snarl in a fury of foam at your passing keel, and if they miss are content to wait a hundred years or a thousand for their next victim.

Rathlin Records

Its grandeur apart, Rathlin can reasonably claim to be the most interesting of all the several hundred islands round the Irish coast in terms of the amount of recorded history and of the number of its distinctive features. The history will speak for itself, but those interested in records might like to note that Rathlin is outstanding in the following ways. It was almost certainly the first Irish island to be inhabited by man, possibly even shortly before the mainland, since Stone Age man first came here some six thousand years ago across the narrows from Scotland. It is, as already mentioned, the only link island between the Scottish Hebrides and the Irish islands, sometimes grouped with one, sometimes the other. It shares with the Blaskets, off Kerry, the distinction of having had the most books written about it. It has the gruesome distinction of half a dozen major massacres of the population, and the most wrecks of any island, and is surrounded by the strongest tides. It is unusual in not having any sort of town or street, since the forty odd remaining inhabited houses are scattered all over its surface. Rathlin is the only "L" shaped Irish island and is the only one with white cliffs, also the only one to have three lighthouses. The biggest single concentration of sea-bird life around the Irish coast occurs during June and July on the rock stacks. It is one of the only two islands which still have in the "big house" the same family who owned the whole island before the Land Acts of the last hundred years.

The three books which have been written in this century on Rathlin have been on the bookshelf in "Wild Goose" for many a season. They are now well thumbed and the bottoms of the covers threadbare from moving to her rolling. I have come across numerous references to the island and to the famous men who have visited it in other works. Many a story of Rathlin has been told round the cabin table by islanders, men from other islands, sailors, ornithologists and antiquarians.

If blood be the price of fame, Rathlin has paid in full. The perimeter of the island, though made strong by nature, has proved time and again impossible to hold successfully against invasion. Attacks have sometimes been repelled after battles ashore but many succeeded, and half a dozen that we know of were the prelude to general massacres, for once an island stronghold falls it becomes a deathtrap.

Rathlin has been fortified for at least three thousand years, as is indicated by the ruins near the north coast of the cyclopean fortress known as Dunmore. Since then Firbolg, Fomorian, Dedanaan and Celt have in turn conquered and occupied Rathlin. The Celtic church was established there soon after the arrival of St. Patrick in Ireland and was driven out five hundred years later by the Vikings. Scotsmen and Norman coveted and fought for the possession of Rathlin. In 1551 the forces of the English government took a hand. In the thirty-five years which followed the island saw battle after battle and changed hands with bewildering rapidity. Since then Rathlin has owed its allegiance to Ireland but the question whether it was truly Irish or Scottish territory was laid before King James I of England in 1617 in a long and complex law suit. Evidence was produced going as far back as St. Patrick's expulsion of all snakes from Ireland. From this it was argued that since no snakes live on Rathlin it must be Irish territory, an argument which would hardly impress a twentieth century judge, but with other evidence it carried the day two hundred and fifty years ago.

The story of Rathlin is the story of Ulster in microcosm. Today the tenure of the land in terms of private ownership is secure but in the international sense, the ownership of Ulster and with it of Rathlin, is still the subject of a dispute that becomes violent at times.

To bring up to date and amplify the island's history is for me the fulfilment of an idea which has built up slowly over the last twenty years. The story begins with the very first arrival of man in Ireland.

CHAPTER 2

THE STRONGHOLD

CIRCA B.C. 6000 TO A.D. 440

"An island with a history more lengthy and illustrious than that of any other Irish or Scottish island excepting only Iona itself."
—Hill, 1873.

Rathlin has had three principal periods of importance in its long history, the first near the beginning of man's arrival in Ireland, the second during the Golden Age of the Celtic Church in the sixth and seventh centuries, and the third in the wars and rebellions of the sixteenth century. It is the earliest with which we are concerned in this chapter.

The main source for pre-history are such volumes as Leabhar Gabala (the Book of Invasions), Cormac's Glossary, the Yellow Book of Leacan, the Book of Ballymote, the Book of the Dun Cow, and one with the unlikely label of MS B502 in the Bodleian Library. I have not been able to read these in the original early Latin or Gaelic but it is clear even in translation that they contain some of the finest Irish literature and comprise written traditions much older than those of any other European nation. The history in them, however, is so interlaced with mythology and what George Russell described as the incandescent imagination of Irish storytellers that even after applying all available critical methods it remains impossible to distinguish fact from fiction with certainty. Later catalogues of events such as the 16th century "Annals of the Four Masters" are not light reading but contain shreds of evidence from near contemporary writers and bards.

The other source for the early history of Rathlin is of course archeology. The spade has not yet more than scratched the surface of the huge bulk of material awaiting discovery in Rathlin, as in so much of the rest of Ireland. A number of small digs have been done and there have been many casual finds. Of the story of Rathlin in pre-Christian days we know only a tiny fraction, but this fraction is enough to provide a reasonably accurate picture of the first three or four thousand years of life on the island.

The first men arrived in Ireland about 6000-5000 B.C., long after the rest of Europe had been populated by the human race. Family groups, living in the fashion of the Middle Stone Age and clad in skins, came across, some from the Baltic, others from Spain; and since the first traces of their occupation have been found along the north Antrim coast and the valley of the River Bann it is supposed that they arrived across the narrow sea gap from

Scotland. This being so, and since we know that the island now began to be inhabited, we may conjecture that in their earliest voyaging they called at Rathlin en route.

Slowly, as the northern ice-cap melted, the climate of Ireland improved and the sea rose. The sea level sites occupied by those first Irishmen are today some twenty five feet above high water, a change which would not however have greatly affected the size of steep-sided Rathlin. A pleasant life those early islanders must have lived in an uncrowded country filled with game and fish. The whole population of Ireland did not exceed two or three thousand people for many generations and since no offensive weapons have been found among their relics, organised warfare may be considered to have been unknown. The bones of the great auk, the bear and the elk and many types of fish and shellfish are found in their kitchen middens, so their diet was, if not Epicurean, at least varied.

By 2,500 B.C. the land was approximately at its present level, society was becoming organised and Rathlin was building up an important export trade. Axes were the product, and the trade was brisk. They were made from a remarkably hard and fine-grained blue stone known as porcellanite[1] found on the island in the townland of Brockley towards the west end. Axe factories in only two other centres in the British Isles were of equal importance, Tievebullieagh in County Antrim and Langdale in the Pennines. Rathlin and Tievebullieagh axes have been found all over Ireland (including one in Tory Island) and in several parts of England. They were mainly used for forestry clearance, for much of the country including most of Rathlin was covered in large trees at that time. The climate was mild, something like the Mediterranean today, and although the tides were probably just as strong then, the passage across the sound in a skin-covered boat loaded with axe heads may have been a little easier in the predictable good weather. If you think of it, the people of those days would not have looked on themselves as primitive; they lived in an outlying part of the

---

1*Porcellanite*

"Two highly metamorphosed rock types have been produced by the plug at Brockley, Rathlin: hornfels, derived from basalt or altered basalt and still showing original igneous texture; and porcellanite, a completely recrystallized bauxitic lithomarge.

The Porcellanite—is a heavy dark-grey to black fine-grained rock. Some examples have pale streaks and some are finely mottled, or speckled white. It is one of the toughest rocks in the world, and despite its small outcrop it was found by Neolithic man who manufactured it in a factory nearby into stone axes which were distributed throughout Ireland, Scotland, Wales and even into S.E. England (Jope, Morey and Sabine 1953). The analysed example is extremely rich in ferrous iron (23.32 per cent.) and alumina (44.67 per cent.) with correspondingly unusual mineralogy."

From "Geology of the country around Ballycastle," 1966, H.M.S.O.

POLISHED STONE AXES FROM TIEVEBULLIAGH AND
RATHLIN FACTORIES

*Distribution of axes of porcellanite of Tievebulliagh and Rathlin type
in the British Isles. The open spots indicate that only the county of
finding is known.*

Prof. E. M. Jope.

known world but kept up with modern ideas by using the tech-
niques of farming and manufacturing instead of hunting which had
been the only means of sustenance in Ireland a few generations
before. From time to time links would have come with the great
civilisations of the eastern Mediterranean in the form of trading
vessels from Tyre or Crete. Four thousand years ago ships of
Tarshish moored in Church Bay or waited for a tide at Illan
Carragh on the east side. Occasionally perhaps a boy from the
island would ship back with the traders, and return two or three
years later with tales of huge cities and of the Pyramids in the
greatest kingdom in the world in Egypt.

Flint, found in abundance in the limestone cliffs, was another
rare raw material, the presence of which was of enormous benefit
to the early generations of islanders. In the soil of Rathlin is an
apparently inexhaustible supply of flint arrowheads and skin
scrapers, as well as axes in all stages of manufacture. The majority
of the artifacts recovered have been found by chance. This happened much more commonly in the days of horse ploughing, as
one of the islanders pointed out to me, when you actually watched
the furrow being turned, than in this age of the tractor, so there
will be a lower rate of return in this way than in the past. The
islands of Oronsay and Colonsay, fifty miles north and much
further from the mainland than Rathlin, have many relics of this
mesolothic period indicating boatmen of some ability, and perhaps some traffic between them and Rathlin.

Rathlin islanders, however, with their corner in raw materials
were men of privilege and position. Anyone who was anyone in
the isles or Ireland had a Raghery axe. Ships trading in these
waters from the south took good care to call early in the voyage
at the island in the narrows to offer their best goods to the ruling
families there who had money to pay for what they fancied, and
were the envy of their less fortunate neighbours. In the summer
days of four thousand years ago the whole island rung to the chip-
chip music of the axe factories.

Ships from Crete visiting Rathlin may sound like a flight of
fancy, but there is archeological evidence, slender but impossible to
ignore, of annual trading voyages to the coast of Western Europe
from the Mediterranean at this period. The main clue is the
dramatic way in which Cretan burial practice, the unique cham-
bered grave, spread during the two to three hundred years preceding 2,000 B.C. to the seacoasts of Spain, France, the Irish
mainland, the Orkney Islands and as far as Scandinavia.[2]

One morning, however, within a generation or so of 1800
B.C. a party of small dark men clad in buckskin rowed their

[2]Cretan craniums in Antrim. U.J.A. 1943. Walmsley.

curraghs homewards across the Sound and landed on the island looking very depressed. They were traders who each year carried axes in their goatskin bags to peddle in England. In answer to the question which faces returning commercial travellers just as inevitably today, "How's business?" they made a sound which was the B.C. equivalent of terrible. Soon all over the island spread stories of a new type of axe now being offered to their customers. It was made by a secret process of a material that could be polished to a bright lustre. Islanders had seen a little of this material in ships but this was the first news of it reaching the home market. The men who sold these copper axes are called by archeologists the Beaker people, and they came from Spain. The sharpness and the durability of the new axes were so much superior to the old that they were soon to finish Rathlin's export trade. Locally, however, axes of stone were to be used for another thousand years at least, for a change of another kind now occurred.

Soon after the Rathlin islanders first heard of copper axes, Ireland was cut off from its main source of world news, for the old Cretan Empire which had sent ships trading to the limits of Western Europe disintegrated and it was to be thirty generations before the Atlantic trade route up the Irish Sea re-opened. Rathlin must have remained a pleasant and secure place to live but very much out of touch with events outside Ireland.

Slowly over the years, however, as commerce had become established and personal fortunes acquired, there had come the beginning of an age of fear. Men looked for a dwelling in a position which was naturally strong and the strength of which could be improved by artificial fortifications. The age of the crannog or lake dwelling was soon to begin, and Rathlin was nothing if not a ready-made crannog, safe from the attacks of landsmen. For internal fortification it has so many suitable hillocks that today, in looking over the surface of the island for early strongholds, almost every hill seems a possibility.

The Beaker coppersmiths did not themselves come to Ireland from England in any great numbers, although their axes did. A new race of men, perhaps from the same stock, reached Ireland five hundred years later, about 1500 B.C., direct from Spain, arriving perhaps after being blown off course on a Biscay fishing trip. They were small and dark and archeologists identify them by their weapon, the long-headed battle axe or halberd. With their superior intelligence and weapons they quickly replaced or absorbed the older race and began to work copper and make use of the vast deposits of gold in the gravel beds of Wicklow, the largest source of that practical and ornamental metal in Europe.

The Irish Annalists call these men the Firbolgs, perhaps translatable as the "bag men" or wearers of trousers. How soon they reached Rathlin we do not know. Finds from their period, which was broadly the Bronze Age, amount on the island to little more than a few spear heads, a couple of gold cloak fasteners and some silver fibulae or pins.[3]

There are in addition many tumulae or burial mounds on the island containing skeletons in stone cists, buried in the fashion of the Bronze Age, which lasted in Ireland very approximately from 2000 to 400 B.C. Their numbers may be indicated by the present day name of one of the districts just south of Church Bay—Ouig, "the place of graves". Islands were, however, sometimes used as burying grounds by people who did not actually live on them. This was the case, for instance, in the Scillies off Cornwall. There was a theory that the spirits of the dead could not cross water, so if you wanted to be sure that mother-in-law was gone for good, you could see her buried on an island and be doubly safe.

That the Bronze Age men in general were seamen of confidence and skill is clear from their regular voyages to the islands and to Spain, but the rule of the Firbolgs on the mainland was not a long one. Perhaps that early gold rush brought fresh invaders, perhaps population pressures in Europe were the cause; whatever it was, the Book of Ballymote records that "the Firbolg were driven out of Ireland by the Tuatha de Danaan and settled in Arn (Arran) and Ile (Islay) and in Rechru (Rathlin), and allied themselves to the Fomorians." This change may be dated to about 1200 B.C. and the arrival from England of a new race, the Tuatha de Danaan (Peoples of the Earth Goddess Danu) armed with swords of bronze, weapons of terrifying efficiency. The change is important as far as Rathlin is concerned as a clue to the date of Dunmore, the great fortress near the highest point of the island at the northwest. All around the coasts of Ireland on islands and promontories are to be seen the remains of fortresses built without mortar, of stones so immense that they are known as cyclopean. They are found in just the sort of places people of the sea would hold on to as a last ditch stand against an invader—an invader so powerful and cunning that only behind the strongest conceivable fortifications was there a chance of survival. When these fortresses can be seen complete, as on the Galway Arans today, they comprise the finest monuments of their kind in Europe, more impressive in their stark strength and endurance than anything else Ireland has to

[3] C. Blake Whelan in 1934 found, in Ballynagard, a small stone rectangular building almost sunk below current surface level, possibly a Neolithic pottery kiln. It was partly roofed by a single large stone. The sherds found near it correspond to those found in North East Scotland. Earlier he had observed small circles of the recumbent stone type which are associated in North East Scotland with late Bronze Age invaders. P.R.I.A., Vol. 42, 1934, Irish Naturalists Journal, Vol. III, No. 1).

show. Rathlin had a fortress like that, possibly two or three. On the Arans they survived because there was such an abundance of stone that the temptation to steal from the fortress walls was small. Elsewhere, including Rathlin, the fortresses have almost invariably been pulled down either by a successful conqueror or in a more mundane fashion by a road contractor or house builder. Marshall records in 1834 that Rathlin had thirty quarries in use at that time, evidence of the pressure on building materials.

It is to this period, about 1000 B.C., that Dunmore, sometimes known on the island as Red Owen's fort, and Doon Beg just west of it, and also the smaller fort of Doon Point near Ushet, can be assigned. The perimeter of Dunmore measures 115 feet by 160 feet, very similar dimensions to those of Dun Formna which is well preserved in Inish Shere, the east island of the Arans, and of the Grianan of Ailech, outside Londonderry. The base of the walls is eleven feet thick suggesting a height of fifteen to twenty feet. In the centre are traces of a building, 30 feet by 40 feet, and the entrance was at the west. To construct it must have taken the slave labour of a whole generation. Only a king of enormous power and organising ability could have caused it to be built. Perhaps he was guarding as well as his life a trading station on what archeologists refer to as the Atlantic Sea Route leading up the Irish Sea, which had become well re-established by this time. Preserved today Dunmore would have made a magnificient and fitting crown to the island; possibly much of it was made with white stone, accounting for the reference to the gleaming white castle of Rathlin in the legend of King Donn (see Appendix One). If you want to see what it looked like (without the white stones), visit the rounded grassy hill three miles north-west of Derry where the Grianan of Ailech stands in timeless grandeur, almost as it was in its days of glory.

The Fomorians, mentioned above in the quotation from the Book of Ballymote, represent another wave of invaders arriving at about this time. Traces of them are found also on Tory Island at the north-west corner of Ireland and on the Scottish island of Colonsay, on Tiree, and again in the south tip of Ireland at Mizzen Head. They were sea pirates by reputation, but from their coastal bases ruled most of Ireland for a period. "There was no smoke rising in Ireland from a house that was not under tribute to them," according to one of the old books. Nothing positive is known of their origin but an interesting suggestion is that they were teutonic and that their name is from the same root as Pomerania. Conaing, one of their legendary leaders who built a tower on Tory Island could be connected with the teutonic word Konig or king. Colonsay has a number of names which commemorate them, like Lorg an Fhomhoir, the giant's footprint and Slochd Fhomhoir, the giant's gully. Rathlin has no such direct references but according to a Colonsay tradition the Calliagh, the mother of the Fomorians, had one eye in the middle of her forehead and ruled the winter. In spring she was supposed to be killed by the lover of a maiden whom she had kept in captivity, whereupon she transformed herself into a grey stone, overlooking the sea and always moist. Perhaps Rathlin's Fomorian heroes are recorded there in names like the Grey Man's Path on Fair Head or the Cave of the Grey Man below the Bull light. At Stack an Fir Lea (the Stack of the Grey Man), at the west end of the island, according to tradition, "the bodies of eleven grey men" were found in ancient times, perhaps an early shipwreck story. Sloak na Calliagh, "the rock creek of the old woman," at the south-west corner of Rathlin, is probably another relic of these occupants. The Colonsay tradition makes an interesting contrast with the Tory story of Balor the King of the Fomorians who lived on that island and also had a single eye and a captive daughter. Little is known of their religion. Balor is probably a personification of the pagan deity we hear so much of in the Old Testament, Baal, a sun god.

The Firbolgs and Fomorians held their islands for some hundreds of years but at length the Tuatha de Danaan took over Rathlin. They, in turn, yielded to the first Celts, whom the archeologists find arriving about 400 B.C., equipped, even more terrifyingly, with swords of iron. According to tradition their leader was Mil and so the Milesians, masterful and warlike, established an ascendancy which gradually became more thorough to reach its peak twelve hundred years later in 800 A.D. They were characterised by being tall with red blonde hair and having considerable artistic genius when they were at peace for long enough for it to be given a chance to develop. They came by sea from France, the centre of a common Celtic culture, which once extended over much of western Europe. Traces of their occupation of Rathlin island in the early days are scanty in the extreme. A few iron age burials have been found and there are stories of swords in the graves but none of these have actually survived. The iron age traces are said to have been confined to the central and lower parts of the island whereas those of bronze and stone age occupation are mainly concentrated in the upper and western areas.

It is not until the fourth century A.D., some seven hundred years after the first arrival of the Celts, that we get into what may be considered a period of history. There are, however, many legends of the intervening period. That of Deirdre mentioned in Chapter I belongs to it. One warms to the human touch in the mention of Bres, one of the Milesian early kings. He was not popular with his own men who complained that "their knives were not greased by him, and however many times they visited him, their breaths did not smell of ale."

In about the first century B.C., Rathlin was ruled by King Donn, great grandson of the Dagda, "of the prime stock of the Tuatha de Danaan." The hand of Taise, his daughter, was coveted by Nabhogdon, the King of Norway, who had just lost his first wife. His scouts had reported Taise as the most beautiful woman in the world, with blue eyes and curling tresses, but unfortunately for Nabhogdon she was already betrothed to Congal ("Long Nails"), high king elect of Ireland, and turned down his proposal. Why Taise preferred her long-nailed Ulsterman to the ardent Norwegian is not recorded—probably because of his unpronounceable name. When Nabhogdon came to attempt to carry her off from the gleaming white palaces, which his ship captains had described on the summit of Rathlin, his army was defeated and he was killed by Congal in a ferocious hand to hand battle.

"For it was indeed a combat of two warriors and it was a mangling of two lions and the madness of two bears and the rage of two huge stags; no one could endure being near them within the space of thirty feet through the bravery of their fighting and the proximity of their breaths, and they were at that fight from the dawn of early morning until the close of day."

Congal, understandably, had to rest for six weeks on Rathlin thereafter, before he was in condition to get married and enjoy his honeymoon with the fair Taise. Her name is perpetuated in Glentaise, the glen on the west side of Knocklayd, by Ballycastle.

This fable is almost certainly based on a folk memory of an unsuccessful attack on the island : the Greenan or "sunny spot," where Taise sat sewing in the story, can be identified with one of the most attractive spots on the north coast of the island, just north of Dunmore; the harbour from which the Norwegians fled after their unsuccessful attack must be Doonagiall, a place where boats can be landed on the coast 500 yards north of the fort. Doonagiall, "the harbour of the fort of the hostages," and Greenan both appear as names on the current 6 inch O.S. map.[4]

Another Rathlin girl of exceptional beauty, from the first century A.D., was Devorgilla, daughter of the King of the island who one day went down to Lough Cuan (now Strangford), hoping for a chance to meet Cuchulain, the handsome hero of the Knights of the Red Branch. All Cuchulain noticed were two large birds flapping across the water in his direction, and he quickly put a stone in his sling and struck one of them. When he came to where they had pitched, he was amazed to find two women, one of them the most beautiful girl in the world, the other her serving maid. Devorgilla reproached the hero bitterly : "It is a bad thing you have

---

[4] Details in "The Martial Career of Conghal Clairingneach." McSweeny, Irish Texts Society. Extracts appear in Appendix one.

done, Cuchulain" she said, "for it was to find you I came and now you have wounded me." He gallantly sucked out the stone and expressed his regret that, being already engaged, he could not marry her. All ended happily, however, for he took upon himself the role of matchmaker and gave Devorgilla in marriage to his companion, Lugaidh of the Red Stripes, and they lived happily to the end. As you stand on the Rathlin shore and watch white swans flying past in pairs it hardly seems strange that folk should believe that among such noble birds is a princess in disguise seeking her lost lover.

Another version of this story, which would be familiar to a student of Greek mythology for its similarity to the meeting of Perseus and Andromeda, tells of the king of Rathlin being unable to pay his annual tribute to his Fomorian masters. He offered instead his daughter, Devorgilla. Cuchulain, returning from a lengthy course in the military arts in Scotland, stopped at Rathlin and found her tied to a post awaiting collection. He slew three Fomorian heroes single handed and rescued her.

There is much complicated symbolism as well as shreds of history wrapped up in the above stories. The change of the seasons and the struggle between winter and summer as well as the attribution by a conquered people, "the Firbolgs," of magical powers, to explain the dramatic success of their new masters. The Firbolgs went "underground," in the modern sense, and since they in certain respects had higher skills than the new lords of Ireland, they in turn were looked on as the shee, the fairies or the wee folk who were only seen in the dusk and had powers of hidden magic.

Perhaps the sword of light, so famous in Gaelic mythology that it now appears on Irish Republican postage stamps, and in some stories slew Balor, King of the Fomorians, is symbolic of the terrifying swords of polished iron which so easily overcame those armed only with bronze.

The early story of Rathlin is that of an island used as an important stronghold for several thousand years in an age of fear. Many different generations of "prisoners of hope" looked to it for safety, it changed hands countless times and was ruled by kings of considerable power. During at least two distinct periods it was an important trading station, the earlier one about 2000 B.C., due to its possession of a hard stone found in only one other place in Ireland, and the second about 1200 B.C., due to its position at the narrows of the Irish Sea on an important sea route.

In the early years of the Christian era one geographer, casting a murky light on the subject of the western isles, deserves a mention. The Roman Solinus, in his *Historia Britonum* written in the third century, gives a description of the Hebudae, by which he meant five islands that probably included Rathlin. According to him the islanders lived on fish and milk, using no grain, and one king ruled over all. To encourage equable rule the king was allowed to have no possessions, not even a wife. He could have relations with any of the wives of his subjects but not acknowledge any of the offspring. Bede also mentions this as a Pictish system but whatever its theoretical advantages, it clearly did not last. The complications resulting from uncontrolled inbreeding in a small community (still a problem on some islands today) would have brought it to an end within two or three generations. One must confess, however, to feeling a little envious of that king, untroubled with earthly goods or domestic problems, exhausted but triumphant, ruling over his many islands uninhabited, and his five with uninhibited inhabitants.

Now, in the fourth century A.D., some seven hundred years after the first arrival of the Celts, we reach what may be counted a period of history.

G. J. A. C.

CHAPTER 3

SHIPWRECK IN THE SOUND

440 A.D.

"The waters are again thrown up so that their belching, roaring and thundering are heard amidst the clouds."

Cormac's Glossary, 900 A.D.

In the fifth century there took place what the newspapers today would headline as "Major Shipping Disaster", "Prince of the Blood feared lost". The "Prince of the Blood" was grandson of Niall of the Nine Hostages, Ireland's most successful warrior king. His name was Brecain and he had built up a steady trade with Scotland—the ancient Irish nobility having no inhibitions about indulging in commerce—until this day when his own vessel and a complete convoy of fifty curraghs were swamped in a great tide rip, since called after him the "Coirevreckan", meaning in Gaelic Brecain's Cauldron.

The curragh is a type of boat which has survived in Ireland in a form unchanged for at least two thousand years. In early days the curragh was built on a framework of light willow branches covered in cow hide. A stock of butter was kept on board to grease the hide and keep it supple. This type of boat has survived in England and Scotland as the coracle, a small round craft to carry one man in a sheltered river. In the West of Ireland the long narrow sea-going curragh is still in use generally. Up until about 1800 it was the main means of sea transport in Rathlin. Today sawn timber has almost everywhere replaced withies, and canvas is used instead of hide. The bird-like hull form and overall dimensions remain the same. The primeval requirements of a boat which can be built where materials and money are scarce still have to be met today. The curragh also fulfils the original demand for a boat that can be launched through surf off a beach where there is no harbour. Its high bow helps to get it through the breakers along the shore and its lightness means that it can quickly be snatched to safety on men's shoulders when it returns. I have rowed many hundreds of miles in these craft on the Irish and Scottish coasts and have learned that, properly handled, a curragh of 25 feet or more in length can be safe at sea in almost any weather. Properly handled means that the crew must be strong enough to keep her head to the wind by rowing, a problem in a long gale, and the curragh must be lightly laden and far enough off shore to be out of the ground swell and tide rips of coastal waters, and must have enough sea room to lie to and drift slowly stern first before the wind.

Even in recent years there have been multiple curragh disasters such as the one at Inishbofin between the wars when a winter gale caught the curragh fleet fishing offshore and swamped any of those which made for harbour. Forty four men were drowned. Some who stayed at sea and rode to their nets survived. The Inishkea disaster took place in 1928 when ten fishermen from that island were lost in a storm that blew up in a few minutes direct on to the shore.

Going back to the fifth century we can picture Brecain's fleet approaching Rathlin Sound from the west with small sails of brown and white set in the bow. Their raw hide skins gleamed almost transparent, as they rode before a strong fair wind that brought them to the narrows and the tide rip a couple of hours too early, while the ebb was still running out of the Irish Sea. Boat after boat was swamped by vertical-sided waves in the maelstrom and bales of hand-woven cloth were spread on the surface of the sea, together with bags of grain and parcels of cow hide, and among them the heads of men, pigs and calves, desperately swimming. The rear boats tried to turn back but tide and wind were too strong. Soon all the debris, human and otherwise, was scattered and lost as it was swept out into the North Channel. A couple of hours later the tide rip would have been quite calm.

The shipwreck took place in about A.D. 440, the same period as St. Patrick's mission to Ireland. Cormac's Glossary, in which the best account appears, was not written until the ninth century so perhaps the numbers lost grew in the interval. The Glossary gives the following account of the tide rip itself:

*"Coire Brecain, a great vortex between Ere and Alba to the
north. It is the conflux of the different seas, the sea which en-
compasses Ere at the north-west, the sea which compasses Alba
at the north-east, and the sea to the south between Ere and Alba.
They rush at each other after the manner of a luaithrinde, and
each is buried into the other like the oircel taireachta, and they
are sucked down into the gulf so as to form a gaping cauldron,
which would receive all Ere into its wide mouth. Brecain, a certain
merchant, the son of Maine, son of Niall of the Nine Hostages
had fifty curraghs trading between Ere and Alba, until they all fell
together into this cauldron, and were swallowed up, so that not
one was ever seen again".*

Luaithrinde appears to mean a swift thing—possibly a shooting star. Oircel taireachta has been translated as the Troughs of
a Water Wheel.

The account of Brecain's disaster gives no positive information as to the position of the tide rip but the relationship of the
seas mentioned and the fact that he was trading from Ireland to
Scotland point to Rathlin Sound as the location.

St. Adomnan in his biography of St. Columba, written about
the year 690 A.D., refers to several narrow escapes in "Charybdis
Brecani". One such incident took place at the beginning, ("trans-
navigare incipiens") of a voyage from Ireland to Iona. Mainly
based on this reference, Dr. Reeves identifies the tide rip described
with Slough-na-more in Rathlin Sound. This location is supported
by three place-names on the island—Brackens probably a corrup-
tion of Brecain's, for a dry cave on the east coast, Altacarry or
Altacoire "the cliff of the cauldron" for the north east point of
the island, possibly also the name Cary (Coire) which is borne by
the Barony of which Rathlin comprises half. The identification
must be correct for early days, but by the Middle Ages the name
Corryvreckan (with numerous variations in spelling) had been
transferred to the much more ferocious tide rip at the north end
of the island of Jura, fifty miles away, and that is where it shows
on the modern chart. It seems probable that this was not a plain
exchange but that "Coire Brecain", first applied to Rathlin Sound
soon after 440 A.D., became by St. Adomnan's time 200 years
later a general term for a bad overfall in the area.[1]

---

[1] A high proportion of the references to shipwrecks and narrow
escapes in those days mention Brecain's cauldron as the location. It
seems unlikely that so many would have happened in exactly the same
place

The most terrifying tidal race on the whole coast lies off the south-
west tip of Islay and has no special name today. A rock in the midst of it
"An Coire", looks like a relic of days when it too was a coire brecain.

Irish emigrants, of whom there were many during the period, first carried the name to the channel between Jura and Scarba. Later at some period when Rathlin was uninhabited the use of the term for the "cross wee spot" (as a fisherman recently described it to me) near there was discontinued. The spread of Norse and later English finally brought to an end the use of "Corryvreckan" as a term for any tide rip and it survived only for the one by Jura. It is curious the way names become transferred. There is a suggestion in the "Battles of Congal Clarineach", an early Irish tract, that Rathlin in the first century B.C. was known as Inish nam Barca, "the isle of ships". "Jura" is of Norse origin meaning Deer Island and the name in use for that island before the eighth century is unknown. This is extraordinary for it is high and conspicuous, much larger than Rathlin and has excellent harbours, so it must have been known and referred to by sailors of every age.

The early geographers do not give much help. Ptolemy, the second century Egyptian, mentions an island at the north end of Ireland as Ricina. He did not draw a map but gave latitudes and longitudes with considerable accuracy based on the Cape Verde Islands as a reference, and this is the only Irish island mentioned apart from Lambay off Dublin. Just at the latitude of the north of Ireland his observations must have become badly distorted for a map based on his position lines places Scotland lying on its back with what we now know as the west coast running along the north. Pliny, the Roman, in his Natural History written in the first century, mentions Ricnea in the same sort of position but one view of his evidence suggests that he was talking of what we now call Islay or Jura. So all that can be deduced from these two accounts is that one of the islands at the north east corner of Ireland had a name beginning with "R". Both accounts were probably based on the voyage of one Pytheas of Marseilles who had sailed around the British Isles in the fourth century B.C., as well as on contemporary accounts by Roman sailors.

When one sees how other island names have changed since 500 A.D., and indeed even on comparatively modern charts during the last two hundred years, it is not very surprising that confusion should exist over the location of the first Corryvreckan and of islands called something like Rathlin. Hinba is an island often referred to in early church writings, but never identified. Some say that it is the old name for Jura, others that it is Eilean Naomh in the Garvallochs. There are at least four other island names between Iona and the north coast of Ireland which remain unidentified, Elen, Oidech, Ommon and Hoine. Rathlin O'Birne off Donegal appears as Inish Telling on eighteenth century charts, the Maidens off Larne appear as the Whillans, and Larne itself has had three different names, Vokings Frith, Olderfleet and its present one during the last thousand years.

Another theory[2], is that the first Corryvreckan and the scene of Brecain's wreck lay north of Rathlin, not south of it in the Sound. This is based on tradition among the islanders but does not appear to have any support in ancient writings, other than through the suggestion that the name came to be applied to any dangerous meeting of currents. The tide rip north of the island has in the last hundred years been called the Race of Skerinoe, and is now on the chart "Mac Donald Race".

It seems unlikely that anyone will ever now untangle the complete tally of names used anciently among the islands; but even if the Scotsmen have now stolen the Corryvreckan from Rathlin, there is one story about it which is worth preserving. Once upon a time Breckan, Prince of Norway, came over to ask for the hand of the daughter of the King of Rathlin in marriage. Papa said that anyone who was to marry his daughter must prove himself a good enough seaman to remain at anchor in his galley in the middle of the gulf for three days and three nights. Breckan took the advice of the wise men of the age and following their instructions carefully put out seven anchors on ropes of flax, seven anchors on ropes of leather, seven on ropes made from the hair of a hundred virgins. On the first night as the maelstrom roared round him the ropes of leather broke, and on the second, when it blew even harder, the ropes of flax, but Breckan was still not worried for the wise men had assured him that ropes made from virgins' hair had never been known to fail. On the third night, however, he noticed a few strands beginning to go in one of the hair ropes. The loss of these few strands put an increased strain on the remainder and at the height of the gale and the full strength of the tide all the hair ropes parted. Breckan was swept away and drowned. Breckan's faithful black dog dragged his master's body ashore and the prince was buried in the cave which still bears his name. (There is one of these on Jura, and one on Rathlin.) The wise men were *bouleversé*, until it was established that one of the girls had not been a virgin.

On this high moral note we may end our brief research into the early whereabouts of the great vortex which the Hydrographer today coldly marks on the chart with a couple of squiggles.

Brecain's commercial enterprise and the disaster which brought it to an end had no doubt stemmed from a movement which started at the beginning of the fifth century. A few of the inhabitants of north east Ireland flitted "across the water" and

[2] U.J.A. 1911, page 46, Morris.

won lands in northern Caledonia where in due course they became known as the Picts. Trade followed the flag, as it did for Britain in the nineteenth century, and Brecain supplied his kinsmen by sea. The trade continued after his death and introduces the period when Rathlin became part of a joint kingdom of islands and mainland bridging the North Channel.

CHAPTER 4

DALRIADA AND THE ISLE OF MONKS

440-795 A.D.

"What joy to sail the crested sea and watch the wave beat white upon the Irish shore".—St. Columba, 560 A.D.

The birth of Christ three thousand miles south eastwards caused hardly even a ripple of interest in Rathlin, or any part of Ireland for that matter, for some four hundred years after the event. Then, gradually, the faith he had preached began to dominate almost the entire being of the country.

For Rathlin the period from the fifth to the eight century is distinguished as the time when it was part of the kingdom of Dalriada and when the Celtic church flourished there during its Golden Age.

To explain the arrival of the monks one must fill in some background. The Romans had never landed as soldiers in Ireland although there is a story in the Histories of Tacitus, that Agricola, his father-in-law, in about the year 80 A.D., looking across the sea from Kintyre gave his opinion that it could be conquered by one legion and a few auxiliaries or native troops. If the story is accurate this great soldier must have looked on the north side of Rathlin and past it to Robogdium, the Roman name for Fair Head. Ireland's stormy history since and her frequent miseries throughout the centuries forces one to the conclusion that it is a great pity that he was not left in Britain to put his plan into execution. A unified system of Roman government and the spread of a common culture might have brought together the inhabitants of England and Ireland in a way that nothing else could possibly have done, with resultant incalculable benefits to both.

Roman merchant skippers were familiar with Irish waters and there are indications that trading stations were established on some of the islands, probably Lambay for one. A find of Romano-British pottery[1] in Bruce's Castle makes Rathlin a second possibility. Perhaps one may picture a portly Roman merchant, dreaming of his far-off olive groves, as he leaned over the walls of the fort which guarded his stock of iron mirrors and pottery bowls, and looked out for the ship from Deva bringing his relief. The legions left Britain, as every schoolboy knows, on the 4.10 boat, that is, more prosaically, in A.D. 410. The emperors had been withdrawing their forces for a couple of generations before that.

[1] U.J.A. Vol. 23. 1960 P.39.

The men who lived in Britain about 350 A.D. found them-selves in a world of change and apparent decay which must have had many similarities with our own times. Every standard, every authority, both military and spiritual, was challenged. The Roman Empire which had ruled almost the entire known world for four hundred years was in decline. The pagans swept into Europe and Christianity which had flourished in the latter days of the empire almost disappeared. Fourth century Ireland was detached from the main stream of events but took advantage of the declining power of the Roman Empire to raid freely across the Irish Sea. Ireland at that time was inhabited by the Scoti and often referred to as Scotia. The Scots who raided the camps of the legions, and the cities of Roman Britain were led from 380-405 by Niall, a splendid hero of the gaelic blood, tall, fair haired and blue eyed. His military success gave him the soubriquet "Of the Nine Hostages", "for no man is a king without hostages".

The British monk Gildas writing 150 years after the event in the middle of the sixth century describes the raids. An early translation runs as follows:

"They (the Romans) were not withstanding no sooner gone home but, as the brownish band of wormes and eamots which in the height of summer and increasing heat do swarming break out of their most straight and darksome dens, the dreadful routes of Scots and Picts aland out of their ships wherein they were trans-ported over the Scithian Vale (St. George's Channel)".

The incursions were so frequent that the Irish Sea is described by the poet Claudian as "foaming with their oars", and in one great expedition the invading host crossing the sea was so numer-ous "that men do affirm that betwixt Ireland and Scotland was a continuous bridge of curraghs".[2] The latter has the familiar ring of the old salt's story picked up by a credulous landsman of a poet. All the same there must have been a lot of boats.

Among the captives which Niall's men brought back was a youth called Patrick, son of a minor Roman official from the west coast of Britain. Patrick at the age of sixteen became a slave under a pagan master tending pigs on Slemish mountain, a day's ride south of Ballycastle. After a few years he escaped, received a religious training on the continent, and in 432 returned to spread the faith beyond the small nucleus of Christians which were already scattered around Ireland.

Five great roads radiating from the royal court of Ireland at Tara had been completed at the end of the second century under King Cormac, and one of them led to Dun Severick about five

2 O'Grady Silva Gadelica II, 352.

miles west of Rathlin, an indication of the importance of the route to Scotland and of the traffic past the island. To Dun Severick came St. Patrick to be entertained at the fort there.[3] and perhaps he visited Rathlin for he was a great traveller and a sailor as well and visited many of the western islands. The name of the townland Kilpatrick may be a witness to this and the harbour of Portadonaghy (the port of the master) on the east side must indicate the landing of some important early churchman, perhaps the patron saint himself. In the hundred years which followed St. Patrick's arrival in Ireland the Christian faith was spread by his efforts and by those of his successors throughout the country, while at the same time in Britain and most of the west of Europe the structure of Christianity was swept away before the pagan invasions.

In 470 Fergus MacArt and his three brothers, Princes of Dalriada in north Antrim, crossed the narrows past Rathlin and founded the kingdom of Argyle (the "eastern Gael"). They retained their Irish lands and the new principality, Dalriada, as it came to be known, remained a joint Irish and Scottish kingdom, including Rathlin and several other islands, for the next three hundred years.

Another Irish Prince, whom we know today as St. Columba, was born ninety years after Patrick's arrival in 521 A.D. and entered the church. A descendant of Niall and a cousin of Brecain of the Whirlpool, he founded many monasteries and became a leading spirit in the great missionary movement which led to the Christian faith being re-introduced into the pagan lands of Europe from Ireland. By his efforts and by the efforts of men like St. Columbanus who followed him, Ireland, instead of remaining a small enclave of Christianity in a pagan world, became the nucleus for the re-establishment of the faith throughout the lands where it had been lost for a hundred years or more.

In 563 St. Columba, with twelve companions, left Derry to sail to Iona and found what was to become the greatest monastery in the western world, pre-eminent in authority and influence for two hundred years. He obtained permission to use Iona, which lay on the boundary between the Scots of Dalriada and the Picts of the north half of Scotland, from his cousin Conall, King of Dalriada and incidentally of Rathlin. When Conall's son Aidan succeeded his father it was to St. Columba and to Iona that he went to be crowned.

Seventeen years later in 580, the first church was established on Rathlin Island by St. Comgall, Abbot of Bangor. The church was known as Teampall Cooil ("the church of Cooil", an abbreviation of Comgall.

3 Abbot McGeoghahan, History of Ireland, page 267.

There was initial resistance by the islanders and in the naive words of the writer of the Life of St. Comgall, "a band of thirty warriors holding his hands led the saint away". On a second visit, however, he was successful in being granted some ground and established his church, a hut of wattles. Perhaps this story is an illustration of the resistance by the older religions, "the Druids", to the landing and the introduction of a new God.

The Celtic Church showed a reasonable degree of accommodation in meeting the older religions and many of its dates of annual celebration and symbolism show traces of the older faith. The Celtic cross, for example, is considered by some authorities to represent a compromise between the circle of the sun worshippers and the cross of Christ.

The rectorial tithes belonged to St. Comgall's successors, the Abbots of Bangor, until the sixteenth century. The Monastical History of Ireland, however, gives the credit to St. Lugadius, for founding "an abbey which is more ancient than the parish church of the same island, for that was not built until about fifty years after by Sigenius who had been Abbot of the Isle of Hu". Hu was a form of the early name of Iona and Sigenius is recorded as Abbot there, dying in 651. The Annals of the Four Masters say that Sigenius founded a church in Rechrainn in 630.

Rathlin at any rate was a late starter as island monasteries went. Aran had had a church community for most of a hundred years by then and Inishmurray, off Donegal, was already long established.

The site of one of the original churches was the same as that of the present parish church close to the sea at Church Bay. This is something of a rarity as there are not more than two other churches in the Diocese of Conor in which Rathlin now lies, where the present day church is on the original site.

"The Saint's Seat", a niche carved out of solid rock in an attractive sheltered cleft just west of the road up the hill past the church, probably dates from this period. The cleft was in more recent times part of the Manor House garden and formed part of the monastery grounds in ancient times.

There are today signs of the foundations of several religious establishments in various parts of the island including two called Kilvoruan, "the church of St. Ruan", or Luan. Undoubtedly several leading churchmen had a hand in the foundation of these establishments which accounts for the apparent confusion of names. Celtic crosses must have been numerous on the island, as they are still on many other Irish isles, but all on Rathlin have been destroyed without trace. The best preserved of the relics is in the townland of Knockans half way along the west leg of the island a quarter of a mile north of the main road. There, on a high heathery hillside, are the bases of a number of circular huts, varying from 12 feet to 36 feet in diameter, possibly of the beehive type which were roofed with successive layers of over-lapping stone to form a rounded dome.[4] Each layer of stones was tilted outwards so that the rain ran off, and on some sites in other islands such huts have survived intact for fifteen hundred years. As an alternative the Rathlin huts may have been of a simpler type with vertical walls roofed with branches drawn up to form a cone in wigwam style. The huts were surrounded by a stone wall whose foundations can still be traced. Such walls were not necessarily for protection but simply to mark the boundary of the monastic territory. In Craigmacagan, south east of Church Bay on a bare elevated area are two huge granite boulders—the only granite to be found on the island. Known as Macatire, or "the Two Wolves", they are said on the island to mark the graves of two Danish princesses and to be able to be rocked with a finger touch at certain seasons. Their significance is probably pre-Christian and perhaps they were deposited during the Ice Age. It has been suggested that they were at one time the entrance to a great stone circle. If so, it is hard so see other traces of it today. An old map, according to O'Laverty, shows "Holy Cross" near them but all traces of anything cruciform have gone. Other beehives known as "Danes' Huts", but more likely to have been monastic, stood east of Ushet until the last century when they were slowly dismantled by boatmen needing ballast.

St. Columba of Iona, the greatest of all the Celtic saints, called at Rathlin on at least one of his voyages, according to his seventh-century biographer, St. Adomnan. Island tradition has it that he landed at Port Cam just north of Portawillin on the east coast. The monastery followed his rule.[5] One of the stories (II 41), included in his biography gives the name of the first private citizen of Rathlin to be handed down. Lugne Tudicla he was, a pilot or helmsman, "who lived in the island of Rechru and whom his wife held in aversion because he was very ugly". St. Columba, acting as Marriage Guidance Counsellor, spoke to the wife who at first said she would prefer to go into a nunnery or accept any punishment the saint might care to put on her rather than share the bed of her hideous husband. After a talk with the saint, however, and a day's fasting, she decided to change her mind.

This is a maddening story in that it leaves out so many details, and the stilted Church Latin is a poor medium for recording the human passions which must have lain behind the incident. Lugne must have been called after the original founder of the

4 For further description see U.J.A. Vol. XVII, 1911, Morris.
5 Colgan.

monastery, but what ships did he pilot? We know from Adomnan's writings, that wine ships from Gaul were common and came every summer to supply the monasteries, unloading at Crinan. The Breton skipper would be able to work up the Irish Sea on his own but would have been glad to pick up a pilot at Rathlin for the intricate passages and tides among the islands. Since sailors are conservative folk, and have not changed their habits in 1500 years, Lugne no doubt had a girlfriend, or perhaps several at his various ports of call, which led to the neglect of his wife and made him seem so unattractive to her.

A narrow escape from drowning by St. Columba in the Slough-na-more has already been mentioned in Chapter II, and Adomnan describes it as follows (II 13):

"*Of another similar danger to him in the sea in Vortice Brecain.*

"*When a very fierce and dangerous storm was blowing and his companions importuned the saint to pray to the Lord for them, he gave them this answer and said, 'On this day it is not for me to pray for you in this danger that you are in, it is for the holy man, the Abbot, Cainech'. I have marvellous things to tell, in the same hour St. Cainnech, being in his own monastery, which is in Latin called 'Field of the Cow', and in Irish Aghaboe, by revelation of the Holy Spirit heard in the inner ear of his heart those words of Saint Columba. And since it chanced that he had begun after the ninth hour to break the holy bread in the refectory, he suddenly abandoned the small table and with one shoe on his foot and the other left behind through the excess of his haste, he went hurriedly to the church with these words, 'We cannot have dinner at this time when St. Columba's ship is in danger on the sea, for at this moment he repeatedly calls on the name of this Cainnech to pray to Christ for him and his companions in peril'. After saying these words he entered the oratory, bowed his knees and prayed for a little while. The Lord heard his prayer and at once the storm ceased and the sea became perfectly calm. Then St. Columba, miraculously seeing in the spirit the hastening of Cainnech to the church, although Cainnech was far away, pronounced these words from his pure heart, saying, 'Now Cainnech I know that God has heard your prayer. Now your swift running to the church wearing one shoe greatly helps us'.*"[6]

This was on a voyage from Ireland to Iona but details other than the dramatic escape are unfortunately not included.

Columbanus also had a narrow escape in the Corryvreckan miraculously sensed by Columba at Iona (I.5).

---

[6] Adomnan, Life of Columba, Anderson.

The biographer, writing about a hundred years after the death of the saint, felt he had a duty to enhance the reputation of the great man, but at the same time he lived in an age of uncompromising faith, when the power of the spirit was strong, and I for one would not like to say that the churchmen of those days were unable to harness powers of telepathy and forecasting to which we have lost the key today.

563 marks the foundation of Iona and the beginning of the Golden Age of the old Celtic Church, a period when almost every island had its monastery. Those on Inistrahull, Tory, Islay, Sanda, Cara, Gigha and the Copelands would have been Rathlin's neighbours. This "Age of Saints" lasted from the late fifth to the late seventh century and is a time of special beauty in early Christianity. The beginning of the Golden Age marks the end of the Heroic Age, and the glimmerings of an age of enlightenment, when it was first in Europe recognised that the mind could have a greater effect on affairs than military strength. A knowledge of the period lies at the basis of any study of Celtic countries, for in its writings are preserved a great deal of the magic genius of the Celts. "Saint" 'in those days meant simply an educated or literate man, not one having special individual virtues. All monks were not saints but the monks of the day were the only educated class and the monasteries the only seat of all the known arts and sciences —history, languages, geography, architecture, farming and boat building, for there was no gap between religion and industry.

The monasteries, unlike the rich establishments of the middle ages, had poverty as their rule, and neither the monastery nor any individual owned any property. Money, if handed to them by rich patrons, was passed to the poor, and when a monastery was visited by a king with his large retinue they ate the same simple fare as the brethren.

A look at the austerity, gentleness, unworldliness and complete spiritual happiness of those island monks is an inspiration. In spite of cold, scanty food and long hours of work, the church in those days had humour as well as a self-discipline, and adventure as well as a sense of catholic order.

The monks lived in individual cells, not communal residences, the abbot's slightly apart from the rest. On Rathlin where wood was scarce the cells were probably of stone. Within the monastic enclosure was also the church, built of oak if it could be got, with a stone altar, sacred vessels and hand bells for summoning the congregation; also the refectory with a long table and beside it the kitchen. The library and scriptorium had manuscripts in leather satchels hanging on the walls, with writing materials. Around the community were the farmlands it owned with probably a forge and a mill.[7] On Inishmurray is preserved a monastic settlement almost exactly as it was one thousand five hundred years ago. All the buildings are in stone and are surrounded by a defensive wall with only a low manhole for crawling through as an entrance.

Fast days when no food could be taken before evening, were frequent, Wednesdays and Fridays throughout the year and every day except Sundays in Lent. The monks wore a white linen tunic underneath and a woollen hooded cape of undyed wool, black since that was the colour of all sheep at the time. Their appearance must have been quite bizarre with the peculiar Irish style of tonsure which consisted of shaving the head bare from the front of the head to the centre line and allowing it to grow long at the back.

Since there was, of course, no way of printing, copying manuscripts was an important part of the work and Columba laid the foundations of a scribal art which led to a style of abstract decoration which was one of the greatest glories of Irish monasteries, unrivalled in its colourful beauty, balance of design and fineness of penmanship at any period anywhere in the world.

The idea of monasteries on islands was in itself an almost unique feature of the Celtic Church. Perhaps St. Patrick picked up the idea from his studies at the Isle of Lerins on the Côte d'Azur in France. But islands were in a way obvious in Ireland as monastic sites both for peace and protection, and there grew up more insulated churches than in any other country.

So we may picture the way of life of Rathlin's monks for some two hundred years. The Celtic monks found peace in the islands and added an embracing benign influence to them. It is an influence which persists to the present day and one can experience it on Rathlin and many other of the Irish islands. Rathlin, on the route between Ireland and Scotland, must have been a most important staging point on boat journeys from one monastic establishment to another. From Rathlin and other islands monks voyaged to Iceland, some even to America. "Pro Christo peregrinare", to go into exile for the love of God was their mystic ambition. They cared not whither.

The Annals of the Four Masters mention the deaths of four Abbots, Cumineus (738), Cobthacus (743), Murgalius (764), Aidus (768) and one Bishop, Flannius (734), of the Rathlin monastery during the Dalriada period. Hardy souls that they were, they deserve to be better remembered on the isle they loved than they are today. I have never heard their names mentioned there or recorded in any noticeable way.

---

[7] Chapter 'The Beginnings of Christianity'. An t-Tthair Tomas O'Feach in The Course of Irish History, Moody and Martin. Mercier Press.

It was one of the peculiarities of the Celtic Church of those days that it was controlled by Abbots rather than Bishops. The Bishop was one of the officers in the Abbey, concerned with certain duties of ordination, but junior to the Abbot. This control by individual Abbots had within it the seeds of its own destruction, for it was a loose system without any strong central authority, and it was partly due to lack of this that after the Synod of Whitby in 690 the Irish Celtic Church declined in influence, losing ground to new missionaries led by St. Augustine pushing northwards from the continent.

The Kingdoms of the Isles

We have not looked much to the temporal background, to those who ruled the isle of monks from afar during its long period of spiritual importance. It must have had for much of the period the status of a sanctuary, for there are many references to the kings of Dalriada in the Annals of Ulster, which are largely a somewhat monotonous recital of battle and death, but Rathlin is not mentioned in any of them. The warlords bypassed the island on their raids and landed often at Murlough Bay, which lies just round the corner from Rathlin, a couple of miles south east of Fair Head. Today it is too small to be of any use as a haven but then it was important enough to give the name "Dalreti of Muirbolg" to the Irish half of the kingdom.

Among the records, the boast of a pagan Ulster hero typifies the period.

"*I swear by that by which my people swear that since I took a spear in my hand I have never been without slaying a Connaughtman every day and plundering by fire every night, and I have never slept without a Connaughtman's head beneath my knee*".[8]

As well as murders, there were founderings.

In 621 Conaing, son of Aedhan, the king of Dalriada, was drowned. The chronicler sung of it as follows:

"The great clear waves of the sea,
and the sand have covered them,
into his frail curragh,
they flung themselves over Conaing.
The woman[9] has cast her white tresses
into his curragh upon Conaing".

[8] R. Thurneysen, Scela Mucce Meic Datho (Medieval and Modern Irish Series VI), P. 15/16.
[9] "The woman" is the sea.

Seaborne raids varied the theme. "In 734 Flaithbertagh led the fleet of Dal-Reti to Ireland and a great slaughter was made of them in the island of Hoine and many were drowned in the river that is called the Bann". This raises the question of nomenclature for Hoine is usually regarded as an unidentified island. Hoine could easily be confused with Moine, similar enough to the root word for monk. It seems possible that Rathlin was sometimes called Moine or "Isle of Monks" at this period. It is the only island near the Bann which would have fitted into Flaithbertagh's raid and the shortage of references to Rathlin at this period makes it probable that it had another name. After all, Iona only got its name as a result of what may have been a similar clerical error. Originally called "I" or "HI", it was given the adjectival form in Latin of Ioua which became by mistake Iona; and so by accident was born one of the loveliest names in our language.

The sanctuaries were not always respected. "In 736 Selbach, the King of Dalriada, seized Brude, the son of Oingus, King of the Picts, from the sanctuary of the monastery of Tory island". Oingus invaded and thoroughly sacked Dalriada in revenge.

In 870 the approaching end of an epoch was marked when the mighty fortress of Dun Severick was sacked for the first time ever. The force which took it must have passed close to Rathlin, but apparently did not attack the island.

Ireland, as already noted, was in those days known as Scotia or Evernia, and her people the Scoti. Those who moved across to live in what is now southern Scotland were referred to as the Scots of Britain or of Alba. Now men referring to Alba began to use the word Britain and for the northern half, the word Scotland. At the same time the kingdom of Dalriada was gradually reduced in size by encroachment from the Picts north of Lough Ness and by the kingdom of Strathclyde from the south. It is an obscure period of Scottish history but it appears that by about 750 the connection between Irish and Scottish Dalriada was severed, Rathlin going with the Irish section.

During this lengthy period, lasting as long as from the American Declaration of Independence to the present day, the monasteries lost some of their early simplicity and poverty, and as successive kings died their gifts of gold cups, jewelled book covers, crucifixes and plate meant that the main stock of portable wealth in the country was held by the church. In the small dark churches the altars, and the tombs of saints gone to their reward must have gleamed with priceless objects of silver, gold and enamel wrought in intricate designs. They were to become dangerous possessions.

G.J.A.C.

CHAPTER 5

THE VIKINGS

795-1180 A.D.

"The wind is rough tonight
tossing the white-combed ocean;
I need not fear the fierce Vikings,
crossing the Irish Sea."
Marginal note in manuscript of St. Gall Priscian.
Translated L. de Paor.

At the end of the eighth century the monasteries of Rathlin, already over two hundred years in existence, seemed an age-old and secure part of island life. On the mainland of Ireland every year brought its battles, burnings and murders, but the island monks were sufficiently isolated to remain untouched. In the battles between local kings, monasteries were not generally considered to be fair game, not so much from an ethical point of view as because of the semi-magical powers, referred to in the last chapter, which were attributed to the churchmen.

In 793 a powerful fleet suddenly appeared out of the North Sea in the darkness of a January morning and landed on the shores of Lindisfarne or Holy Island, off the Northumberland coast. They killed many of the monks, ate up all the cattle and sailed away with a rich horde of gold, jewels and sacred emblems, plus as many of the monks as were strong enough to be likely to fetch a good price as slaves. *"Lo, it is three hundred and fifty years that*

*we and our forefathers have dwelt in this fair land and never
has such a horror before appeared in Britain such as we have
suffered from the heathen; it was not thought possible that they
could have made such a voyage."* So wrote Alcuin, the Northumbrian, who was living at the court of Charlemangne in France, condoling with his countrymen. Not only was this raid in the close
season but it broke the local conventions of warfare. The news of
the atrocity travelled far and wide, not only in England, but all
over Ireland, and the Coarbs and Abbots of Rathlin must have
heard that a new terror stalked the sea. They warned their lookouts
to be on the alert and hoped that their communities would be
spared.

Two years later when the keels of long high-prowed ships
grated on the beach at Church Bay and fierce mailed men waded
out of them, there must have been little the monks could do to
protect themselves, although they were not averse to taking arms
in self defence when the occasion warranted. The Vikings had
arrived. "Rechrannia per Gentiles Pirates Flammis Exuritur Eiusque Scrinia destruuntur." "Rathlin was scorched with fire by
pirates from overseas and the shrines destroyed."

Iona was raided the next year and three more times in the
following decade. Derry was burned in 812. With immense
patience and bravery the monks returned again and again to rebuild their precious shrines and they were often successful in hiding
some of their belongings before the Vikings arrived. Even so by
810 it was decided to abandon Iona and move the sacred relics to
Kells in County Meath, where the monks built themselves a new
headquarters. To be inland, however, was not much safer, for the
monastery at Kildare was sacked no less than sixteen times during
the next hundred years, and those at Armagh and Clonmacnoise,
eleven or twelve times.

On Rathlin there must have been some survivors from the
first raid, for the death of an Abbot Freradacus, the son of
Seginius, is recorded the year after.

Fifty years later the monks were still there. In 848 "the death
of blessed Tuathalius, the son of Freradacus, the Abbot of
Rathlin" is recorded. Either the Rathlin monks had acquired a
reputation of putting up such a strong resistance that they were
not worth raiding, or they had made a deal with the Vikings.
However it was, the Rathlin monasteries survived when on other
islands every monk had been slain. In 924 death passed close by
when the Vikings of Strangford sailed through Rathlin Sound to
storm Dun Severick but apparently did not touch the island.[1]

Possibly the records are incomplete but it is not until 973,
a hundred and eighty years after the first raid, that the Annals

[1] Annals of Four Masters.

give a reference to a further slaughter on Rathlin. Another Frerdacus, Abbot of Rathlin, possibly a great-great-grandson, although we are not told as much, was "crowned as a martyr by Northmen or Danes" in that year.

Terrible deeds they were but on the other hand those very characteristics of the monks that today appeal to us would have irritated the pagan sea rovers, who probably hardly even thought of the monks as human, as they hewed them down or carried them into slavery. The chanting of monks' voices and a preoccupation with things spiritual can be annoying if you are not in a religious mood, so perhaps one should have some sympathy with the Vikings as well. The bravery and endurance of the men of God was not however wasted. Two centuries after these attacks started the bulk of the Vikings had themselves become Christians. The monks in their own way had overcome.

For four hundred years from the middle of the ninth century the Scottish islands were a separate political entity, known to the Irish as Innisgal, the isles of the foreigners, and to the Vikings as the Nordreys and Sudreys. They were ruled at times by the King of Norway as an overseas empire and at other times were independent under a strong Earl. Rathlin at this time was considered part of the Sudreys or South isles which comprised all the Hebrides and the Isle of Man, a group name which survives today only in the title of the Bishopric of Sodor and Man. At the same time Orkney and Shetland were known as the Nordreys.

There is no written record of Rathlin having been occupied by the Vikings and little in its place names of the Viking words so common in the isles farther north. The word "Bo" (the Clachen Bo, the Bo reef in Church Bay) meaning sunken rock is the only one I recognise. No Viking burial mounds have yet been found there to compare with the three excavated on Colonsay where a chieftain was interred with his wife, his ship and his horse. Perhaps all linguistic traces, and the blue eyes and fair hair of the people, which usually go with the Viking blood, were obliterated by the sixteenth century massacres; or possibly their absence is a tribute to the stoutness of the resistance put up by the islanders, and the Vikings never really occupied Rathlin. Rathlin could not have been by-passed or ignored by any sea chief for it is a key stronghold at the entrance to the Irish Sea, one which no overlord could afford not to control. Any ship on passage might be held up by a tide while passing through the narrows between Scotland and Ireland and have to rest at Rathlin until it could again make headway.[2]

[2] In 1897 near Ballycastle a hoard was found containing Hiberno-Norse coins of a period about A.D. 1035. The site, Carnsampson, was traditionally the headquarters of the Danes of North Antrim. U.J.A. Vol. 24, Third Series P.88. 1962.

The absence of any mention of Rathlin by name in the Nordic writings of this period supports the theory suggested in Chapter 4 that at this time it had a different or perhaps an alternative name to that which it bears today. The reference to the burnings of monasteries in Irish writings might in each case refer to Lambay, then called Rechra, but on balance of evidence our Rathlin is the most likely to have been the one meant by the scribes.

A vivid contemporary description of Viking activities in islands in the same part of the world is contained in the Saga of Burnt Njal, as translated by Sir George Dasent, which tells of a family blood feud started by a woman's jealousy, and the eventual burning of a homestead in Iceland. One chapter is of how Njal's sons, Grim and Helgi, took passage from Iceland one summer in a trading vessel to sail to Scotland.

"*They got so strong a wind from the north that they were driven south into the main and so thick a mist came over them that they could not tell whither they were driving and they were out a long while, but at last they came to where the great ground sea was running and thought they must be near land. 'Many lands there are here,' said the pilot, 'which we might hit, with the weather we have had, the Orkneys or Scotland or Ireland.' Two nights after they saw land on both boards and a great surf running up the Firth. They cast anchor outside the breakers and the wind began to fall and next morning it was calm.*"

Then they see thirteen ships coming out to demand the surrender of their goods or their lives. Helgi persuaded the "chapmen," or traders, to fight even against these great odds. The fight ran very warm and men were killed on both sides until someone looked seaward in a pause and the Saga goes on as follows:

"*There they see ships coming from the south round the Ness and there were not fewer than ten and they row hard, and steer thitherwards. Along their sides were shield on shield but on that ship that came first there was a man by the mast who was clad in a silken kirtle and had a gilded helm, and his hair was both fair and thick, and that man had a spear inlaid with gold in his hand. He asked, 'Who have here such an uneven game?' Helgi tells him his name and that against him are Gritgard and Snowcolf. 'Who are thou?' asks Helgi. 'My name is Kari, Solmund's son.' 'Then thou art welcome,' said Helgi, 'if thou wilt give us a little help.' 'I will give you all the help ye need, but what do you ask?' 'To fall on our enemies,' said Helgi. Kari said, 'So shall it be,' and they pulled up to them and then the battle began the second time and when they had fought a while Kari springs up on Snowcolf's ship, he turns to meet him and smites him with his sword. Kari leaps nimbly backwards over a beam that lay athwart the ship and Snowcolf smote the beam so that both edges of the*" *sword were hidden. Then Kari smites at him and the sword fell on his shoulder and the stroke was so mighty that he cleft in twain shoulder, arm and all, and Snowcolf got his death there and then. Gritgard hurled a spear at Kari but Kari saw it and sprang up aloft and the spear missed him. Just then Helgi and Grim came up both to meet Kari and Helgi springs on Gritgard and thrusts his spear through him and that was his death blow, and after that they went around the whole ship on both boards and then men begged for mercy, so they gave them all peace but took all their goods and after that they ran all the ships out to the islands."*

The bay where this took place must have been on the Scottish mainland but cannot be identified.

Kari was one of the bodyguards of Earl Sigurd, Ruler of all the Scottish and Irish islands, and had just then been gathering scats or tribute in the southern isles possibly including Rathlin from Earl Gilli.

"When the next spring came Kari asked Njal's sons to go on warfare with him but Grim said that they would only do so if he would fare with them afterwards out to Iceland. Kari gave his word to do that and then they fared with him a-sea roving. They harried south about Anglesey and all the southern isles. Thence they held on to Kintyre and landed there and fought with the landsmen and got thence much goods and so fared to their ship. Whence they fared south to Wales and harried there, then they held on far Man and there they met Godred and fought with him and got the victory and slew Dungal, the King's son; there they took great spoil. Thence they headed on north to Kola (probably Coll) and found Earl Gilli there and he greeted them well and there they stayed with him a while. The Earl fared with them to the Orkneys to meet Earl Sigurd but next spring Earl Sigurd gave away his sister Nereida to Earl Gilli and then he fared back to the southern isles."[3]

Kari's raid took place about 980, that is at roughly the same period as the second raid on Rathlin described in the Annals of the Four Masters.

I was told a story on the island only a year or two ago of how one of the islanders used to outwit "the Danes" which is the common Irish name nowadays for the Norsemen or Vikings.

" Dan na Doon used to keep a lookout for the Danes at the high point on the road out to the west; that's near where the Forestry plantation is now. When he saw them coming he would run out to the west end, climb up to the top of Dunmore, the big rock stack near the Bull. He used to pull up two skins

[3] Everyman's Library, Dent, The Story of Burnt Njal.

of water after him, then he would wait there until the Danes were gone. But one time he was asleep when they came and they took him and killed him. He was buried in the heather with a wee thorn tree at his head, and it was always unlucky to touch it. A few years ago a boy pulled the thorn tree up for devilment and he died a few days later when he was climbing on the cliffs for sea birds' eggs, and the rope broke."

The Viking invasions had by this time lost their original character of incursions by a foreign race and now partook more of the nature of a great civil war as the Irish sided sometimes with one band of Vikings, sometimes with another. For instance in 1018 a force of Norsemen under Eyuind Urarhorn, assisted the Irish King Conor at the battle of Ulfreks Fjord (Larne) against Einar, Earl of Orkney. In 1036 an Irish division travelled to Scotland to assist Earl Muddan against Thorfinn at the battle of Torfnes.

Sigurd the Stout, Kari's leader, Lord of all the Irish and Scottish islands, Earl of Orkney, was killed at the battle of Clontarf in 1014. This was the most serious defeat the Vikings suffered in the entire history of their incursions and it put Dublin, for a period, back in the hands of the Irish, but in the islands the Viking power remained strong for another two hundred years at least.

Sigurd and his successor Thorfinn who was also "Lord of All the Islands" must often have landed on Rathlin, but the McQuillans, rulers of the north-east Ulster province of Ulidia, retained some sort of control of Rathlin, for in 1038 Randal Eochada their King there fought the Vikings under Imar. Imar was the son of Harold who had been killed at the battle of Clontarf, and "the Landwaster," the Viking flag of the raven, brought him victory that day for Eochada and three hundred of his men were slain. This is the last recorded Viking raid on Rathlin, and resulted at last in the expulsion of the monks, for from that date on there is no record of any regular religious observances on the island for seven hundred years.

Magnus Barefoot, King of Norway, from 1093 to 1103, had all the old Viking temperament and reinforced the authority of the Norwegian crown over the Scottish and Irish islands. He anchored his fleet inside the Skerries off Portrush in 1103 and fought a great battle in the sandhills in a place still called the War Hollow, but he died fighting in Ulster himself the same year.

Many of the Scottish islands still paid tribute to the King of Norway at this period but in 1266 King Haakon was defeated at the battle of Largs in Arran, by Alexander, King of Scotland. In the truce which followed the Norwegians handed over to the Scots the overlordship of the Isle of Man and all the Sudreys in return for a payment of four thousand marks, and this brought to an end a period of more than four hundred years of Viking rule of the islands. Rathlin was, however, specifically left out of this arrangement as it was by then firmly in Anglo-Norman hands. Whether it was part of the Kingdom of Ireland or Scotland continued to be disputed at intervals during the following centuries but as the structure of the Church grew up on a diocesan basis in Ireland under the Normans, the spiritual care of Rathlin remained throughout with the Irish Bishop of Connor. There is little evidence that he took his duties in that respect very seriously.

In completing the story of the Vikings in the isles we have by-passed by more than a hundred years great events which took place in the twelfth century which were to shape the future of Rathlin and Ireland for centuries to come.

CHAPTER 6

THE EARLDOM OF ULSTER

1180—1242 A.D.

"So was the kingdom of the isles ruined from the time the sons of Somerled took possession of it."—Manx Chronicle.

Soon after 1100 a child was born in Argyll who was given the unmistakably Norse name of Somerled and after a long struggle became a great Thane or chieftain. He was probably descended on his mother's side from Sigurd the Stout, the Orkney Earl, but raised the standard of revolt against the Norwegians in the Isles, and in 1156 met them in a great fight on the night of Epiphany. Both sides lost heavily yet neither could achieve complete victory. In the morning a peace was reached by which the Kingdom of the isles was split between Somerled's son, Dugald, and Godred, the Viking King of the Isle of Man. Dugald took Kintyre, Bute and the Sudreys, including Rathlin, while Godred retained Man, Arran and the Nordreys. The Manx sea empire was split in two, but in 1164 Somerled was assassinated and Godred for a time came into his own again taking to himself all the islands with the exception of Skye and Bute. From Somerled's son, Donald, descended the McDonalds of the Isles.

In the same way that Rathlin was in dispute the land boundaries of the whole of Ireland were forever changing in the perpetual warfare between one Celtic chief and another. The strong central authority of the feudal system which many European nations were developing could have brought peace, power and prosperity to all, but instead the Irish continued to rob the country of its wealth and power by their total inability to live at peace. It was inevitable in such circumstances that the Normans, the warlike race who during the last three generations had conquered England and Wales, should sooner or later be asked to come in on the side of one or other of the many protagonists in this thousand years' war. The Normans landed under the great Earl Strongbow near Wexford in 1169 , and soon reached Dublin. In the north, however, the impact of their coming was not felt until eight years later. Henry II, King of England, granted in that year to John de Courcy as much of Ulster as he could lay hands on, to enjoy without charge or tribute save homage to the king. De Courcy was an attractive character to those who admire the military virtues. Tall and fair haired, strong and energetic, he often forgot his role of commander in his eagerness to be in the thick of the battle. Riding a white charger, he was careful to fulfil an ancient prophecy about the appearance of the conqueror of Ulster. His rule

was a period of brilliance and achievement in the fields of administration and agriculture, building of church and castle such as had
never been seen before in Ulster and was not to be repeated for
another four hundred years. The Earl of Ulster, as he later became,
after five battles and several narrow escapes conquered a large part
of the north east and by 1180 was ruling one sixth of all Ireland,
one of the largest seigneuries in all the king's territories. One
of his concerns was to develop and secure sea communications
direct with Britain rather than have to make all his connections of
trade and diplomacy via Dublin. To do this he built many castles
on the sea coast of County Down and Antrim, a greater concentration of fortification than was seen in any other part of Ireland
except Wexford in Norman times. In Antrim he fortified Dunluce,
a position of great natural strength, on a flat topped rocky pinnacle, which had been occupied from the earliest times, fifteen
miles west of Rathlin on the mainland coast. The pinnacle is
separated by a deep gully some 40 feet wide from the neighbouring
cliffs so that the castle could be approached only by a drawbridge.
Underneath is a seacave with a boat harbour and an entrance on
the land side.

The fortunes of Dunluce were often closely linked with those
of Rathlin and it will come into our story a good many times.
Dunseverick,[1] five miles further east, was another site where De
Courcy improved old fortifications, and it is probable that he also
occupied Donananie immediately south of Rathlin. The name of
the seaport below it, Brittas, is believed to come from the Norman
word "bretasche" for a wooden palisade. On the east coast of
Antrim he fortified Glenarm, and as his principal fortress built the
immense square keep of Carrickfergus which was to remain the
stronghold of the English in Ulster for the next six centuries. Even
today with so much modern construction all round Belfast Lough,
this great keep is still the most striking building on its shores. In
1180 John married Affreca, daughter of Godred, the King of Man,
a stroke of great diplomacy. Godred ten years before had sailed
over with thirty ships to help the Irish besieging Strongbow in
Dublin and escaped when Strongbow turned the tables dramatically on his attackers. Affreca's brother, Reginald, who succeeded
his father as king in 1186, was described in the Orkney Saga as
"greatest Viking in all the western lands. For three winters he remained on his ship without once entering a smoky house." Lucky
man to be able to do it. Perhaps Port Mananan, "the landing place
of the Manxmen," shown on old maps of Rathlin, on the east side
recalls visits by Reginald to his Norman brother-in-law, and
famous parties in long ships anchored off. Certainly De Courcy,

---

[1] The Anglo Norman Invasion of Ulster by James J. Phillips, P.R.A.I.,
1896.

by ensuring the friendship of this family, acquired at once freedom
of the sea and powerful Viking allies, a considerable step towards
independence from the Viceroy in Dublin. De Courcy began to rule
Ulster like a king, striking his own coin, making external treaties
and creating his own barons.

Bruce's Castle

Two Cathedrals, five monasteries and a hundred and ninety
one churches and chapels are recorded as having been built by the
great earl, but island monasteries were out of fashion. Many of
the priests who filled his religious establishments were English with
no tradition of serving God in remote places, and he did nothing to
restore the church on Rathlin. A man of his all-encompassing
energy and enterprise must have visited the island and appreciated
the strategic value of what was at once the only large sea isle and
the remotest spot in his kingdom. Traditionally the castle now
known as " Bruces' " near the north-east corner of the island was
built during the reign of King John which coincided with the later
years of De Courcy's reign in Ulster, but the point has never been
proved. At any rate this is a suitable place to include a description
of a fortress which has been the scene of high drama out of all
proportion to its size. It is in a position of considerable natural
strength with the inner keep sited on top of a rock stack 80 feet
high with sheer walls on all sides separated from the main island
by a gully some 15 feet deep. The top of the stack measures about
40 feet by 60 feet and the building on it was about the size of a
squash court. Across the gully, as at Donananie on the mainland
at Ballycastle, there was a drawbridge leading to the outer bailey.
The bailey was rectangular, 70 yards by 50 yards, and gave access
through a gate and second drawbridge. Its south and north sides
used natural cliffs for protection and were virtually unassailable.
On the west side a deep artificial ditch was dug out. There is today
only a short length of the north wall of the keep and a corner of
the bailey to be seen. Many additions and alterations must have
been made over the years.

Below the keep on the seaward side is a flat rock where boats
can land and south of it a cove where they could be pulled up.
In the prevailing west wind galleys could anchor off the castle in
safety for most of the summer. The view from the walls of the
indented east coast of the island, of Kintyre to the east, of the
pyramid of Torr Point to the south, of sea everywhere, is just the
sort of thing a sea chief should see from his bedroom window.

The castle was built with mortar, fired with coal, which is
unusual at that early date. Some portions of this mortar, still rock
hard and showing the coal, are in the Museum at Trinity College,
Dublin. Dr. Hamilton who first reported this curiosity described the

material used as "seacoal," but this does not indicate any different substance from what we know as coal today. It was a term used in early days to indicate coal which had been transported across the sea. When Dr. Hamilton visited Rathlin at the end of the eighteenth century the coal mines were in use at Ballycastle and traces had recently been found by miners breaking through accidentally into an old shaft of well-planned workings which must have been in use several hundreds of years earlier.[2] In the south of England and London, coal was only beginning to be known shortly after the reign of King John so its use on such a remote spot as Rathlin at a similar period indicates an unexpected degree of technical advance. It is just the sort of practical ingenuity one might expect from De Courcy who could have picked up the idea on one of his visits to court in London. None of his other castles in Ireland show a similar use of coal but that can be explained by the lack of deposits near by.

De Lacy takes over

In 1205 Hugh de Lacy the Viceroy, succeeded in turning King John against the Conqueror of Ulster whom he greatly envied. De Courcy was deposed from the Earldom and de Lacy installed in his place, but John's policy towards his barons was the erratic one that was to lead him a year or two later to Runnymede and the signing in submission of the Magna Carta. Five years later the greedy de Lacy had overstepped the limits of independent action which King John set for an Ulster earl, and the king came over in

---

[2] Note on mortar sample, taken from Bruce's Castle in 1970. Examined by Mr. H. E. Wilson of the Geological Survey of Northern Ireland. He writes:

"The specimens of mortar from Bruce's Castle do not contain any obvious coal, but I append this note I made on the field map when I mapped the area in 1952.

"The mortar from Bruce's Castle is often quoted as a criterion for establishing the age of the Ballycastle coal workings because of the presence of fragments of Ballycastle coal which was allegedly used for burning the lime. There are certainly pieces of carbonaceous material in the mortar some of which are apparently mineral coal but some of which are like charcoal. The sand used is coarse and gritty with well-rounded and sub-angular fragments of flint, basalt and chalk. It is unlike any seen on the island and if imported from the mainland the coal might have been detrital."

The specimen you provide is not quite like this—the sand is mainly angular flint and chalk with little quartz or basalt and might well be local in origin. It is doubtful, however, if coal would survive lime-burning—certainly I have never seen any in modern lime and I would not like to accept the evidence as certain proof of coal working when the castle was built, though I think it likely." For reference to this subject see the 'Geology of the Country around Ballycastle' p. 289. H.M.S.O.

person to put things in order. De Courcy had the satisfaction of accompanying the expedition and driving the usurper out of his territories. On the 16th June, 1210, King John himself who showed extraordinary energy and ability at times, was outside the walls of Carrickfergus when the castle surrendered. He found that de Lacy with his wife had fled secretly by boat to Scotland and sent De Courcy after him. The fugitives were, however, captured by Duncan of Carrick, of the family of the Earls of Galloway, and duly handed over.

The further fate of De Courcy after this period remains obscure; he had begotten no sons but was according to a tradition reinstated as Earl of Ulster. Bad weather held him up on fifteen occasions when trying to return to his fief and he eventually died in obscurity in France. De Lacy was starved to death in the dungeons of Carrickfergus by order of the King, having been Lord of Rathlin, in title at least, for a period of five years.

In the resettlement of lands which followed King John's three month blitzkrieg, Duncan of Carrick was given large grants of land in north eastern Ireland in return for his help. As well as capturing de Lacy he had assisted Lord de Gray, the King's Justiciar in a raid on Innishowen, the peninsula between Lough Foyle and Lough Swilly, by bringing over a fleet of seventy six ships. To Duncan's kinsman, Alan Earl of Galloway, went Rathlin—in the grant to him in 1213 comes the first mention of this form of the name. Confirmatory deeds of 1215 and 1220, however, call it Rachrunn.[3] In going to the Galloway family the island became once more for a short period, as it had been in the days of Dalriada, part of a joint Irish Scottish kingdom bridging the North Channel, ruled by sea kings with much Viking blood in their veins. This was not for more than three or four years, however, for in the final year of his life in 1216 John, erratic to the last, restored Rathlin to the de Lacy family.

The De Burgos, another Norman family, who controlled Connaught, married into the de Lacy family and a few years later Rathlin was part of the fief of Richard de Burgo, Brown Earl of Ulster, who thus acquired it by the time honoured method of becoming son-in-law of the owner.

Rathlin was too remote for the great Earl to administer in person and he let it to tenants who were anything but domesticated.

[3] Hardy's Rot. Tur. Lond. quoted by Reeves.

CHAPTER 7

THE BYSSETS AND THE BRUCE

1242-1401 A.D.

"The most celebrated spider known to history".

Sir Winston Churchill.

In 1242, an important date in island history, John and Walter Bysset, members of a Scottish family, were accused of the murder of Patrick, Earl of Atholl, at Haddington. Patrick was a grandson of Alan of Galloway who had briefly owned Rathlin twenty six years earlier. The Byssets, whose name was sometimes spelt Bisset or even Mysset, were a family said to be of Greek origin who had come to England with the Normans, had moved north to Scotland, and who had feuded over many years with the Atholls. When Patrick Earl of Atholl died, smothered in his burning castle, the two brothers were summoned to Edinburgh. Although they alleged that they had been sixty miles away on the night of the fire, their servants had been seen in the vicinity, and they decided to make a run for it. They fled to Ireland where some of their family were already established and acquired from De Burgo lands in the Glynnes, nowadays the Glens of Antrim. These lands included Rathlin and were to be held by the family for five generations. In 1279 it was found by inquisition that John Bysset, son and heir of the first John to arrive in Ireland, held from De Burgo "Insulam de Racry, Quae Valet IV Lib. VIII. 5 VD et duas partes unius denarii"; in other words the rent was £4 8s. 5½d.[1]

To what extent, if any, Byssets lived in Rathlin is obscure; probably very little. Their main castle was down the east coast at Glenarm. Wild men themselves, the Byssets in turn had trouble with their sub-tenants, for Cox, in his seventeenth century History of Ireland, states that in 1274, "the islanders and Scots made a successful raid on the Irish mainland". By way of reprisal Sir Richard de Burgo and Sir Eustace la Poer entered the "isles", burned the cottages, slaughtered the inhabitants and smoked out those who had hidden themselves in caves, "after the manner of smoking a fox out of his earth". To our ears it sounds like a day's snipe shooting or ferreting, involving about as little danger and as much sport for the armoured Norman commanders. Counting the Viking attacks, it was Rathlin's fourth massacre.

Another incident of this period,[2] was when Scottish marauders seized the castle and proceeded to treat the islanders, who consisted

[1] Inq. P.M. 7 Ed. I No. 28 Tur. Lond.
[2] Seawrack, Campbell.

of McDonalds and Blacks, very harshly, forcing them into bringing daily provisions to the castle. One day it happened to be the duty of Turloch Mac Ilieve (anglice Charles Black) to convey these provisions. At the usual hour the laden creels were carried over the drawbridge and placed in the castle hall to remain until evening. The chief and his warriors proceeded to feast as usual in the hall while their prisoners looked on, fettered to their seats. But, inside each creel, instead of provisions, was a cramped warrior, Turloch and his brave followers, listening to all that passed and biding their time. At a prepared signal they leapt out, dirk in hand and slew all their enemies, the castle becoming a scene of appalling bloodshed. Having liberated the islanders, they set the castle on fire.

The intaking of the castle was a fine feat of arms, but why they should have proceeded to burn their prize, instead of retaining it for protection, is hard to make out. Perhaps they looked on it as a symbol of the power of the Byssets from the mainland, whom they disliked almost as much as the Scottish invaders.

At the beginning of the fourteenth century Sir Hugh Bysset ruled the Antrim coast but still took an interest in affairs in Scotland, and the struggle for the kingship taking place there. So it was that when the main contender for the crown, Robert the Bruce, needed a winter hideout at a time when his fortunes were at a particularly low ebb, Sir Hugh said to him, "I have just the place for you, do come to Rathlin". It was a safe offer. If Bruce prospered he was the man who had helped him. If Bruce failed he could say that a renegade landing in Rathlin was nothing to do with him.

Robert Bruce was not the first man or the last to come there "on the run". One of Scotland's greatest heroes, he is principally famed for having freed his country from the hated rule of the English. Like most of the other great soldiers of the period he came from a Norman family. He had a claim through his grandfather to the throne of Scotland, but Edward I of England arbitrated in favour of John Balliol and had him crowned in 1292. Robert Bruce took part in a number of struggles against the English but it was not until early in 1306 that he began to lead his country openly against King Edward and Balliol. Early that year he killed one of Balliol's chief supporters, the Red Comyn, during a conference in a church at Dumfries. He came out of the sanctuary saying "I doubt me I have killed the Red Comyn." One of his men replied "I'll mak' siccar!" and re-entered the building. This deed made Bruce an enemy to both English and Scottish kings and an outcast from the church. He gathered his supporters together and marched to Scone where he was crowned king in March of that year. He was soon badly defeated by the English and had to escape and hide at Saddell, the Kintyre stronghold of his ally, Angus McDonald Og of the Isles. Angus, for fear of traitors in his own party, advised Bruce not to stay there and got in touch with Hugh Bysset. Bruce passed on to Dunaverty, a fort on the south tip of Kintyre, and arrived at Rathlin in the autumn of 1306 accompanied by Sir James "the Black" Douglas, and Sir Robert Boyd. The islanders were at first terrified at the appearance of this armed party of outlaws and drove their cattle for safety to "a rycht stalwart castell".[3] Well they might, for it was an age of blood and turmoil in Scotland. William Wallace, another great national hero, the year before had led his rebellion wearing a sword scabbard bound with the skin of a slaughtered English tax gatherer, until he was captured, hung, drawn and quartered. Giving shelter to such men was a risky business but the islanders had not much room for argument against Bruce's force of three galleys and three hundred men. They soon got used to the idea and took a liking to the party. Later Hugh Bysset came over to see that they were as comfortable as possible.

On Rathlin,[4] according to tradition, Bruce drew inspiration to renew his struggles for the Scottish crown from watching a spider in the sea cave near the Castle, a spider which Sir Winston Churchill referred to as the most celebrated known to history. Seven times the spider tried to get its web hooked across from one rock to another on the roof, and only succeeded at the last attempt. Why he should have been in such a place only accessible by boat in calm weather is a difficulty in accepting the location of the story. Perhaps the Castle was over-crowded and Bruce had rowed round to the cave to get peace and quiet to make his plans for the next summer's campaign. Perhaps it was at the time when the king's men traced him to Rathlin and according to tradition he had to flee even from there in a small boat and hide until they were gone. Whatever Bruce did on Rathlin he certainly made his mark there for the castle and cave have both been called after him almost ever since, and he remains today the most familiar of any historical figure on the island. There is no evidence that he built the castle, but possibly his men did some masonry work to pass the winter days and recompense Hugh Bysset for their keep. Bruce at this time was thirty two and must have been impatient to see those winter days pass. With the assistance of Angus MacDonald he collected a force of thirty three ships to be commanded by Douglas when the campaigning season opened. This was the same Douglas who was later to be the hero of one of the most famous stories of medieval chivalry. He was Bruce's faithful henchman

[3] Barbour.

[4] Other isles from the Orkneys to Arran claim to be the wintering place of Bruce. Barbour in his early poem, "The Brus," gave Rathlin the honour and on balance it has much the best title.

for twenty years and when in 1329 the king died Douglas took his master's heart to be buried in the Holy Land. The ship touched in a Spanish port on the voyage and Douglas responding to a sudden call for help joined the hard pressed Christians in a battle with the Moors. Charging into the heathen army he threw far ahead in among their warriors the silver casket containing the heart of Bruce, "Forward brave heart as thou wert wont, Douglas will follow thee or die". He was killed in the moment of victory. Such were the men who wintered on Rathlin in 1306.

Douglas left first and won a victory at Brodick on Arran, where incidentally there is another "Bruce's Cave", complete with spider. Tradition on Rathlin has it that as Bruce was leaving to join him, a wise woman or "pythoness" predicted his winning the throne of Scotland, and requested that her two sons from the island should accompany him.

One thing led to another as far as Hugh Bysset was concerned. Robert the Bruce triumphed and won the Scottish crown. When a few years later a strong man was needed to head a combination against the Normans in Ireland Hugh supported Robert's brother Edward, Earl of Carrick in Galloway, for the post. In fact there are indications that it was he who gave the invitation. At Larne close to Hugh's manor at Glenarm Edward Bruce landed on the 25th May, 1315, with the victors of Bannockburn and at first all went brilliantly. In May 1316 Edward was crowned King of Ireland and Hugh with several of his family stood at his right hand. Robert Bruce himself came over to help in further campaigning but in 1318 at Faughart Edward was defeated and slain. Sir Hugh Bysset had backed the wrong horse this time and forfeited his lands including Rathlin to John D'Athy,[5] the winner of the battle.

However, Byssets were not to be put down so easily and after a few years in the cold obtained the return of their lands from Edward III.[6] By the year 1400 the Byssets were in such a position of influence that the hand of Margery, the only daughter of the head of the family, was sought by John Mor McDonnell, descendant of Somerled and son of the first formal holder of that magnificent title, Lord of the Isles.

Margery apart from her personal charms which are stated to have been considerable, was heiress to the seven Lordships of the Glynnes, an area running from Ballycastle to Larne including Rathlin, and when her father died in a fight with a neighbour they passed with her to Clan Donnell. The McDonnell Earls of Antrim, descended in the female line from John Mor, still hold a good deal of the same ground today.

[5] Rot. Pat. 13 Edw. II, page 28.
[6] Rot. Pat. page 53.

CHAPTER 8

CLAN DONNELL PUSHES SOUTH

1401-1551 A.D.

"Upon the coast of Ireland by four myle to land layes ane iyle callit Rachlaine pertaining to Ireland and possessit this many yeirs by Clan Donald of Kyntire, four myle lang and two myle braide, guid land, inhabit and manurit".—Dean Munro, 1549.

During the hundred years following their marriage into the Bysset family, the McDonnells gradually increased their hold on Rathlin and north east Antrim. The land was much more fertile there than in the isles and this was probably the main motive. They changed their name from McDonald to the more Irish form used by their kinsmen, the O'Donnells of Donegal, but the exact spelling remained at the choice of the user and was as often written as McConnell. Marriages into the great Ulster families of O'Neill of Tyrone, and of McQuillan who ruled north-west Antrim helped to consolidate their gains. A strong castle, part of which still stands today on Kenbane Head, a mile west of Ballycastle became their Irish headquarters. Scotland remained more or less constantly in a state of warfare; the Lords of the Isles were for ever in strife with the King. There were major rebellions in 1429 and 1475. Several attempts at settlements were made to reach a state of peace based on the mainland remaining Royal territory and the isles staying with the clans, but no treaty lasted for long. As often as the McDonald fortunes ebbed, a tide of refugees and exiles came from the more northerly isles to Rathlin and Antrim.

In 1470 Angus McDonnell emerged as leader, famed for his handsome figure, courage, skill in hunting and lavish hospitality. He gained widespread following throughout the islands and might have secured their independence for several generations, but in 1490 his dashing career came to an end when he was stabbed to death by an Irish harper who was said to have been bribed by his enemies. With his death came the end of the independent lordship, for his successor was an old man, unwilling to control the situation. In 1493 the affairs of the isles were brought before Scottish Parliament by James IV, where the lordship of the isles was declared forfeit and the title invested in the crown.

This still did not put an end to the fighting; the islesmen continued to elect their lord, and there was a further rebellion in 1504 led by Donald Dubh, a son of Angus born after his father's death, another by Donald Gallda in 1511 and a final one in 1545, when Donald Dubh escaped, with incredible tenacity of purpose, after thirty seven years in prison. He allied himself to King Henry

VIII, whose ambition it was by intrigue or force to control all Ireland and Scotland as no English king had ever done. Donald Dubh disposed of such powerful forces that he could send four thousand men and one hundred and eighty galleys to help the English forces in Ulster while retaining a similar number near home to fight the Campbells, and managed to preserve his independence for two years until his sudden death brought the rising to an end.

During the years the rivalry between the clans of Campbell, led by the Earl of Argyll, and McDonnell, led by the Lord of the Isles, had been steadily building up. The McDonnells were still much the more powerful and the Campbells generally took the royal part. Many a battle and murder took place in the name of this inter-clan feud over a period of several hundred years. James McDonnell of Islay, however, was shrewd enough to keep clear of the Donald Dubh rising and make a pact with the Campbells, sealed by his marriage to Agnes, daughter of the third earl of Argyll. He became head of the clan on Donald Dubh's death and steadily pursued his ambition of making larger and more secure his Irish possession.

There is a tradition that Rathlin was held by the McQuillans for a period early in the sixteenth century, but this cannot be properly established. They were a Norman family who had adopted Irish ways and ruled The Route, a district west of the Glynns roughly from the Bush to the Bann including Dunluce Castle. The exact boundaries of Route and Glynns changed a good deal over the centuries.

Piracy flourished in the North Channel. During the fifteenth century wool and wines were carried on an increasing scale on English bottoms to most parts of Europe, to Iceland and to Southern Ireland, but merchants still had to shun the north of Ireland due to the risk of capture. If the pirates were not McDonnells, at least the seizures must have been carried out with their connivance, and Rathlin used as a base.

The sailors of Italy, however, had an interest in coming to these waters and were prepared to risk the pirates, for Rathlin achieves a curious prominence during the fifteenth century on the Portolan charts, which were produced in Venice at that period. In a chart of 1422 by Jacobus de Giroldis of Venice, Rathlin appears as Ragrani or Ragram, with an amount of detail out of all proportion to its size. Other islands in the area of similar size are simply shown as a blur, but Rathlin is quite a distinct triangular shape with a bay shown in the position of Couraghy. Navigators in those days kept information as to good anchorages and sources of supply of rare commodities strictly private, and the charts which we can see today in collections, were far from being available to the public at the time when they were first drawn. It is possible that fine sand for use in the manufacture of Venetian glass was obtained at Rathlin or at Ballycastle. A glass industry did flourish in Ballycastle for a short time in the eighteenth century.[1]

Apart from occasional references like these, one hundred and fifty years of what may have been one of the most interesting periods of island history remain quite obscure, mostly because to the Scottish chieftain the ability to write was not a desirable accomplishment. It was something for which he hired a clerk, and that as rarely as possible. The Scottish islesmen, swift and brave like the seabirds who are probably in their own view the real owners of Rathlin, came and went careless of records, and un-recorded.

But soon they were to face a second group of powerful contenders for their Irish territories, contenders who kept records and who provide us with accounts, one-sided but fairly detailed, of the turbulent years following 1551. These were the English.

[1] Paper by Michael C. Andrews, Fellow of the Society of Antiquaries of Scotland, 28th October, 1924, in P.R.O. Belfast.

Galley incised on wall of Gatehouse of Dunluce Castle

CHAPTER 9

THE TUDORS VERSUS THE SCOTS

1551—1573 A.D.

"This Raghlins is the greatest enemy that Ireland hath."—
Smith, 1560.

From about the year 1520 James McDonnell of the Dunnyveg
or Islay branch of the family, began with his brothers, Colla,
Alexander and Sorley, to extend the Scots' colonies in Ulster until
these formed a thin but almost continuous line from the Bann to
Glenarm. James had been reared at the Scottish court where he
learned to write and quickly absorbed the arts of diplomacy. He
refrained from taking part in the rising in 1543 but in spite of the
unpopularity which this must have earned him at the time and the
fact that he belonged to a junior branch of the family, he was
elected Lord of the Isles by the clansmen on the death of Donald
Dubh two years later. At the same time as accepting this now
illegal title, he retained the support of the royal party and further
secured his position by the marriage already mentioned to Agnes
Campbell, daughter of Colin, 3rd Earl of Argyll, thus sealing the
friendship of her clan, his traditional enemies. As well as being a
skilled diplomat James was a fearless sailor and bold warrior. For
the first time the Lordship had fallen to the branch of the family
most interested in the Irish colony. The next brother, the mighty
Colla, was swarthy, and bow-legged from his long hours in the
saddle for he was a great horseman. James had appointed him
Captain of the Route and of Rathlin and he lived constantly in
Ireland where he held his castle of Kenbane, except for one short
incident in his absence in 1551, against all comers.

The colonists fought hard for supremacy with the McQuillans and constantly raided and expanded into the territories of the O'Cahans and O'Neills. Many an Irish and Scottish hillside echoed to their way cry, "Eilean Fraoch," "The Heather Isle." This was taken from an islet of that name in the Sound of Islay which the family used as a prison, as necessary in these times as a spare bedroom might be today.

There is a tale[1] of Colla raiding against the O'Cahans with the McQuillans in the Route and being invited to spend the winter quartered at Dunluce Castle. He there succeeded in winning the affection of Eva McQuillan, daughter of the head of the clan, but had to clear out with her and his men in a hurry when a plot by McQuillan was discovered at the last minute for a wholesale slaughter of his Scottish guests. Colla went to Rathlin, found it uninhabited and had to live on colt's flesh during his stay. This and other stories indicate that Rathlin during this century was almost exclusively a fortress and that there was only a very small resident population, at times none at all.

The Scots made more use as residences of their castles on the mainland, Waterfoot, Donananie just west of Ballycastle, Kenbane and Dunseverick.

Ireland was governed during these times by a Viceroy appointed by the King of England. He bore the title of Lord Deputy, or in exceptional circumstances the higher one of Lord Lieutenant. The only difference in effect was that the Lord Lieutenant could leave the country while in office, whereas a Deputy could not.

Ireland at this time appeared to the ordinary Englishman as remote as China seems to us today, a country "somewhere east of Suez, where the best is like the worst, where there ain't no ten commandments, and a man can raise a thirst". The image was also like that of the wild west in the nineteenth century, a land of quick fortune or sudden death. The hardships of campaigning were considerable. For the Irish and the Scots the most successful tactics were to avoid setpiece battles other than very occasionally in circumstances highly favourable to themselves, but constantly to harass the English, cut off stragglers, intercept food supplies, fight in fact a guerilla war. The only effective counter for the English commanders was to starve the Irish in return by burning corn and slaughtering cattle. It was a thoroughly dirty war. The present day solaces of soldiers on active service, tobacco and hot drinks such as tea and coffee, had not been introduced. A campaigning breakfast might consist of a handful of meal, mixed with a little cold water in the heel of a shoe, eaten with the point of a

[1] Footnote by Hill on page 52.

dagger. Hot food and waterproof shelter was a rarity outside the garrison town. Wealth and position could produce for officers and commanders spices and wine, whiskey and beef, but for the common soldier these things were so rare that it is not surprising that he looted and stole whenever he got a chance. Mortality from sickness was up to 30 per cent. in some campaigns.

In the late 1540's, with James and his redoubtable brothers hungry for expansion into good lands southward, and the English equally determined to rule supreme in Ireland, trouble looked inevitable, and Rathlin was bound to be in it. It was not, however, until 1550 that the English government became so concerned about the Scots as a powerful and growing element in the Irish balance of power, that they decided on a determined attempt to wipe it out.

Sorley Boy McDonnell, the youngest brother, was captured in that year by Sir James Crofts, the Deputy, and held prisoner in Dublin. In 1551 Crofts accompanied by Captain Cuffe and Sir Ralph Bagenal, set off from Carrickfergus to attack the Scots with four ships and several hundred men. It was the first time for many years that a Deputy had come so far north. As the land forces drew near the north coast, Scottish prisoners, questioned by methods which are best not thought about, revealed the strength and disposition of the forces commanded by James in person on Rathlin. Crofts had enough boats to land one hundred men on the island but not the three to four hundred which he estimated as required to kill the Scots there, so it seemed a good idea first to capture one or two of the Scottish galleys which were either drawn up or anchored off the east shore at Port Sassenach (the Port of the Englishman),[2] near Bruce's Castle. The land forces marched on and waited at Ballycastle while Cuffe, commanding the English ships approached Rathlin and anchored off in the strong tide which runs past the port. They put springs on their cables so that they could haul themselves broadside on to the coast to open fire in the most effective way, but in spite of "the great gonne shot that was shott out of the shippes", the Scots disobligingly refused to fall back. It was a difficult target for the gunners, for they could not fire at or close to the galleys found to be all on land or they would defeat their own object by damaging them. Then, according to Lord Chancellor Sir Thomas Cusake's account, one of the English boats was thrown on the shore and capsized by a sudden swell.

The eruption of a swell or "shore" as the tide turns east is something well known to anyone who has sailed around Rathlin, and need not take an experienced sailor by surprise, certainly not

---

[2] There are two ports of this name, one 50 yards south of the castle, the other near Rue Point.

on the east side. It is nothing that Elizabethan seamen could not
have coped with, unless they were in the best naval tradition
"landing in the smoke", using the fog of the gun fire to try to
confuse the enemy's bowmen; with very thick smoke and a gentle
wind in the right direction, visibility might well have been so low
that the sailors misjudged the swell.

Cuffe perhaps attempted a landing against nautical advice,
and then blamed the sailors. There is a tendency for soldiers
and sailors to misunderstand each other and the Elizabethans were
no more immune to this than anyone since. In reporting what
followed the boat's upsetting Cusake was concerned to cover up
an ill-directed fiasco.

At any rate, it is clear that James and Colla McDonnell
seized their chance and swept down upon the stranded boat.

The outcome was that all its crew were killed or captured,
and the attack was a complete failure. Cuffe and Bagenal were
among the captives. In the exchange of prisoners which followed,
Sorley Boy was released from Dublin.

The Annals of the Four Masters record that every man who
landed was killed except the commander; they do not mention
the number involved but indicate a much heavier defeat than
Cusake admits.

First round to the Scots. This is also the first time we learn
anything of the character of Sorley, who was to become famous
as Captain of the Route on the death of his brother Colla, seven
years later. At this time Sorley, aged forty-five, was an experienced
warrior and had led his clan in a score of violent fights. He was
fifth in line of direct descent from Margery Bysset and his name
was a gaelic edition of that of his forbear Somerled, founder of
the Gaelic Kingdom of the Isles. The suffix "boy" came from
Sorley's yellow hair. One can picture him at that time as shaggy,
tall and broad shouldered, wielding his great two-handed sword
in battle with the agility of a twenty year old. "He walked the
ling like a buck in spring, and looked like a lance at rest".
Sorley celebrated his freedom with a raid on Carrickfergus the
next year, during which he carried off Walter Floddy, the Constable, and when he returned him on payment of ransom, sent a
message which many Irishmen today would applaud, "Playnly
that Inglishe men had no ryght to Yrland".

These raids in 1551 and 1552 mark the beginning of a period
of thirty five years of bloodshed and warfare with widely varying
fortunes between the English and the McDonnells. Holding the
ring were McQuillans, O'Neills and the Donegal O'Donnells who
came in sometimes on one side, sometimes the other. The
bewildering shuffles of alliance and numerous inter-clan marriages
make the motivations and train of events somewhat difficult to

follow at times but Rathlin held throughout a key position as an offshore island or base. As long as the Scots held it they could pick their time to raid the mainland. Sea power was all important. England commanded the sea, but the Scots could generally infiltrate. The main fighting strength of the Scots lay in Kintyre and the isles where they always had enemies to contend with. The survival of the Irish colony depended on their ability to reinforce it quickly by sea.

The Scottish galleys were five hundred years behind the English ships in design, but in the narrow waters had a number of advantages. The larger ones known as lymphads had ten oars or more aside and could carry a hundred men. Barlinns or birlings were smaller, usually six oars aside. Pointed at both ends and undecked, the galleys were descended directly from the ships of the Vikings, but were shorter and beamier. They carried a single mast amidship with a square sail, and the chieftain's banner on a staff at the bow. Few other details have survived, and pictures occur only on a few coats of arms, seven on sculptured stones on Islay and one in a crude sketch scratched on the stone work at the entrance to Dunluce Castle. It is clear that the galleys could make the passage from Scotland to Ireland in almost any weather and fast too, for a signal fire on a hill on Fair Head would bring over two thousand men from Kintyre within seven hours. The weakness of the Scots' ships lay in their light timbers which meant inability to carry guns, or stand up to gunfire. Even the hardiest commanders avoided, if at all possible, an encounter with the smallest English ship. On the few occasions when they met and the English could get their guns to bear, the Scots' galleys were quickly sunk or captured.

The English, however, due to the government's chronic shortage of money, never had enough ships to maintain a proper blockade and suffered the disadvantage of lack of harbours near the landing places used by the Scots. There was no port between the River Bann and Larne where a deep keeled ship could remain at anchor in winter, and the same applied to most of the Kintyre peninsula. The Scots' galley could use any creek or beach and be pulled up into safety. In calm weather too the Scots with their ability to row, also had the best of it and could pass the English ships unattacked. The English attempted to counter this advantage by sending up in 1563 a couple of smaller craft known as brigantines, the Makeshift and the Post, oar/sail warships, capable of carrying several light guns and up to sixty men each but they were short ranged, difficult to manage in heavy seas and do not seem to have achieved a great deal.

Essex in 1575 brought similar light draft ships which served him well. From about 1562 onwards it was customary to have one royal ship on the coast which became known as the Irish

Galley, and as wars flared up extra ships were sent from time to time. Their names are evocative. The Saker was the first Irish Galley succeeded in 1572 by the Handmaid, newly built of ninety tons; she was succeeded in turn by the Popinjay in 1587 and by the Tramontana in 1601.

On land the Scots were highly effective. Sir Francis Knollys in 1566 estimated that "three hundred of the Scots are harder to be vanquished than six hundred of the Irish."

The Irish had no seagoing ships at this time other than the small fleet of the chieftainess Granuaile in faraway Clare Island in the west so Rathlin was a secure bank for any stores looted from them by the Scots.

Crofts made two further expeditions against the Scots, neither effective enough to reach Rathlin. His relief, St. Leger, did little better. In 1555 the Scots, under James, were strong enough to besiege Carrickfergus for several weeks. In 1556 the Earl of Sussex was appointed Deputy. He had as his Captain, his brother-in-law, Sir Henry Sidney.

In 1557 Sir Henry succeeded in landing on Rathlin "more politiquelly and saufly," in his own terms, than had Cuffe, and slaughtered the entire population, "all mankind, corn and cattle in it." One account says that a son of Sorley traitorously assisted Sydney and was rewarded with a gold mounted sword and spurs for his help. Perhaps this is what Sydney meant by politically, but there is no confirmation in his own reports. Little mention of this masscre is made in the Irish Annals; the incident is generally condoned by historians, perhaps because, like the housemaid's baby, it was a small one. Sussex followed up this success with a raid to the McDonnell home country. Flying his pennant of the Ragged Staff in the Mary Willoughby of 140 tons, he sailed up the Clyde, burned James McDonnell's castle of Saddel on Kintyre and incidentally destroyed all the McDonnell archives. Then he devastated Arran, and had not bad weather set in James' lands in Islay, Gigha and the lesser isles would have been raided.

Miskimmin's "History of Carrickfergus" places this raid in 1558 and states that a garrison and colony were placed on the island but Sussex "lost one of his ships on its rocks during a storm, in which were some citizens of Dublin." If this is accurate it is the first shipwreck on Rathlin of which we have a record. There was certainly no attempt by the English to maintain a post on Rathlin for long. Sydney had estimated that it would cost three hundred pounds a year to maintain a force there, far too much for the Royal exchequer.

Sydney was one of the most able men England has ever sent to Ireland and in most ways the beau ideal of an Elizabethan aristocrat. Polished courtier, good and witty conversationalist, competent soldier and fair administrator, he was brave but when occasion demanded it ruthless, even cruel. His son, Sir Phillip, who accompanied his father on some of his Irish expeditions, achieved a more lasting fame as a poet.

Sir Henry's great ambition was an Earldom of which he felt the need to obtain social equality with the Deputy, his brother-in-law. For this he served four terms in Ireland in various capacities and no doubt would have been allowed to serve more continuously and get his reward, but for the fact that he was looked on as an extremely expensive man. He did things on the grand scale and travelled with such a large retinue that as soon as things became peaceful Elizabeth tended to recall him and put in a cheaper man. His only recorded failings were a certain tendency to gluttony and lechery.

Some accounts and several maps of the period, including Speede's, suggest that Sorley at this period built a castle called Donananie on the island, near where Bruce's castle stood, but this seems a confusion with his stronghold of that name which had been constructed some years earlier on the mainland cliffs just west of the present site of Ballycastle.[3]

Another mystery on Elizabethan maps is a rock called Dundelbhuny, shown as lying off the east coast of Rathlin near Doon Point. There is no detached rock there but perhaps this was a name for the old fortification on the point which was also at some later period called "Castle Voodish" (O'Laverty). Sorley had an Italian lieutenant who acted as his adviser on fortification and no doubt was responsible for some modifications to Bruce's castle and Donananie.

The next year, 1558, Queen Elizabeth came to the throne. In the same year Colla McDonald died at Kenbane, as also did Conn Bacagh (the Lame), head of the O'Neills—his last words a curse on any or all of his posterity who should learn English, sow wheat or build a stone house. He was succeeded by his son, Shane O'Neill, a man of some military ability but repulsive and overbearing character, whom the Irish nicknamed "The Proud." James appointed Sorley Captain of the Route.

Queen Elizabeth's policy, soon after she came to the throne, was to support Shane (whose sister Mary incidentally was Sorley's wife) against the Scots. Perhaps she was influenced by the

---

[3] Donananie. This fortress, of which the gate posts and defensive ditch are all that remain today, lies just to seaward of the wire fence which surrounds the caravan site recently constructed at Ballycastle. It must have been of considerable strength, a mini-Dunluce in fact, and had access to the sea by a steep path on the west side. The name is said to mean "the place of the fairground."

McDonnell victory at Aura in 1559 which gave them a superiority over the McQuillans for many years and would have left them free for further expansion if unchecked. Sorley had commanded the McDonnells in that battle and when charged by the enemy horsemen retreated over a path of rushes he had secretly laid down in a bog to his rear. The horsemen pursued at full speed and because they were tied to the saddle in accordance with the custom of the time, they became engulfed, and were quickly slaughtered.[4]

James McDonnell must have felt confident of his ability to hold his Irish territory for he sent a hundred carpenters across the water and built for himself a mansion counted the finest in Ulster at Red Bay.

At the same time Elizabeth began to think of plans for an English plantation, a second Pale, in the north-east. One of her advisers was John Smyth whose remarks in so far as Rathlin was concerned, went as follows:

1. *First for the quietness of Ulster and Connaught is to take away the Isle of the Raghlins from the Scots and there to place 25 soldiers in the castell that one Sorly Boy now keeps, for this Raghlins is the greatest enemy that Ireland hath, it is the only succour of the Scots for thither they bring their spoils out of Ireland, and there keep them until they can well convey them into Scotland.*

2. *For when the Scots come out of Scotland, and make raids into Ireland there they lie lurking until by their espialles they may understand where to do the most mischief.*

3. *Therefore to prevent them if it please the Queen's Majesty to have there a pinnace or galley well furnished to scour the Scots galleys as well about the isles of Scotland as Olderfleet (Larne), the river of the Bann, Lough Foyle, Lough Swilly, Sheephaven and Esroy (Assaroe), so shall the said pinnace or galley do the Scots much mischief on their own coast and also keep them from fishing off the Bann and other places of the country where they have such commodity as they cannot well live without.*

The plan was sound enough but little could be done about it until the power of the McDonnells was weakened. Shane, relieved of pressure by the English forces and helped by an efficient intelligence service, succeeded in picking, in April, 1568, a moment when the clans were scattered getting their crops sown, and Sorley had only four hundred men holding the Route.

Shane first burned James McDonnell's new house at Red Bay. He then pursued the Scots whom he outnumbered by two to one,

---

[4] Gage account.

and cornered them up the coast at Glentaise, the glen that contains the westerly of the two rivers running into the sea at Ballycastle. James McDonnell, on seeing Sorley's signal, fires and the smoke from his burning mansion took a few men and jumped quickly into the first boat available, telling brother Alexander to gather the main forces and follow as quickly as possible. Strong south-westerly winds made it a slow passage for James but after weary hours of rowing to windward he succeeded in landing and making contact with Sorley. However, his force was not enough to effect the outcome of the battle which began at 5 a.m. next morning and ended in a victory for Shane with about five hundred dead on the Scottish side. James, severely wounded, and Sorley Boy were captured. Shane, who was an extremely timorous man, must have been scarcely able to believe his good fortune. The Lord of the Isles was his captive, begging to purchase his release for the price of all his lands in Ireland and Scotland and promising not to seek revenge.

The only part Rathlin played in this horrific battle was as a refuge for a few survivors and a stopping place for Alexander who arrived with nine galleys, a hundred men in each, a day too late. He was tempted to attack but knew that this meant death for the captives, so sent messages offering ransom, which Shane accepted for some of the less important. Sorley he kept and James in particular he refused to part with, saying that it was for Queen Elizabeth to decide his fate. The problem was solved by the death of that great leader; his obituary by the Four Masters described him as "a paragon of hospitality and prowess, a festive man of many troops, bountiful and munificent". Now James and Colla were dead and Sorley a prisoner, the command of the Route fell to Alexander.

Shane proceeded to capture Dunseverick and lay siege to Dunluce. To encourage the garrison to surrender, he told them that Sorley Boy would be starved until they gave in. Sorley stoutly told them not to mind him but after three days the gates were opened. Shane massacred the defenders to a man.

The fortunes of Shane had reached their high water. By having ransomed his Scottish prisoners, twenty or more in number, instead of handing them over to Dublin, he lost the favour of the Queen. Then he proceeded to make a raid on the English strong-hold of Newry. Defeats followed at the hands of Sydney and the Donegal O'Donnells. In his hour of extremity Shane released Sorley Boy and sought refuge with a force of McDonnells, com-manded by Alexander at Cushendall. This seemed the act of a madman; perhaps failure had deranged him. A great dinner was held to celebrate this apparent union of the clans but when both sides were heated with drink a brawl developed and Shane was stabbed to death. James was avenged and another phase in the Irish wars had come to an end.

As soon as Shane was dead, Elizabeth began to think again of her plan for an Ulster plantation. The Scots in the interim reoccupied much of their lost land. The Queen sent Captain Piers, Constable of Carrickfergus, to conclude a pact with the McDonnells, making over to them Rathlin and what land they could get from the O'Neills west of the Bann, on the understanding that they would evacuate all the Route and the Glens. Sorley appears to have honoured his part of the bargain for he kept out of Ireland for four years from 1567, being pleasantly occupied with family feuding in Kintyre.

During this truce period, a remarkable social event took place on Rathlin. In July 1569 there were fourteen days of feasting to celebrate the long planned wedding of Turlough Luineach O'Neill, Shane's cousin and now his successor as head of the clan, and Lady Agnes Campbell, widow of James McDonnell. She was described by Sydney as of high culture, speaking English, Gaelic and French with equal fluency, and Bagenal found her "a very nobell, weyse woman". Her marriage portion was three thousand Scottish Redshanks, the name then used for the hardy bare-footed Scottish mercenaries of the day. Elizabeth sent Captain Thornton to try to intercept the bride at sea but he missed making a capture. She arrived with her escort and never did a bridegroom make a better bargain. Sorley presided at the festivities and since the wedding of King Donn's daughter to Congall, King of Ireland, one thousand five hundred years earlier, such a party had not been seen on the island. The Castle was of considerable size at this time, able to accommodate two hundred and fifty people and in addition Sorley had been to the mainland to cut withies to repair the walls and build extra temporary shelters for the guests. The ceremony itself must have taken place on the site of the present parish church, the holiest ground on the island.

Much good material must have been provided for the gossip columns of the day by the happy couple. Argyll, the bride's brother, had sent Turlough "a steeple-crowned taffeta hat set with bugles"[5] to mark the occasion, which, however, the bridegroom refused to accept. Perhaps it would not fit on over his Irish glib, the long hair which could be shaken down over the eyes to hide the expression, or perhaps it spoiled the look of his beard for he was "meadowed from chin to his navel in an acre of black man hair".

Scots at this wedding would have worn a multi-coloured garment hanging in folds to the calf of the leg belted at the waist,

[5] Bugles—"tube shaped beads of glass usually black in colour."

and borne huge horn-hafted two-handed swords which hung from the shoulder. (The kilt was only introduced by a road contractor two hundred years later, as a more practical working garment.) Others would have carried polished longbows with twanging leather strings and quivers of arrows "which whizzed in flight". Turlough's escort of gallowglasses would have had battle axes on their shoulders and been bare headed with flowing curls, yellow shirts dyed with saffron with large sleeves, short tunics and rough fur cloaks.

Among the guests was Agnes' offspring, Fiona, usually known as Ineenduv, "the dark-haired daughter." She had been betrothed in the same deal to the O'Donnell of Donegal and in a few months time was to become the mother of Red Hugh, one of the leaders of the revolt at the end of the century. Ineenduv is one of the most famous figures in Ulster history with a streak of vicious purposefulness in her character which she did not inherit from her mother. The company mingled against a background of high prows of the galleys, bright with the banners of the chieftains, pulled up flank by flank around the semi-circle of Church Bay. There were the usual gleemen and story-tellers, jugglers and jesters, all the colourful trappings of a Celtic court, with highland games, bull baiting, horse racing and much drinking of usquebaugh. Truth to tell there was little romance in this match, marking an important dynastic event, between a widower, who was rarely sober after midday, and a middle-aged widow. Traditionally, Lady Agnes had a mansion built on Crocknascreidlin, a flat topped hill with traces of walls round its edge lying in the valley east of Church Bay, and had in her garden the finest apple trees in northern Ireland, but historically it seems unlikely that she spent very long on the island, for she went off to live with Turlough at Dunalong Castle on the Foyle. There she continued to intrigue with the Scottish and English courts on behalf of Angus, her son by James, for many a year.

CHAPTER 10

ESSEX, DRAKE AND A MASSACRE
1573-1575

"First for the quietness of Ulster . . . . take away the Isle of the Raghlins and there to place 25 soldiers in the castell that one Sorly Boy now keeps."—John Smith, 1566.

The truce arranged by Captain Piers in 1567 was brought to an end by the arrival in 1573 of Walter Devereux, Earl of Essex. Aged 34, he was a man of the highest honour, but at the same time a keen speculator, rash and autocratic. In his first dealings with the Irish he showed fairness, even generosity, but this was taken as a sign of weakness, an inevitable conclusion from the Irish point of view. His confidences were abused and he became embittered and harsh.

Captain Smyth's feeble attempt at administration had left the English Colony in the North in such a state of weakness and despair that Essex, a favourite of Queen Elizabeth's, had had little difficulty in persuading her to revoke Smyth's grant and turn it over to him. He was, from his own purse, to meet the expenses of the Plantation and of the armed forces necessary to start and safeguard it, in return for personal grants of large areas at Farney in Monaghan and Island Magee near Larne. Sydney had had four ships to enforce the truce, the Saker, the Hare a small barque, the Makeshift and the Post. Essex now had to provide his own, and solved the problem in an effective way, as we shall see.

Elizabeth appointed Essex Governor of Ulster which gave him much wider powers than his predecessor. The change might not have been much for the worse as far as the Scots were concerned had not Elizabeth also on no grounds whatsoever included Rathlin in the territories granted to Essex for plantation. Only six years before, the specific allocation of the island to Sorley in the agreement made by Captain Piers had been ratified by the Government. Sorley had apparently more than carried out his side of the bargain and the inclusion of the island in the grant had all the appearance of flagrant breach of faith.

Essex had learned enough, after some early reverses, to suggest to Elizabeth a pact with the Scots allowing them to re-occupy the Glynns, but this Elizabeth firmly, and as it turned out for herself most unfortunately, refused to do.

Possibly the wedding of Turlough to Lady Agnes three years before and rumours of a combination of the Donegal and Scottish clans to turn Ulster into a second Scotland were the reasons for her decision. Hatred of her cousin, Mary Queen of

Scots, and fear of her escape from imprisonment to seize the English throne were others.

By 1575 the Elizabethan Ulster plantation scheme had finally failed. In the case of Rathlin this was hardly surprising for any planter who undertook to work a holding there would have been committing a painful form of suicide. The Scots, outraged at the loss of what they regarded as their rightful property by ancient inheritance as well as by recent agreement with the Queen, would have been free to pick any time of the year, day or night, for a raid to wipe out new arrivals. There were no bidders for this part of the plantation territory but even those prospective planters who had been offered grants nearer Carrickfergus had long since lost heart and returned to England. For Essex, the already great difficulties of carrying out the scheme had been made much greater by the jealous enmity of Fitzwilliam, the Deputy, and the highly contradictory instructions issued at various times by Elizabeth. She wrote on the 22nd May, 1575 : —

"Right trusty and right well beloved Cousin, we greet you well. Whereas it may seem somewhat strange unto you, considering our late commandment given unto you to resume the government of Ulster lately given over by you, as also to proceed in your former enterprize, that we should now be of another opinion; we thought good, for your better satisfaction in this behalf, to discover unto you that in very deed, notwithstanding our said commandment, we had no meaning that you should proceed in the service, otherwise than we thought it necessary for a time, in respect of the danger you laid before us of a general revolt, to will you to resume the said government, and to proceed in the enterprize; which thing we would not have concealed from you, but that we doubted that the knowledge thereof might have quite discouraged you from proceeding therein; whereof there might have followed presently some dangerous issue, if, by a new resumption of the government of that province, the same should not have been prevented. But now having more just occasion of late to look more inwardly into our estate at home, and finding great cause for us to forbear the prosecution of your enterprize, not for that we have any cause at all to mislike the same, or to doubt of the likelihood of the good success thereof, either for that the matter was not well digested, or should not be by you well executed, if other respects did not most necessarily draw us from the proceeding therein; we thought it very convenient to dispatch this bearer secretly unto you, to give you notice thereof, to the end you may, upon knowledge of the same, direct the course of your proceedings in such sort, as the enterprize may yet be so given over as our honor may best be salved : the safety of such as depend on us in some good sort provided for : and that province

*left in that state, so far forth as shall lie in you, as there may
follow no such alteration as may disquiet the rest of that our
realm . . .
Given at our manor of St. James, the 22nd May, 1575."*

Wrapped up in admirable verbiage, the Queen had told
Essex that she had changed her mind. Her numerous changes of
policy on Ulster at this period depended as to whether she heeded
the advice of Burghley, Essex's close friend and adviser, or the
Earl of Leicester, an even closer friend of Essex's wife. Leicester's
object which he pursued with considerable success was to keep
Essex employed as far away from London as possible, busy but
achieving nothing which would advance him either financially or
in the favours of the Queen. Meanwhile he, Leicester, enjoyed the
charms of the white arms and red lips of the fair Lettice, Lady
Essex. He also had an eye on the hand of the Queen herself.

This was the summer of the revels at Leicester's great house
of Kenilworth where the Queen was richly entertained. Perhaps it
was of this period the schoolboy was thinking when he summarized
by saying "Elizabeth was known as the virgin Queen; as a Queen
she was a great success".

These amours of the Court of St. James may seem little
connected with a far distant stormbeaten island in the North
Channel on which neither Essex nor Leicester ever looked, but
the turn of mind of Essex that sunny Irish June was to have a
horrific effect on the fate of its inhabitants. Walter Devereux was
in a state of frustration bordering on despair, blaming everybody
except himself for his failures. He was deep in debt having in-
cautiously pawned his lands in far away England to the Queen
to raise funds for the Irish expedition which was costing far more
than he had calculated. Now it had failed.

Desperation

He had lost his reputation as a soldier and administrator and
was in the process of losing his wife to the man he hated. His
ambition of becoming Deputy in place of Fitzwilliam had finally
been blocked. The only escape from ruin lay in ensuring that he
obtained the Irish estates which he had been half promised. To
get them confirmed was a matter of regaining the Queen's favour,
something which seemed less and less likely with each failure
reported to her, each one exaggerated by his enemies at court.
Without the lands, the gay, the bold, the successful Essex, the
man who pranced where others plodded, would be reduced to
bankruptcy, to selling the family seat at Penshurst, to the status
of a landless man begging his bread. It was a horrifying prospect.
What sudden stroke could he devise to put himself back in the
royal favour?

At the end of June, Essex, desperate as ever, set off to try to carry out the Queen's final instructions, which were to leave Ulster as peaceful as possible and cover up the loss of face involved in the abandonment of the Plantation. He had already made a treaty with Turlough Luineach O'Neill which covered the western part and now marched north up to the Bann to show the flag in the east. Sorley Boy moved out to meet him to defend his inland territories with the main force which he had in Ulster at the time. In doing so he left on Rathlin a garrison of forty men which he knew to be inadequate to stand for long against a concentrated English attack, but it was a risk he had to take, for with his loosely disciplined islesmen he could not possibly keep on Rathlin all the time the three or four hundred men necessary to ensure its absolute safety when there were well-manned English ships on the coast. It caused him a little more worry than usual this time as he marched inland for there were more people on the island than at other times just then, harvest labour from Scotland, and he had had reports of three English ships in the area.

Sorley and Essex met inland near Coleraine, and in the skirmishing the honours were even. Essex no doubt had hoped to corner him and score a victory, but after the first day's fighting the Scots forces melted away into the forests, leaving only scouts to watch the English camp. Essex scoured the countryside for several days, then found that due to an onshore gale the ships ordered to come up the Bann with supplies to meet him had been unable to get over the bar. His force had used up their rations and he would have to call off the campaign. Another failure. With him, serving as a Captain, was John Norris, whose father had held the position of Groom of the Stole and been executed almost forty years before for alleged adultery with Anne Boleyn, Henry VIII's second wife. Norris knew the glitter of court life and the intrigues and ruthlessness which it covered, the sudden changes from oblivion to giddy success and back to disaster, which followed changes in the royal favour. He could sympathise with Essex. Together in the camp the night before the force was to withdraw they hatched a scheme for their joint advancement. The one place where they could be sure that the Scots would have to stand and fight, where sea power would give them complete superiority, was Rathlin. The ships having failed to land in the Bann, should be back by now at Carrickfergus. The capture of Rathlin would have little or no strategic value but a report on it could be made to look good.

Next day, Essex fell back southwards, doing his best to draw Sorley Boy after him and as far away from the coast as possible. His next letter to the Queen of the 22nd July from Dundalk contains a rosy account of the land operation and no reference to any further projected attacks on the Scots. Indeed, it mentions that Sorley Boy "doth send me in manner daily for peace". It was far better not to spoil the good news he soon hoped to have by any anticipation. If it did not come off, the less said about it the better. Nine days later, on the 31st July, by which time he had moved north to Newry, Essex had every reason to be in a high state of excitement in describing what had happened after he had left his camp near Coleraine. As he marched south with the main force, he "appointed Captain John Norris, Constable of Belfast, with three hundred footmen and eighty horse to return to Carrick-fergus to reinforce the garrison there", and gave him in addition some secret instructions. On arrival at Carrick, Norris summoned the captains of three frigates, which lay at anchor off the town, to a conference in De Courcy's great castle to decide whether wind and weather were suitable for a raid on "The Rathlins". The admiral, as the flagship was referred to in those days, was called the Falcon and commanded by a certain Francis Drake, whom Essex according to accounts which have been preserved, paid the un-princely sum of forty-two shillings a month for his command. [1] Champernowne, a famous privateer, was probably another of the captains. These frigates had been brought back by Drake from the West Indies and purchased by Essex[2] as they were of shallow draft and light construction so that they could overcome the disadvantages of the heavier ships and overtake the Scots' galleys as they fled into the shallowest creek or harbour, yet still "brooke a sea and carry 300 soldiers".

Norris' secret instructions, Essex wrote to the Queen, con-tained a letter to each of the three frigate captains. They greeted the idea of the raid with enthusiasm. No one knew better than Francis Drake how to run a combined operation, how to make a surprise landing at dawn, sack a town and capture its portable wealth, for he had only the year before succeeded after several failures in taking the Spanish treasure convoy on its way by mule across the Isthmus of Panama to Nombre de Dios. He was aged 30 and as yet a comparatively unknown figure who had taken part in one slaving expedition, which he clearly did not like for he never joined another, and he had established a reputation most unusual in those times for humanity to those who fell into his hands. He had earned too the adulation of his fellow townsmen. On his last return to Plymouth with holds full of Spanish gold he had arrived on a Sunday morning, and when the whisper went round the pews in church that Frankie Drake was back, the entire congre-

[1] Captain John Norris was paid 180s. per month. The smallness of Drake's wage may have been because he was a shareholder in the enterprise.

[2] B.M. Additional Mss. 48015 Folio 311 probably Jan., 1574, Essex to Privy Council.

gation left their seats in the middle of the sermon and dashed down
to the quayside to greet him. The treasure was looted from a
country with which England was nominally at peace, and Burghley,
the Queen's adviser, to minimise diplomatic difficulties with Philip
II of Spain, had sent Drake off to Ireland to assist Essex and lie
low for a couple of years. In the idle moments of his service in the
cold grey northern waters he must have dreamed and planned his
round-the-world voyage which was to begin in 1577.

The Fleet Sails for Rathlin

The frigate captains gathered all the boats from Carrickfergus
and towing the larger ones astern, set out together on the 20th
July. Outside the lough they found winds light and variable and
became separated on the sixty-mile passage up the coast which in
good conditions would have taken less than twelve hours. They
managed to rendez-vous forty-eight hours later on the morning of
the 22nd in Arkill Bay (which means in Irish anchorage), on the
east side of Rathlin, but were promptly spotted by the fighting men
of the island who took up arms to prepare to resist the landing.
However, in the words of Essex,

> "the captains and soldiers nothing regarding, did with
> valiant minds leap to land, and charged them so hotly, as they
> drave them to retire with speed, chasing them to a castle which
> they had of very great strength; and at the first charge was slain
> only one soldier. The Scots, being thus put into their fort, were
> presently environed with your Majesty's force; and thereupon the
> captains landed two pieces of great ordnance, which they brought
> with them for that purpose, and approached them to the castle,
> which they battered right upon the gate, where they made a
> breach."

Drake had a great reputation for doing things for himself. On
his round-the-world voyage two years later, he insisted from the
beginning that the "gentlemen must haul and draw with the
mariners," so it is quite likely that he personally saw to the landing
of the great culverin cannon in Church Bay, and hauled at the
tackles as they were dragged into position.

West of the fort the ground falls away for some hundred yards
to a boggy depression before rising in a heathery ridge running
parallel to the main wall. Near the top is a small area where the
ground is made firm by rock close under the sod, and it must have
been here that the guns were placed, protected by earthen banks
from the Scottish bowmen. From just above the guns Norris and
Drake could look down into the outer courtyard of the fort and
see how it was protected by a sea cliff in the north and a dry cliff
in the south, so that only in the west could it be attacked and there
a deep ditch had been dug in front of a strong wall of large stones.

Together they directed the gunners to concentrate on breaking down the gate. By the afternoon of the third day, the 25th July, the breach was made. Norris' men made their assault, fought their way over the drawbridge and through the gate but were not able to get past the temporary barricades of wood erected inside by the Scots from timber torn from the hutments inside. Two soldiers were killed and eight wounded but the loss of the Scots was much more serious for the Captain of the island was among the dead. Three of his men fell with him and six others were wounded, a severe loss for a garrison totalling only forty fighting men. The English fell back to their own lines, not displeased with the afternoon's work.

During the evening they succeeded in setting fire to the wooden ramparts, perhaps with red hot shot, and it became clear to the defenders that an assault which they would have little chance of beating off, would come in at dawn. In fact as soon as they had seen the siege guns brought up two days before they must have known that it would not be possible to hold out for long. There was no well in the castle. Two hundred and forty people were packed into an area about the size of a double tennis court and in the overcrowded conditions shortage of water and food was an additional worry for the commander. He had no guns with which to reply and no strength for a sortie to disable those of the enemy. It could be but a matter of time until the walls were breached. The only hope lay in delaying as much as possible on the chance of a gale scattering the ships, or Sorley creating a diversion.

During the short July night, there was little sleep for any of those inside the walls, where women and children outnumbered the fighting men by four to one. Two or three days before the bare-footed bairns had been delighted with the excitement of their temporary sojourn in the fort and had fingered the soldiers' great swords and bows, and fought mock battles with each other with wooden spears. Now terrified at the gunfire and the grim expressions of the garrison, they crouched whimpering in the arms of their fearful mothers. Other women bound up wounds or helped in scratching up soil and stones to repair the defences. A quarter of a mile to the west just out of bowshot could be seen the encircling watch fires of the English camp and to seaward in the half light the dark shape of a frigate at anchor with lookouts peering over her rail and men lying beside her guns ready to prevent any attempt to escape by sea. The other frigates could be glimpsed occasionally as they patrolled to the north and west of the island guarding against any reinforcement which might arrive from Scotland.

"If only Sorley would come; if only Sorley were here," they said to each other in the garrison, knowing in their hearts that even if he was, there was little or nothing he could do in face of the complete superiority of Drake's ships to his galleys.

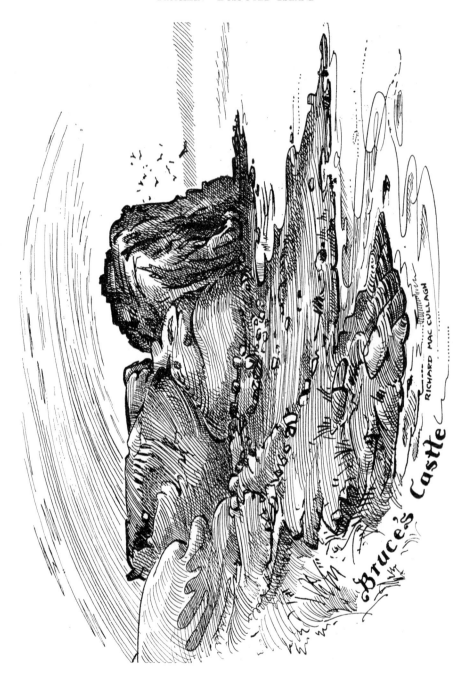

Bruce's Castle

RICHARD MAC CULLAGH

In the fort the bolder spirits were all for holding out to the last and shedding as much enemy blood as possible, others were for making a deal with the Sassenach. At last the Constable shouted over the walls that he wanted to parley. Norris would make no guarantee even for the safe return of an envoy and insisted that the Constable came alone, so this man, whose name is not recorded, slipped over the wall and walked off into the darkness watched by hundreds of anxious eyes. The bargaining was tough and lengthy. An hour later the Constable came back white-faced to announce that he had arranged a truce. The castle was to be handed over, the garrison to lay down its arms and they, with all the inmates, to be given a safe conduct back to Scotland. The weary defenders could scarcely believe such good news but leaving a few sentries on the walls snatched some rest in the short remaining period of darkness. In the cold 4 a.m. dawn, Norris came forward under a flag of truce and was heard to arrange with the Constable that all arms were to be piled at the gate, and the people were to come out in parties of ten at a time, with the garrison first. They were to march over towards the ships which he said were waiting in Church Bay, out of sight over the hills.

The Constable with his wife and child went with the first party accompanied by his one hostage, the son of Alexander Oge McDonnell of the Glynns. This lad was being held by Sorley to ensure his father's good behaviour; being a hostage was usually a matter of pleasurable dalliance but he must have wished many times in the last few days that someone else had been sent in his place. The Constable's party were promptly led away separately; after that each little group as they passed over the hill top and out of sight of their comrades were, without warning, surrounded and silently butchered, man, woman and child, by the English soldiers. A few of the younger women were kept, and a few of the men as labourers, for a few days. The pitiful bodies were stripped of their garments and articles of value by the soldiers, for whom pay day was never much of a certainty. Some of the bodies were thrown into the sea and others piled into a huge common grave dug by the captives at the point of the sword.[3] The moonfaced English boys fresh from the shires who comprised a good proportion of the land forces, must have looked with feelings of revulsion at the slaughter carried out by older men hardened in the Spanish wars. Drake, we may be sure, found some urgent business to be attended to on his ship, while it was being carried out, for he never in his career showed any taste for taking life wantonly.

A clammy silence fell over the whole fort which a few hours before had been the scene of such violent activity and emotion.

---

[3]Some years ago great quantities of human bones were found in a piece of boggy ground a few perches west of the castle—O'Laverty.

Later in the day the soldiers were told off in parties, a large one to garrison the fort and repair the defences, others to search every hiding place, every bothy, bush, thicket, cave or galley where more Scots might be hiding. The Rathlin residents were good at hiding, they had had quite a lot of practice, so it all took a long time. A line of men, three or four yards apart, was drawn up stretching from one cliff to the other across the width of the island to beat the ground from end to end. Boats keeping pace along the shore landed parties to peer into the sea caves, fifty or more of them, and haul out any inmates they could find there, to be stripped of their possessions and slaughtered. Other parties cut down the green corn and gathered up three hundred cattle, three thousand sheep and a hundred stud mares which they found in the pastures. The soldiers, little knowing when they would see meat again, gorged themselves on stolen beef and mutton.

The Aftermath

A few days later the ships withdrew leaving a garrison of eighty men in the fort. If Norris kept his secret bargain with the Constable, that pitiable man, his wife and child were taken away with him, to be released after a month in prison. It must have been hard for him to know where to go afterwards.

To divide a garrison against itself by offering favourable terms to those who would sell their comrades was not uncommon tactics in Ireland in those days. On Tory Island in 1608 Ffolliott, the Governor of Ballyshannon, granted a McSwiney, who came out to negotiate, his life on the condition that he yielded up the garrison with seven dead men in it, which McSwiney promptly did; the same tactics served at the island in Lough Veagh, County Donegal that year. The possibility of a secret deal was no doubt in Norris' mind when he insisted on the Constable coming out alone. That unfortunate man yielded to the most terrible temptation put before him to save the life of his wife, his child and himself. The alternatives were death for all in the fort plus a few English soldiers they would kill in the final assault, or death for everyone in the fort and life for himself and his family.

Essex's letter to the Queen describing and exulting in the victory appears in full in the Appendix; a second letter to Walsyngham the same day, adds the following postscript:

"I do now understand this day by a spy coming from Sorley Boy's camp, that upon my late journey made against him he then put most of his plate, most of his children and the children of most part of the gentlemen with him, and their wives, into the Raghlins, with all his pledges (hostages), which be all taken and executed, as the spy sayeth, and in all to the number of six hundred. Sorley then stood also upon the mainland of the Glynns and saw the

taking of the island and was like to run mad with sorrow, tearing and tormenting himself, saying that he then lost all that he ever had."

One can well imagine the anguish of the Scottish chieftains who had hurried back a long day's ride from Glenconkein at the first news of the attack, standing at Donananie Castle from where they could clearly see the Falcon and her consorts at anchor and cruising along the shore, hear the gunfire, later boats plying to and fro and landing parties to search the caves, the smoke and the fires and perhaps even little groups of fugitives dashing across the green uplands trying to find refuge. There would be a terrible feeling of impotence, for probably their own galleys lay at their feet in Port Brittas but to venture across the waters, and try to give help or provide rescue parties would have brought them under the guns of the English frigates which had already accounted for eleven ashore and afloat during the operation. Even if Sorley dashed off and attacked Carrickfergus he would never draw off the enemy forces in time. He was too wise an old fox to jump into some impromptu suicidal action and bided his time for a satisfactory revenge.

There are a number of curious features about the reports of this raid. It is clear why Essex planned it and carried it out, and why he had to do so, although its military value was almost nil. But as to the number killed and their standing in the clan there were grave doubts. If Sorley had wanted to put his women, children, best animals and treasure into safety, the place to move them to would have been not Rathlin but Kintyre, only an extra three hours once on shipboard. On Rathlin they were in much greater danger than on the mainland in view of the English supremacy at sea. Even if he had for some exceptional reason wanted to leave the families of the leading members of the clan on Rathlin for a short while, such an experienced warrior would have brought over an adequate garrison from Scotland for their protection. We know that none of Sorley's sons or his wife were on the island. In the family tree two daughters are unaccounted for, but if one of them had been slain in the raid, Essex could hardly have resisted telling the Queen. If the families of his leading chieftains had been there, why were some not mentioned by name in Essex's report, or indeed why, if taken, were they not held as hostages for ransom instead of being butchered. Of the "plate" mentioned as being sent to the island in the letter to Walsyngham there is no other mention as to capture or disposal.

Whatever the real numbers slain may have been, Essex would surely have added a hundred or so for good measure. Miskimmin in his "History of Carrickfergus" gives the number as two hundred and forty, a much more likely figure; it was probably based on reports brought back after the raid by sailors who had no particular reason to twist the total. Then Essex mentions hostages or pledges in the plural in his letter to Walsyngham, but only names one in the report to the Queen. The bit about Sorley "running mad" as he watched, vivid though it is, may have been pure embroidery.

The indications are that his account was greatly exaggerated as regards the importance and numbers of those slain and the value of goods taken. It is more probable that on the island was just the garrison and their families, say a hundred to a hundred and fifty, a few resident crofters and a body of harvest labourers in transit. There are references in correspondence of the time to the movement of such people backwards and forwards depending on the time the crop ripened on each side of the water. The amount of livestock reported taken in the raid is no larger than one would normally expect the island to carry; nowadays it has about a thousand acres of arable land and on a recent count nearly 800 head of cattle.

In putting together the story so many of the pieces of the jigsaw puzzle are missing that one cannot be positive, but the interpretation I have suggested fits the known facts.

The Queen, who took an intense personal interest in the island, replied to Essex as follows:

By your letters of 31st July you advise us of the taking of the island of the Raughlins, the common receipt and harbour of such Scots as to do infest that realm of Ireland; and that your proceeding against Sarleboy has taken happy success. Give the young gentleman John Norrice, the executioner of your well devised enterprise, to understand that we will not be unmindful of his good services. You shall receive our resolution touching the keeping of the Raughlins at Sir Henry Sidney's hands, who means within eight days after the date hereof to be at the sea side, there to embark, whom after his arrival and acceptation of the charge of government there, we have appointed immediately to repair into the North, there to confer with you for the stay of that Porvince.

In the meantime we think it very convenient, according to your own opinion and allowance, that there be continued a ward of thirty soldiers in the fort lately taken in the said island; and if you shall see any necessary continuance for the entertaining of the frigates until you shall confer with our said servant and counsellor Henry Sidney, we can be content to allow thereof."

Dudley Castle, 12 August, 1575, 17 Eliz.

The Queen was as delighted as Essex had intended her to be and added mincingly in her own hand,

If lines could value life; or thanks could answer praise, I should esteem my pen's labour the best employed time that many years has lent me . . . Deem therefore, cousin mine, that the search of your honour, with the deanger of your breath, hath not been bestowed on so ungrateful a prince that will not both consider the one and reward the other. You most loving cousin and sovereign E.R."

The ethics of the massacre caused no comment. In the Irish wars prisoners of low degree were almost invariably butchered. Life was cheap. When a force of Irish kerne were used by Henry VIII in France their elemental methods of warfare had brought forth indignant protests from the French king. Even allowing for the lower than average standards of military conduct in Ireland, one would have expected better from Essex had he been in any state of mind short of desperation. The cold ferocity of this deed has made it stand out as the blackest event in the annals of the century.

As soon as the main force was gone the Scots began to slip over to the island. They landed at first with muffled oars in the darkness to search for their dead and take their revenge. They found one adult survivor only, a woman named McCurdy who had managed to remain hidden in a cave when the others hiding in it were dragged forth.[4] The McCurdy family is still on the island. One child is also supposed to have survived according to a story told on the island. A small boy, he was hiding under a wooden bench gnawing a raw "crubeen" or pig's trotter when spotted by an English soldier. The soldier was so horrified at seeing a child reduced to such straits that he managed to have his life spared and the boy grew up to live on the island.

Rebuilding the Castle

Norris sent from Carrickfergus lime, bricks, timber and a squad of workmen to repair the castle to a total cost, as reported to the Privy Council, of £37. The civilian victuallers who competed to supply the army and other stations refused to take the risk of visiting the Rathlin garrison, so Norris bought a hoy and a dinghy for unloading her, especially for this service at a cost of a further £60.

As the autumn approached, every night or two a sentry on the walls would fall back choking, with a Scottish arrow through his throat; even in daylight foraging parties were liable to be ambushed and wiped out unless twenty strong at least. Any English soldier who straggled was never seen again. After a while

4 Hill P., 186.

the soldiers did not dare to leave the walls of the fort and had to rely solely on food and water coming in by sea. The ravens and crows from the cliffs of Rathlin had many a grisly feast during those weeks.

Sorley produced in a very short time a spectacular riposte. Most of the troops who had taken part in the Rathlin island expedition had returned to Carrickfergus. On the 6th September, just six weeks later, Sorley Boy at the head of a force mainly composed of the fathers, brothers and sons of the island victims, led an attack of the most extraordinary daring. For the first time in the history of Ireland a strong English garrison was assaulted in its own fortress. Animated with intense fury at the thought of the butchery, the Scotsmen hurled themselves against the walls of Carrickfergus. The garrison bravely sortied to meet the attack but broke before the Scottish charge. Captain Baker and some hundred soldiers who had taken part in the raid were killed, and Sorley managed to carry off all the cattle which the town possessed.

The events which followed are a testimonial to the personality of Sir Henry Sydney, back in Ireland for the fourth time, and of the calming influence his reputation for fair play was able to bring to bear on events of the time. Taking over from Fitzwilliam as Deputy, he landed on September 22nd with his son Philip at Skerries to avoid the plague then raging in Dublin. Recognising the terrible consequences which could follow from the massacre, he set off northwards with the absurdly small force of six hundred men and reached the Glynns early in October.

At this point there seems to have been some poor staff work for Drake and his frigates were paid off, leaving no naval forces in the area, but advice of this move was not sent to Norris who remained responsible for the island garrison. The Scots, in contrast, learned about the departure of the escorts at once and the hoy on her next victualling trip to Rathlin was taken and burned. We learn of this through correspondence in which Norris wrote pointing out the circumstances and asking to be relieved of the cost of the loss of the hoy.[5]

Sorley, who could probably have crushed Sydney's little force without difficulty, was soothed into a calmer frame of mind by the news of his approach and agreed to meet him. Sydney seemed to be entirely sensible to the old man's grievance and at once withdrew the garrison on Rathlin. He produced to the Queen the somewhat feeble excuse that the castle had no well; this seemed, however, good enough to please her.

"The Fort of the Raghlins I cawsed to be abandoned," said he, *"for that I saw little purpose for the present to keep it; so small*

[5] CSP 63/54/43.

commodite at so great a charge to her majestie, being a place so difficult to be victualled; they within the Piece having no fresh water to relieve them, which, with greate danger to themselves, they are forced to fetch abroade. The soldiers I cawsed to be brought hence, being forty in number; they confessed that in this small tyme of their continuance there, they were driven to kill their horses and eat them, and to feed on theim, and young colts' flesh, one moneth before they came away, soch extremities they endured for victuals; it is a Piece veri easy to be wonne at any tyme, but very chardgious and hard to be held".

Essex was made Earl Marshal of Ireland for life, not just "at the Queen's pleasure" as was usual, and his grants of land confirmed. Ironically, he did not live to enjoy his office, for he had only just been appointed when he fell ill. He died on September 22nd the following year, of dysentery; a death of three weeks' agony during which he displayed the greatest piety. Some said he had been poisoned, but the balance of evidence favours natural causes. Leicester promptly abandoned his efforts to become Consort to the Queen and much to her fury married Essex's widow.

Norris, although described by the Queen as "the young gentleman," was older than Essex and at thirty-nine not all that youthful by the standards of the times, when boys of fifteen went to the wars. He must have had what might be termed a special relationship with the Queen as a result of his father's fatal affection for her short-lived mother. His career is another example of how many of the main figures in the Ulster wars and Rathlin raids were, when not campaigning, familiar with the colourful panoply of court life. Others were Captain Piers who had saved Queen Elizabeth when her life was in danger before her accession, Crofts the Deputy, who finished his days as Comptroller of the Royal household, Essex himself, Sydney and Sussex. Norris was knighted and appointed to the lucrative post of President of Munster for his part in the raid.

Sydney's presence maintained the peace apart from some minor raiding until 1578, when he left Ireland forever, a very much poorer man, by his own account, than he had come.

CHAPTER 11

THE McDONNELLS WIN RATHLIN AT LAST
1575-1605

"The island of Raghlens is very barren, full of heath and rocks and there is not any woods in it at all".

John Price to Walsyngham, 1st May, 1586.

As a result of Sydney's peacekeeping arrangements Rathlin remained in Scottish hands but the Queen grew suspicious and in January 1580 the coastal patrol was renewed. Her ships, Handmaid and Achates, were commissioned to stop and seize all Scottish ships except those chartered by merchants of corporate towns. A new turn of events had showed with the arrival of a certain Captain Crawford in support of Sorley, who, with the apparent approval of Argyll, set about the fortification of Rathlin. It was significant that he appeared to be doing this in the name of Scottish King James VI, although Edinburgh denied any knowledge of the matter. An unusual feature was that Crawford's force was described as being made up of "inland Scots", that is men from the mainland, not from the islands. The King was then but fourteen years old and Sir Nicholas White reported that Tirlough Luineach was arranging to take the young Scottish king as a foster son. This sounded most unlikely but there were other indications that a serious attempt was being made to combine the kingdoms of Scotland and Ulster. Agnes O'Neill, née Campbell, Turlough's wife, had been to Stirling to negotiate with the Scottish government.

Rathlin did not again figure in the news until 1585 when Sir John Perrot, one of the most active of Irish Deputies, began yet another raid north against the Scots. Said to be an illegitimate son of Henry VIII, he was respected and liked by the Irish for his fairness but he had been criticised by Elizabeth for inaction and perhaps this move north was mainly an effort at self justification. While the land party was slowly marching north the Handmaid and Achates were sent ahead with the idea of intercepting any attempt on the part of the Scots to escape by sea. Under the direction of Captain Thornton, they captured six Scots galleys on passage, but missed others in the Foyle by a couple of hours only. Thornton, who was Commander of the Irish Galley and in effect Admiral of the Irish Sea for something like thirty one years, must have been one of the most interesting characters of the century. He first appears arrested for piracy in the John of London in 1561 but somehow succeeded in saving his neck and joining the royal service, a case of poacher turned gamekeeper! How one would like to have watched him beating through Rathlin Sound in his unwieldy war worn ship in the dusk of an autumn evening or dropping his huge wooden stocked anchor thankfully in the lee of the cliffs at Ballycastle during a summer gale. Perhaps instead, as some of us do these things today in yachts or small craft, it is he who is watching us. His log books are lost but despatches from a succession of land commanders have nothing but praise for him "as always ready at first call faithfully to prosecute any service committed to him." It is pleasant to be able to record that in that century of injustice and disorder, he got his reward and retired as Sir John Thornton to a royal pension, large grants of land near Limerick, and the post of Provost-Marshal of Munster, all "for his service at sea".

By their flags and gilded upperworks as well as by their numerous gunports, the royal ships were readily identifiable and embodied in themselves the image of the Crown. To add to this moral ascendancy was the fact that most of them were real war-ships heavily constructed and with much flatter decks than merchantmen of the period to facilitate the handling of guns. There is no record that any Spaniard, Scotsman, Irish rebel or pirate dared attack a royal ship in Irish waters during Elizabeth's reign.[1]

Perrot camped before Dunluce on the mainland ten miles west of Rathlin on September 15, 1584. He succeeded, with Thornton's help, in landing a culverin and two brass sakers on the rocks near the castle which he described as "the strongest piece in the realm". A culverin was a very big gun by Irish standards and weighed 4,500 lbs., firing a $17\frac{1}{2}$ lb. shot, and a saker about 2,000 lbs. with a 6 lb. ball. It must have required very calm weather and good seamanship to get them ashore on the flat rocks at the base of the cliffs and haul them into position for there is no port nearby. When Perrot called on the garrison to surrender, Randal McDonnell boldly answered that he would hold it to the last man for the King of Scotland. No McDonnell would have said that a few years earlier. Perrot started his bombardment and after two days the castle was taken but only after every man in the garrison had been killed. Among the booty was St. Columba's pectoral cross of gold, a thousand years old, probably the most prized possession of the McDonnell clan. This Jack Perrot dispatched with a facetious note to a lady friend in London. Its subsequent whereabouts is unknown.

Perrot then planned a follow-up attack on Rathlin, but like many an expedition to the island before and since, it had to be put off due to bad weather. The Deputy reported that this was because he was worried about not being able to get back rather

[1] Tom Glasgow, Jr., "The Irish Sword," Vol. VII, 1966.

than about good enough weather to get there. Many visitors to Rathlin know the feeling.

When the Deputy marched south he left large forces on the north coast, greater than had wintered there for many a year. Up to two thousand men had to be victualled by sea, the ships landing the stores on the beach at Ballycastle for lack of any better harbour. The commanders in their correspondence complained bitterly to Perrot of the conditions. The swell was often too heavy to allow the employment of boats and the supplies had to be floated in on long ropes on rafts guided by sailors wading up to their necks in the freezing winter seas. Of course many of the stores were lost or spoiled.

All winter the opposing forces glared at each other across the no man's land of Rathlin Sound.

The Raid on the Abbey

On the 1st January, 1585, Sir William Stanley, summoned from Munster in the south, marched his company from Bushmills to Ballycastle. There was a plan for him within the next two or three days to meet Henry Bagenal, his cousin, who was at that time lying at Glenarm, at a midway point so making a pincer movement to clear out any remaining Scots' forces from the coast. At Ballycastle he found Captain Carleill encamped at Bonemargy Abbey with forty seven men, and with him Captain Warren commanding a troop of cavalry. The horses were stabled in the Abbey nave which was thatch-roofed. This was not a matter of sacrilege, just practical soldiering. The horses had to be clipped for campaigning and their commander must have been delighted at the chance to get them under cover for the frosty nights. The Abbey was the burial ground of the McDonnells but the monks had been cleared out a good many years before on the Dissolution in the time of Henry VIII. It was then the only stone building, apart from the castles, for miles around and stood behind the sandhills about two hundred yards from the sea beside what is now the main road running east from Ballycastle. Today, in ruined condition, it suffers from missiles no more lethal than an occasional hooked golf ball. The ground around it is flat running down to the Margy river on the west.

During the evening Captain Bowens came in with his company and was allotted quarters at Donananie Castle, about a mile to the west. Sir William Stanley, tired after the day's march, turned in leaving Captain Carleill to take the first watch. What neither Captain knew was that the night before a strong party of Scots with several horses had rowed across the Sound from Rathlin and landed a few miles down the coast. They had avoided being seen by the English ships anchored off and by the woodkerne, the light armed Irish troops used by Perrot as scouts. An hour before midnight when the full moon was high in the sky the whistle of arrows was the first sign that the camp was under attack. At the first volley several of the guard were wounded. A further "camisado" of arrows followed, and then forward galloped horse-men carrying long staves tipped with bundles of burning tow. They thundered into the camp, and threw their incendiary sticks on to the roof of the Abbey which promptly caught fire. As Sir William awoke and turned out of his tent in his shirt, it must have been a weird scene; in the flickering light of the flames under the winter moon the whizz of arrows, the clash of sword on shield and the yells of the Scots mingled with the terrified squeals of the horses trapped in the Abbey and the shouts of the English officers rallying their men. Sir William set himself to organise the defenders but as he turned round to urge them on, was wounded in the back by an arrow. The Scots kept up the attack for nearly an hour and succeeded in killing three of the soldiers. Sir William managed to organise parties of musket men to return the fire, but while doing so was wounded again in the arm, the side and the thigh. The Scots' gidon or standard bearer was killed at the head of the attack and his comrades fought hard but unsuccessfully to recover his body. By the time the attack was beaten off twenty one Englishmen were wounded, in addition to the three dead. Seven horses had been burned to death in the abbey and with them most of the cavalry equipment. Next day Sir William had to get replacement lances from the barque Hare which was lying off in the bay. English morale fell in much greater proportion than the physical losses.

On the same night a few miles southward, another Scots' force had attacked the company which was coming up to meet Stanley, and Bagenal (according to Captain Lee) only saved his skin by a "precipitate" flight back to Carrickfergus. There were many adverse comments on his behaviour on that occasion. Sir William wrote his account from Donananie three days later when he was recovering from his wounds.[2]

Perhaps the aura of the abbey had cast a spell on him for he turned Roman Catholic a year or so later, and this stout warrior became a traitor, taking his whole company over to the Spanish side at Deventer in the Low Countries.

The raid on the camp was just the sort of attack which the Scots could launch in a highly effective fashion as long as they held Rathlin. They did not, however, always get the best of the winter's skirmishing. A few weeks later a party of fifty-two of them were ambushed by the English as a result of good intelligence

[2] C.S.P., Stanley to Bagenal.

while embarking for Rathlin, and every one of them slain, including Donald Ballagh, a captain who had played a great part in the successful attack on Carrickfergus nine years earlier.

Two days after the attack on the camp on the 4th January, twenty-four galleys "out of Kintyre" were seen passing Ballycastle. An impressive sight they must have been. "Our shipping here had sighted them but it was so calm that they could not bouge", as Sir William Stanley reported. Perhaps on this occasion discretion rather than lack of wind played some part in the decision for inaction. He calculated that there were two thousand five hundred men on board the galleys. Sorley was in command and his fleet duly landed at Cushendun. The Scots still had ample reserves.[3]

Henry Bagenal captures Rathlin

The assault Perrot had planned on Rathlin took place at the beginning of March, early in the season for combined operations. A formidable force commanded by Sir Henry Bagenal, including his nephew Ralph, Sir William Stanley, Captains Henshaw and Berkeley and Arthur Savage did a sweep through the Glynnes, and finding little Scotch opposition arrived at Ballycastle on the 9th. There, in Stanley's words, "*they concluded to take the opportunity to attempt the Rathlins having Captain Thornton and his shipping ready who afore our coming thither and after in the service behaved himself so sufficiently as we judge no man in this land could so well have discharged the place. With all this help he gave us he put himself in great adventure and took a Scottish galley which stood us in no little stead for the landing of our men on the Island where we found few people but great store of all sorts whereof we made as great spoil as we could.*"[4] The Scots did not attempt to hold the castle which was half ruined, for Crawford's attempt to rebuild must have been thwarted. They set light to their dwellings on the island, sent away their women folk and made a stand in the old fortress of Dunmore near the north end of the island. Some sharp fighting took place, in which Sorley Boy, aged eighty, took an active part. His nephew, Donald Gorm, was wounded. On the English side Sir William Stanley was again wounded, and young Ralph Bagenal distinguished himself, so doing something to recover the military reputation of the family.

The number of officers involved on the English side is explained by the fact that the force consisted mainly of the garrisons, with their commanders, of all the forts held by Perrot in

---

[3] Stanley to Bagenal.
[4] CSP 63/115/37.

the neighbourhood. It was the second visit to Rathlin by the Bagenals. Two brothers, Nicholas and Ralph, had first come to Ireland from Yorkshire in 1542 to avoid a charge of manslaughter. They received a pardon from Henry VIII and both were knighted. Ralph, captured in Cuffe's raid on Rathlin in 1551, became a member of the Privy Council and Nicholas, the Marshal of Ireland, each acquiring large estates. Sir Henry, Nicholas' son, who commanded the 1585 attack, succeeded his father as Marshal but was killed in 1598 at the defeat of the Yellow Ford. These were just the sort of swashbuckling adventurous careers open to men with ability and not too many scruples in Elizabethan Ireland.

The Scots had a number of galleys in readiness close by at Doonigiall and when the pressure of the English became too severe, made off to Kintyre. It must have been a well-planned withdrawal to avoid Thornton's ships. One might sum up the attack by saying, like the umpire on the Field Day, that both sides deserved great credit. The result was that the Scots had lost Rathlin for the third time in thirty years. On it the English captured between two and three hundred cows and some five hundred sheep with some corn and butter hidden in the ground. A garrison under Captain Henshaw with Arthur Savage as his lieutenant was left on the island. They must have been relieved to have as company Captain Thornton with forty men manning a barque and a pinnace.

There was considerable doubt as to whether to hold the island, *"My Lord Deputy is not fully resolved whether any garrison shall remain in the Rathlins"*, wrote Mr. Secretary Wallop to Walsyngham on 22nd March, *"but as far as I see he mindeth to revoke them and for my part unless Her Majesty would fortify there and keep a continual strong garrison in it I take it to small purpose to keep it. It is the same island that my Lordship took eleven or twelve years ago."*

Perrot was highly delighted with the capture and wrote to the Council in England that the Scots were driven out of the Route, and Ulster finally cleared of them. He was over-optimistic, and to add insult to injury, the Munster poet, Eugene McGrath, selected the Duke of Ormonde who had accompanied him, to be given the credit for the success of the campaign.

> "He took from Rathlin in the land of Alba
> After hard fought combats a prey of cattle.
> Thrice he set Glen Conkein on fire
> This wealthy tender-hearted chieftain,
> He left no herds round Lough Neagh.
> The seer so provident and bountiful".

The Scots might not have agreed about his kindliness, but perhaps his bountiful nature is shown in the open-handed way in which he distributed other people's cattle to his supporters, and his foresight in gathering his food supplies at Lough Neagh because the north was swept so bare.

In the autumn, the Scots attacked Dunluce. With some assistance from inside, eighty men landed in boats by night and were hauled up the walls. The garrison was quickly overwhelmed, and Peter Cary, the Constable, driven into one of the towers. He had been warned by Perrot to employ no Irish in the castle and so paid the penalty for breaking his instructions. After fighting to the last he was captured and hanged over the walls on one of the withies used in the assault. There was no quarter. Perrot was mortally upset at the loss of the castle and made an effort to have Sorley poisoned. The attempt was reported in a veiled reference in the official correspondence after it had failed.

Meanwhile there had been a division among the McDonnells. Angus, James' son, and Sorley's nephew, was trying to obtain a grant of the Glynns by interceding directly with Elizabeth at court, through the good offices of his mother, Agnes O'Neill, née Campbell, Tirlough's wife. Sorley was not to be outdone although the part of courtier or suppliant can hardly have come naturally to him. He was now over eighty, but as soon as he heard the news he summoned a clerk to write a letter promising eternal loyalty to the Queen if the grant could be given to him instead. He slipped across from Kintyre to Rathlin in a small boat and bribed one of Captain Henshaw's soldiers to get the letter conveyed to Perrot in Dublin.

Perhaps Elizabeth realised that with the Armada beginning to assemble in the ports of Spain, she would soon have more use for her ships than chasing Scotsmen. In May, 1585, she authorised a pact between the Scots and Perrot by which Angus and Sorley were given substantial grants, including the island. Sorley got Dunluce and the western part of the Route but they seem to have made some mutual rearrangement of the territories. The Queen was careful to include in the rent several casts of hawks from the Rathlin.

This episode marks the close of the long conflict between Elizabeth and the Ulster McDonnells. Sorley's wife had died about 1582, and nothing daunted the old man remarried the next year a daughter of Tirlough Luineach. In 1588 when the Armada at last came and was forced to flee round the west of Ireland Sorley benefited by acquiring a fortune in gold and jewellery, as well as three guns, salvaged from the Gerona which was wrecked near the Giant's Causeway. His men assisted a number of survivors from this and other wrecks to escape to Scotland but there is no reference to Rathlin in accounts of their adventures.

If only Sorley had hired himself an attractive young ammanuensis and spent his declining years writing his memoirs and having his portrait painted, many of the incidents in the preceding pages would have been recorded in a very different light. He died in 1590 at the age of eight-five in his beloved castle of Donananie and in control of Rathlin. The most picturesque figure in sixteenth century Ireland, he had an abundant fund of resource and courage. There is something which stirs the sympathy in thought of the old man, his long yellow locks turned white, as he fought one Deputy after another, losing many battles and yet never crushed, never seeking favour by means of false pretences, and finally enjoying for the last four years of his life the lands for which he had fought for half a century.

During the rebellion of Hugh O'Neill which occupied the remaining years of the century, Angus McDonnell was one of the very few chiefs to remain loyal to the Queen. Other Scots, however, joined the rebels and the threat of large reinforcements coming over from the islands was always present. In 1599 Captain James Carlisle, a specially employed government spy, recommended that two galleys "not pinnaces or barks" be stationed at Rathlin to prevent the Scots reinforcing Hugh O'Neill but the plan was not put into effect.

Sir Arthur Chichester seems to imply in a letter quoted in the next chapter that he had made a number of expeditions to the island during the O'Neill rebellion but there is no record elsewhere of any of them.

In 1603, within days of the end of Hugh O'Neill's rebellion, Elizabeth came to an end. She was not as much given to displaying her personal griefs as had been her sister, Mary, but if she had talked of a word to be found written on her heart when she died, it might well have been "Raughlin."

CHAPTER 12

IRISH OR SCOTTISH? THE LEGAL CASE
1605-1642 A.D.

"If it be of Scotland, we have run into great error, for in the time of the rebellion we have often wasted it, and destroyed the inhabitants by the sword and by the halter as we did the rebels of Ireland."—Sir Arthur Chichester

With the death of Queen Elizabeth and the end of the O'Neill rebellion in 1603 came the beginning of a Stuart monarchy in England. The Scots of Antrim found themselves in a much better position to court royal favours. Sorley's son Randal was knighted and given a grant of The Glynns. Sir Randal, however, soon found that the patent document did not include Rathlin. Being his father's son he gave the government officials no rest in his efforts to get the grant put right. In April, 1604, James I wrote to Sir George Carew, the Irish Deputy, requiring him to accept Sir Randal's surrender of the old grant and to have a new one prepared and to be careful to include the island of Rathlyns. Carew passed on the instructions to Sir John Davys, the Attorney-General for Ireland, adding that by reason of the sudden departure of the Lord Lieutenant (Mountjoy) the grant was drawn in haste and did not include the island of Raughlin, "always esteemed one of the seven tuoghs (territories) of the Glyns."

So in 1605 the island was formally and correctly made over to Sir Randal.

The Scottish government were still involved in efforts to reduce the isles to obedience. In 1615 Sir James McDonnell, who had been imprisoned in Edinburgh, escaped and raised once again the standards of revolt. He joined forces with Coll Kittach McDonnell who had been roaming the waters of the islands in piratical fashion for a considerable time, commanding a fleet which comprised a bark and several birlings manned by eighty men. Earlier that year Coll took an Irish fishing boat laden with oats and a Glasgow bark bound for Lough Foyle with salt, wine, beer and spirits, close off the north coast of Rathlin after considerable fighting and loss of life. Sir James joined Coll's forces on the island of Eigg, and they enjoyed success for a while. Their first object was to free Kintyre from seven years of oppressive rule by the Campbells and Coll made his base on Cara and Gigha, but Argyll's forces proved too strong for them. Cara was taken while Coll was away up the coast, and Sir James defeated on the mainland. Coll fled to Islay but Sir James came first to Rathlin. He only stayed there a few days in September, 1916, and then went on to the island of Orsay off the Rhinns of Islay to try and gather fresh forces, but further resistance proved useless, and when Argyll's fleet hove in sight a few days later Sir James and most of the leaders fled to Inistrahull and later the Irish mainland, abandoning their followers to their fate.

Randal had taken no part in the rebellion of his cousin but was not clear of trouble for in 1617 a legal action was commenced against him for the ownership of Rathlin by a Scotsman named Crawford of Lisnorris on the ground that Rathlin had been granted to his ancestor in the year 1500 by James IV of Scotland. Randal sought advice and it was pointed out that this action immediately raised the question as to what Kingdom, Ireland or Scotland, did Rathlin really belong? If to Scotland, then Crawford's claim appeared reasonable enough, but if to Ireland, James IV had clearly no right to grant it to any of his subjects under any circumstances.

Sir Arthur Chichester, who at this time was governor of Carrickfergus, readily gave his opinion on the matter when asked for help and in a letter written on March 10th, 1617, made the following points:

"The Bearer, Sir Randal McDonnel, is by the King's letter required to appear before him about the 6th April to answer a suit commenced by one George Crawford of Lochnorrise for the island of Raughlins, to which he pretends as a parcel of Scotland and of his inheritance, which to me seems a strange proposition. If it be of Scotland, we have run into great error, for in the time of the rebellion (of Hugh O'Neill) we have often wasted it, and destroyed the inhabitants by the sword and by the halter as we did the rebels of Ireland. So did Sir John Perrott in his time, of whom no complaint was made by any subject of Scotland. It has been taken and reputed for half a tuogh of the Glynns in the County Antrime, ever since it was a county, and was so found by inquisition taken by commission the first year of the King (James I), and is passed to Sir Randal McDonnell and his heirs by letters patent. The dismembering of it from the Crown of Ireland is a matter of State, and not to be mined as a private debate. I have declared my knowledge of it to the Lord Deputy, who will open it to the Lords at large. It lies not past three miles from the mainlands of Ireland, and 24 miles from Scotland. In the maps of Scotland I have not seen any mention made of it, and on all those of Ireland it is set down as a member of this County."

At the hearing said to have been in the royal presence Randal first began by an argument drawn from the situation of the island "because it lies within a league from the firm land of Ireland, seven leagues and more from the firm land of Scotland and not so near (as a league) to any of the isles that are of the Scottish dominion."

The importance of being snakeless

The next evidence produced for the defendant to show that Rathlin was a "parcel of Ireland" was drawn from the "nature of its soil which neither breeds nor nourishes any living thing venomous, but is as clear of them as Ireland, where the isles of the Scottish and of the English in the same sea, breed and nourish the snakes which was thought to be a proof that the isle Man was British, as appears by Giraldus."

This argument is curious and learned, if not very conclusive. Giraldus Cambrensis, or Gerald de Barry, who came with the first Norman invaders in 1170, referring to the question had written:

"*Man stretches midway between the Northern parts of Ireland and Britain. It was formerly a matter of great dispute to which of the two it belonged. The controversy was at length decided in the following manner: venomous reptiles were brought there on trial; they lived and as a matter of course the island was on this account unanimously adjudged to Britain.*"

Giraldus adds:

"*I am not astonished that there should be some natural property in the earth destructive to reptiles, as there is in other lands to certain birds and fishes; but what astounds me beyond measure is that this island is destructive to poisonous animals if introduced from other countries. In old writings on the saints of the land, we read that serpents were sometimes brought, for experiment's sake, in brazen pots, but as soon as the ship had reached the middle of the Irish sea, the animals were found dead. It is manifest, therefore, that either from the merits of the Scots (the ancient Irish), which is a common opinion through the world; or from some strange and unprecedented, but most benignant quality of the climate, or hidden virtue of the soil, no poisonous animals can live there.*"

The Drumceat Declaration

Further to assist his case Sir Randal obtained the services of a distinguished Irish archivist of his time, Peregrine or Cucogry O'Duigenan, a member of the family who had compiled the Annals of Kilronan. O'Duigenan had also assisted the O'Clerys in preparing the great historical record known as the Annals of the Four Masters. Sir Randal brought him to Dunluce where he suggested the use in evidence of the judgment of Columbanus in the great Dalriadic controversy of 575. This is preserved in the ancient Irish manuscript known as the Leabhar na Uidhre. In the sixth century there had been an argument to the point of war between the colonists of the Scottish portion of Dalriada and the parent community in Ireland as to whether the Scottish side owed dues or military service to the High King of Ireland. To discuss it a conference was held at Drumceat near Limavady and St. Columba himself presided although the judgment was actually given by his younger colleague, Columbanus. The decision was simple, that the Irish Dalriada "including the island of Rathlin" was to be considered Irish ground and to continue under the dominion of the Irish king while Scottish Dalriada was from that day to remain allied but independent, free from all future tributes or services to the mother country. It was an early case of a colony's complaints being settled by negotiation.

Sir Randal visited London and Dublin in his searches for historical record. The marriage between John Mor McDonnell and Margaret Bysset, mentioned in Chapter 5 as giving the ownership of Rathlin to the McDonnells, was quoted in support of the argument that Rathlin was Irish territory. The granting by King John of the island to Alan of Galloway was also quoted, as well as the Norman Earls of Ulster's overlordship of the island, and the exclusion of Rathlin from the settlement, after the battle of Largs, for the subdivision of the Hebrides as being Irish territory.

Randal's researches in Dublin show up in a letter from Oliver St. John, the Irish Deputy, to Sir George Carew:

"Concerning of Rathlin of the records here, what he could discover Sir Randal carried with him. The Bishop's records are utterly lost by the mutiny of former times. I found a Registrar here who has executed the office under the last four Bishops. He affirms that the people of the island of Rathlyn, always with readiness, appeared upon summons in the Bishop's Court of Connor, underwent their censures, paid their portion according to the statute towards the maintenance of the schoolmaster and neither the people nor anyone else ever heard so much as of a claim being made by the Bishop of the Isles. The Justices of Assize and of the Peace always called them to their assemblies without gain saying, and they have ever felt the hand of justice both by the civil magistrate and marshal and it is close joined to the land of Ireland and therefore are possessioned continual without interruption unless other proof be made to the contrary which I can hardly believe it can be. Besides there is one Donell O'Murrey, yet living, that was Bishop of Connor in the time of popery; he affirms that in those times he ever recovered twelve shillings yearly of procuration due on to him out of the island of Rathlin".

Sir Randal's arguments were lengthy and complicated, and finished up by stating that he and his elder brother, Sir James of Dunluce, had frequently been in Scotland and visited at the Scottish court before the king was called to occupy the throne of England but they had never heard any challenge or pretence of right made by anyone to the island of Rathlin saving except the complaint presented by Crawford at the time of the king's last visit to the north.

The Case for Scotland

Crawford's case began with quotations from Solinus, the Roman geographer, whose description of the habits of the dwellers in the Hebudae was mentioned in Chapter 2. "All cosmographers," argued Crawford, "account the Hebrides or Aemonae Insulae belonging to Scotland, like as all of them consider Raughlin to be one of the same." Cosmographers who took the same general line as Solinus were Ptolemy, Marcianus and Stephanus. However, the inclusion of such ancient evidence, based on the inaccurate surveys of fourteen hundred years earlier, showed the weakness, as regards historical evidence, of Crawford's case.

He next endeavoured to sustain his claim on the authority of a grant of several lands, including the island, made by James IV to Adam Rede in the year 1500. This was following the surrender of the island kingdom by John, Lord of the Isles, in 1493. Rathlin had not been held by the deposed Lord but by Alexander, (the father of James, Lord of the Isles, and of Sorley), a chieftain representing a different branch of the McDonnells and owning the island in virtue of his descent from Margery Bysset, to whom it belonged, as parcel of her estate of the Glynns. As Alexander's family, however, was involved in the struggle and fall of the island kingdom his Scottish lands were forfeit, and in this forfeiture Rathlin was for a time included, although it was in reality a part of his Irish, and not his Scottish, property. Adam Rede was one of James IV's most active servitors in the work of suppressing the Kingdom of the Isles; and Rede's descendants kept up a nominal claim, at least as owners, for a hundred years, although the McDonnells of Antrim and occasionally the McDonnells of Kintyre were the virtual possessors. Adam Rede died in 1537 and his son Bernard procured the regular document of seizin, but does not appear to have had actual possession of the island. Bernard died about the year 1571 and his son Adam appears to have held Rathlin by no firmer grasp than his father and grandfather. He died in 1575 leaving four daughters.

Henry Stewart of Barskymmen who had married the eldest daughter established his wife's title to a share and claimed Rathlin in about 1585 from Angus McDonnell of Kintyre, the son of James of the Isles, who is mentioned as then holding it as swordland. It seems probable that the Captain Crawford mentioned in the last chapter as assisting with the fortifications was really there to stake this claim. In answer to Stewart's legal manoeuvres, Randal of Dunluce, Sorley's son, seized and held the island. So matters rested for twenty years. In 1605 Margaret and Jane, daughters of Adam Rede of Barskymmen, and their children, Hugh Wallace and John Spottiswoode, were regularly served as joint-heirs in the lands of "Ranchnie." Suddenly the several claimants were made aware for the first time that the Seventh Earl of Argyll had secretly obtained a grant of "the non-entry of the island." Henry Stewart made some arrangement with Argyll and in 1606 purchased out the interest of his wife's sisters. He then disposed of his rights whatever they might have been, to his nephew, George Crawford, and it was the latter's petition to the King in 1617 for possession, describing himself as having "the best right and title to the same," which started the case in the English courts.

The Sheriffdom of Tarbet

The Laird of Lisnorris appears to have attached much importance to the fact that Rathlin was reckoned in Scottish authorities as part of the Sheriffdom of Tarbet in Cantire, and that the Sheriff of Tarbet had made payment of its rents into the Exchequer of Scotland. Among the Carew MSS., there is a note in the handwriting of Sir George Carew which contains the following significant reference to this point:

> "*Whereas it is alleged that the Rathlins belong to the jurisdiction of the Sheriffdom of Tarbar it is to be understood that the South Isles of Scotland were assigned to that jurisdiction; but not before the year 1503. For at that time James IV enacted in the 6th parliament cap. 59 'for that there is a great abusion in the North and South isles for lack of justices and Sheriffs, and therefore the people are almost gone wild—it is ordained that there should be a Sheriff made for the South Isles, and to have his place in the Tarbar of Loch Kilkeran'. So that this new institution of the Sheriffdom of Tarbar cannot prejudice the right of the Crown of England to the Rathlin which, since the conquest of Ulster, was annexed to the County of Antrim, both for temporal and spiritual jurisdiction*".

The Laird of Lisnorris ridiculed the idea that Rathlin could be considered as part and parcel of Irish territory.

> "*For whereas,*" it was argued, "*they would have this island comprehended under the Glennes lying in the continent of Ireland, as it is against sense to make an island, four or five miles from any land, to be a part of the Glennes in the main, which designeth no shire, county or place of one jurisdiction but which (Glennes) are hills, with valleys between them bounded with woods; so doth it appear likewise in the grant made of old by the Kings of England that Raughlin hath ever been granted as*

several territory by itself, and not comprehended under the Glennes."

Snakes again

Finally Crawford attempted to refute Sir Randal's argument based on the absence of snakes on Rathlin, by pointing out that a number of the Scottish islands enjoyed the same immunity.

This line was in turn defeated by Sir Randal pointing out that the extension of the immunity to the Scottish islands simply derived from missionary activities by Irish monks. It is said even today that snakes and toads, numerous on Islay, do not live on such smaller islands as have Columban chapels on them, like Nave Island off Islay and Iona.[1]

The verdict

Crawford lost his case.   Had he been a more successful courtier Randal's arguments might have been disregarded and the verdict gone the other way.   Rathlin might now be in the County of Argyll and benefitting from the care of the Highlands and Islands Development Board.   James I reinforced the favourable decision by making a baron out of Randal who was a man of many parts and clearly popular at court. He had married Alice, a daughter of Hugh O'Neill from whom he must have learnt some of the arts of diplomacy.

Perhaps the main interest in the proceedings lies in the historical details and references which were dug up by the two parties in putsuit of their claims.

Crawford had picked a good time for his lawsuit for it was in the sixteenth century more than at any other time that Rathlin was regarded as Scottish soil. Since then the island has been looked upon firmly as part of Irish territory.

In that stormy century no one had much time to worry about church affairs on the island but in theory at least on the Dissolution of the Monasteries by Henry VIII the tithes of the Raghlins were transferred from the Abbey of Bangor to one Rice Aphugh; later from him to John Thomas Hibbots and in 1605 to Sir James Hamilton.[2] From him the tithes were to pass to the McDonnells, as they became in the years that followed, Earls of Antrim. This was a process which made them highly respectable

---

[1] Most of the details in this Chapter are obtained from an article by the Rev. G. Hill, the author of "The McDonnells of Antrim," which appeared in the Coleraine Chronicle, but he does not there quote any of his sources, other than those mentioned in the above text.

[2] Reeves.

but before they settled down to that dullness which so often follows joining the Establishment there was more bloodshed on Rathlin.

Sloat na Calliagh

CHAPTER 13

THE CAMPBELL MASSACRE, AND RECOVERY
1642-1746 A.D.

"The most disgraceful outrage of which even the mean vindictive spirit of Argyll and his bloody associates are capable".

Sir James Turner, 1646.

Shortly after the lawsuit, Randal McDonnell was made a baron as Lord Dunluce, and later became the Earl of Antrim. Meanwhile the plantation of Ulster proceeded apace. Grants of land were made to settlers from England and Scotland based on huge confiscations from the Irish occupants. The O'Neill and Donegal O'Donnell chiefs, fearing arrest and execution, had fled the country, leaving their luckless followers to endure the penalties of military defeat. Feelings ran high and in 1639 began a great rising in which many thousands of people were killed on both sides. In the spring of 1642 King Charles I of England, in desperation, made an agreement with the Scots to raise an army to help quell the rebellion. Archibald, Eighth Earl of Argyll, was appointed commander and took the opportunity to pay off old scores with his traditional enemy—Clan Donnell. Nicknamed Grumach or "Grim", he had a squint and an appropriately sinister expression. Part of the deal was that the Earl himself was to be made Governor of Rathlin. The island had little or no strategic value in this purely land campaign and Argyll's reason for seeking the Governorship can only have been clan and religious hatred. On the pretext of securing the lines of communication for his army, he sent his cousin, Sir Duncan Campbell of Auckenbreck, to land there with sixteen hundred troops, their one aim to kill as many McDonnells as quickly as possible. The fighting took place in a hollow in the centre of the island known as Lag-na-vista-vor, "the field of the great battle". The McDonnell forces were no more than two or three hundred strong and the result a foregone conclusion. Above it is Crock-na-screedlin, "the hill of screaming", the spot from which the women watched the battle and keened as their menfolk were cut down. It was the first time that a battle in the name of religion had been fought on the island, and the massacre was the more thorough for that. The Presbyterian Scots fighting in the name of the Covenant, which many of them had signed in blood four years before, proceeded to put the entire population to the sword. Many women and children were thrown over the cliffs in a gully since known as Sloak-na-calliagh near the highest point of the south end. This is a dark sinister funnel in black cliffs where there are rocks at the bottom of the fall at low water, covered by the flood tide. The Campbells picked it with professional skill.

The fact that a few stories are still told on the island about the massacre indicates that it was not quite one-hundred-per-cent successful. One tale is of a young woman, whose husband had been slain in the battle, being "rescued" by a Campbell clansman who took a fancy to her and carried her to Islay as his wife. Another one is of an older woman who saved herself by quick thinking when she was ordered to take her clothes off before being thrown over. "If you were a gentleman you would turn round while I undress", she gibed at a soldier who was watching. As soon as he did so, she seized him and carried him with her over the cliff; he was killed, but she managed to fall on some bodies and survive. Returning to the island twenty years later she found her son, whom she had assumed to be dead, inhabiting the old family farm. Another islander escaped in his curragh to one of the caves whose mouth is hidden on the north side and hid there for months, living on shellfish: "when he came out he was only able to squeak like a seagull". A hoard of coins dating from 1533-1641, found in 1931 by Mr. William Curry of Rathlin, doubtless belonged to some pathetic islander who did not escape.

Apart from these few survivors the Campbells did a thorough job, and up until fairly recent times the name of Campbell was so hated on the island that no one of that name dared to set foot on it. Now they have become well established there, one of the more recent arrivals being my godson Rory, of Peter Port beside the church.

Island massacres were something of a specialty of the 18th century Campbell clan. In 1647, under the same commander, they raided Islay, and having captured by treachery eighty-year-old Coll Kittach, the ally of James in the 1615 rising, they proceeded to hang him with devilish irony from the mast of his own galley set across a cleft in the rock. On the same expedition they went on to Mull and murdered most of the population in spite of the fact that they offered no resistance. As a postscript the head of the Clan MacLean was forced to hand over "fourteen very prettie Irishmen" who were in his service, on the threat of the death of his heir whom Argyll held captive. The Irishmen were promptly hanged. Such were the Campbell standards of the times.

The beginning of better times

After 1642 the story of Rathlin mercifully becomes less blood-soaked, and many of the incidents are of domestic interest only, less dramatic to write of but pleasanter to live in.

The Earl of Antrim forfeited his estates including the island as a result of his part in the Rising. For a while they fell to Argyll, later to a Dr. Ralph King to whom they were granted by the Cromwellian party.[1] But the Earl regained them in 1662 at the time of the Restoration of the Stuart monarchy. The island must have become gradually repopulated and at least three of the names which appear in the Hearth Rolls of the late seventeenth century, McCurdy, Black and McCuaig are still common on the island today. There are, however, no McDonnells on the island now although they were represented in the nineteenth century.

The first named tombstone in the churchyard is that of a fugitive, this time from the Montrose rebellion of 1646. James Boyd, fourth son of the Bishop of Lismore, fled from home and was "excommunicated" for his part in that brave, brilliant campaign. It seems a curious fate for a Protestant but that is what the records say.[2] He died an exile on Rathlin in 1665.

There must have been plenty of beef reared, for in June, 1689 a fleet commanded by Captain George Rooke in H.M. Frigate Deptford came to anchor in Church Bay and took in a hundred head of cattle. These were intended for the beseiged garrison in Derry. The captain was the same Rooke who was later to capture a Spanish treasure fleet in Lisbon and storm Gibraltar, but in his attempt to relieve Derry he showed little signs of the dash he was later to develop. He reached the Foyle on the 11th June but starving Derry was not relieved for another six weeks. The cattle

[1] O'Laverty.
[2] Law.

were probably what we would call today West Highlands, of which there was a half-wild herd on the island in the walled enclosure in Kilpatrick up until about 1890. When a round-up was due most of the population used to take the day off and make an occasion of it, and the animals had to be shot or lassoed in the Wild West style. The only relic of them today is a fine bull's head mounted in the Manor House.

Piracy remained widespread and thirty years later in the reign of Queen Anne a French privateer used Church Bay as a base and maintained a look-out for shipping from a high point on the island. A watch of another sort was kept in the townland of Kilpatrick from "The Look-Out Stone", on which are etched crude drawings of sailing ships. Near here in a natural amphitheatre Roman Catholic services used to be held in the open air secretly for fear of persecution and a look-out was needed to disperse the congregation on the approach of any stranger. The Mass rock or altar can still be seen and a stone where the chalice was hidden beside it. There were seven other such open-air altars on the island some of which were still in use after the penal days for lack of a proper building. The first record of a Roman Catholic priest being appointed to the island dates back to 1740. Before that there had been visits every five or six weeks by a Friar Bradley, whose name was remembered on the island for a hundred years thereafter.

In 1722, as a result of the keen interest and efforts of an Englishman, Bishop Hutchinson of Connor and Dromore, the Parish of Rathlin was separated from the mainland union of Ballintoy and Billy to which it had long belonged. St. Thomas' Church, on the site of the present building and on the ruins of the original one,[3] was completed and consecrated for use by the Anglican community in that year. The date on the chalice still in use, 1719, suggests that services were held before this by Archibald Stewart, Rector of Ballintoy. Bishop Hutchinson, who noted that at this time there were four hundred and ninety souls on the island, was also instrumental in getting a schoolmaster appointed, a library of books put together for the island, and instituting a phonetic alphabet for the better instruction of the Irish-speaking inhabitants in English, so that they might hear the word in that language.[4] A King's customs officer at that time stationed on the island was one of the board of management of the school. This system of education continued for a good many years but was discontinued sometime before the end of the century. Rev. John Martin, curate of Ballintoy, was the first Rector, and held the

[3] Wares Works, Vol. I.P. 215.

[4] The Rathlin catechism was another of his brain children—quite celebrated at the time as it showed Irish on one page and English opposite.

incumbency until he died in 1740 at the age of eighty. A skull-and-cross-bones are the apparently inappropriate symbol on the memorial tablet erected by his son, still to be seen in the church today. Different ages have different symbolisms. The Church itself was named not after one of the fairly numerous saints associated with the island but to honour the Christian name of the then Primate of All Ireland.

A few years later came a change which must have made Sorley Boy revolve in his tomb in the vault of Bonemargy.

VIEW • FROM • THE • MANOR • HOUSE • GARDEN

G. J. A. C.

CHAPTER 14

RATHLIN UNDER THE GAGES
1746—1820 A.D.

"An island gives pleasure twice in your life; once when you buy it and once when you sell it."—Breton saying.

In 1746 the fifth Earl of Antrim, whose carefree generosity had led to the overspending of his income, was forced by his creditors to look for a purchaser for Rathlin.

The Rev. John Gage, who at that time was Prebendary of Aghadowey, 20 miles inland in Co. Derry, bought the island at a price of £1,750. His wife had inherited some money and this went into the deal. It is interesting to speculate what caused a country clergyman, son of Queen Anne's private chaplain, at the age of fifty to make such a purchase. One might think that it was looked on initially as a good commercial speculation, since Ballycastle at this period was beginning to recover from the ravages of the two previous centuries. In the Indenture dated the 10th March 1745, which is preserved in the Public Records Office in Belfast referring to Raghlin otherwise Raghery, Lord Antrim retained rights of fishing, airies of hawks, coal pits, mines of coal and culm. John Gage, however, in addition to the land acquired a mill, quarries and rights to stone, limestone, slate and marble. Coalmines and salt pans of considerable importance were being got into production under the direction of Mr. Boyd; a much improved pier was under construction to be completed in 1748. There were indications of similar possibilities on the island. John Gage's attention might have been drawn to that direction by the marriage a few years earlier of one of his nieces to a McNeill of Gigha, or by the purchase by the Governors of Queen Anne's bounty of the great tithes of the island, during his father's time as the Queen's chaplain.[1] On the other hand, to discourage him would have been the fact that 1745 was still a time of unrest in the isles, for Bonnie Prince Charlie, the Young Pretender, had just that year launched his ill-planned expedition into England. The Prince's handsome presence and gay bearing gave an appearance of popularity to his cause and led him to embark on one of the most audacious and irresponsible enterprises in British history. In April 1746 on Culloden Moor the last chances of a Restoration were swept away forever. The '45 was to be the final rising but that can scarcely have been clear at the time. Plenty of rumours must have been in circulation on Rathlin for the pattern of the last century repeated and many of Prince Charlie's supporters fled there after their defeat. The Prince himself, according to a hard dying local tradition, spent some weeks at Glencolumbkille on the north west coast of Ireland waiting for a ship in the course of his flight to France. If he had put in at Rathlin he could have been sure of meeting steadfast friends who would have proudly harboured him and served him at the risk of their lives on his way to Ireland.

In acquiring Rathlin John Gage re-established the long tradition of Norman ownership started by De Courcy and continued by the Byssets, for his family, like theirs, were associated with William the Conqueror's invasion of England. Since then the Gages have continued to produce many distinguished soldiers and sailors, and have loved and served Rathlin faithfully for seven generations.

John Gage did not live there for there was no house fit for a gentleman on the island, but visited it regularly, staying in Ballynoe House—now a barn. In 1758, twelve years after the purchase, he presented a Petition to Parliament directed towards the improvement of the island's facilities. He pointed out that many ships having worked up the Irish Sea had to wait at the island for a fair wind out to the west. While ships of three hundred tons and upwards could ride out a gale on the east side, small vessels were

[1] Reeves, page 288.

124

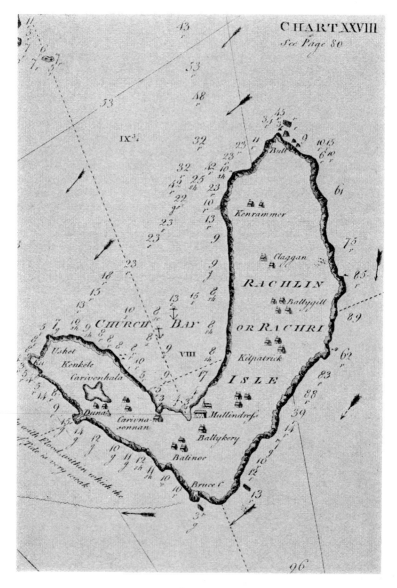

1″=1 mile

From a Maritime Survey of Ireland by M. Mackanzie, London 1776.

frequently lost for want of a harbour. Estimates were shown for the construction of piers in Church Bay and at Ushet, and the point made that facilities here would assist vessels in carrying away coal from the colliery which was being worked on the mainland, and in fishing the cod and herring which were in abundance nearby. He also suggested that since coal had been found on the north face of the island it was quite possible that a worthwhile seam existed there and that this should be investigated; he asked for a king's ship to be stationed at the island to suppress piracy and intercept smugglers who were using it as a base "on a vast scale." A more unusual suggestion was that Rathlin should be used *"as a public granary where great stores of corn in cheap seasons might be brought from the islands and continent of Scotland where rents are mostly paid in grain and in scarce years might supply the northern parts of this Kingdom at moderate price."* He also proposed that a lighthouse be erected on the island similar to those already in existence on Howth Head and the Copeland Island. It was a good report, probably submitted because the Irish Parliament had announced a surplus of £500,000 that year. Similar requests from all over the country poured in as soon as the news got abroad. Rathlin's case was turned down and it was to be another hundred years before the island obtained a lighthouse. Today, two hundred years later, Rathlin is still waiting for an adequate harbour. Kintyre, however, got a lighthouse before the end of the eighteenth century, so at least one side of the narrows was marked.

In those days of sail and oar the boat trip from Ballycastle, now usually over in fifty minutes, often took four or five hours. Curraghs were in use on the island up until the nineteenth century, but though they remain common on the west today, they have not been seen on Rathlin or elsewhere east of the Swilly for seventy years. There must have been a good many tragedies; one is recorded in 1772 when the Rector, Mr. Cuppage, and one of John Gage's sons were drowned in Slough-na-more with the loss of a whole boat's crew.

Robert the First

John Gage died in 1763. His eldest son Robert regularly visited the island and in his later years began to reside there permanently. It was he who built the long two-storied Georgian manor house which still stands today within a few yards of the sea on the west side of Church Bay; one of the most delightful houses I know. With its narrow cobbled yard behind and walled garden to the west, it nestles comfortably into the hillside under some of the few trees to be found on the island. The light from the water, dappled as it reflects from the tangles of maidenhair seaweed at the edge of the bay, shines into the deep windows all along the south side.

Robert had earlier brought weavers to the island and the older part at the east of the Manor House is the remains of their work rooms—as an export industry it did not last long but cloth for use on the island was woven from flax and wool in handlooms until fifty years ago. Joiners and a mason came from the mainland to build the house—their rates of pay are recorded in an accounts' book in the Belfast Public Records.

About 1780 one of the first independent accounts of the island which goes into any detail has been preserved in a letter of the Rev. William Hamilton, a Church of Ireland rector in County Donegal. His description runs as follows:

"The little skiff in which I navigated was built of very slight materials and did not seem to be well calculated to buffet the stormy seas of the Sound. I observed that we had received a good deal of water into it and on expressing my uneasiness that there was no visible means of throwing it out one of the boatmen instantly took off his brogue with which he soon cleared the vessel of water and put it on his foot again without seeming to feel the slightest inconvenience from the wetness, leaving me quite at ease on the subject of pumping the vessel.

Rathlin contains about twelve hundred inhabitants, and is rather over-peopled, as there is no considerable manufacture which might give employment to any superfluous hands.

The cultivated land is kindly enough, and produces excellent barley. In a plentiful year, grain of this kind has been exported to the value of six hundred pounds. The craggy pasturage fattens a small, but delicious breed of sheep. The horses, as well as the sheep, are small in kind, but extremely serviceable and surefooted beyond conception. Of this I had a strong proof in a little expedition which I made through the island in company with Mr. Gage, the hospitable proprietor of it. You must know it was but the other day the people of Raghery recollected that a road might be some convenience to them, so that in our excursion we were obliged to follow the old custom of riding over precipices, which would not appear contemptible, even to a man who enjoyed the full use of his legs.

It seems my horse, though fifteen or sixteen years old, had seldom before felt a bridle in his mouth, and after many attempts to shake it off, in a very critical situation, on the top of a rugged precipice, he refused to proceed one step further, while this troublesome incumbrance impeded him. Having no other resource, I was obliged to comply, and was carried over an exceedingly dangerous heap of rocks, with a degree of caution which amazed me in the midst of my terrors.

It seems singular that this island should not contain any native quadruped, except those universal travellers the rats, and the little shrew mouse, which is sometimes found. But the various tribes of foxes, hares, rabbits, badgers, etc., for which it might afford excellent shelter, and which abound on the opposite shore, are here unknown. A few brace of hares indeed were lately introduced by the proprietor, which bid fair to produce a large increase.

A good many years ago, Lord Antrim gave orders to his huntsman to transport a couple of foxes into the island, for the purposes of propagating that precious breed of animals. But the inhabitants assembled in consternation, and having subscribed each a hank of yarn, prevailed on the huntsman to disobey orders. However he was sharp enough to take the hint, and for some years paid his annual visit to Raghery, for the purpose of raising a regular tribute, to save the poor islanders from those desolating invaders.

The inhabitants are a simple, laborious and honest race of people, and possess a degree of affection for their island which may very much surprise a stranger. In conversation they always talk of Ireland as a foreign kingdom, and really scarcely have any intercourse with it, except in the way of their little trade. A common and heavy curse among them is—'May Ireland be your hinder end.'

From this amor patriae arises their great population, notwithstanding the perils which attend their turbulent coast, as they never entertain a thought of trying to better their fortune, by settling in any of the neighbouring towns of Antrim.

The tedious process of civil law are little known in Raghery; and indeed the affection which the inhabitants bear to their landlord, whom they always speak of by the endearing name of master, together with their own simplicity of manners, renders the interference of the civil magistrates very unnecessary. The seizure of a cow or a horse, for a few days, to bring the defaulter to a sense of duty; or a copious draught of salt water from the surrounding ocean, in criminal cases, forms the greater part of the sanctions and punishments of the island. If the offender be wicked beyond hope, banishment to Ireland is the dernier resort, and soon frees the community from this pestilential member.

The chief desideratum of the islanders is a physician, the want of whom they seem to consider as their greatest misfortune, though their master appears to be of a very different sentiment; and indeed, the remarkable population of Raghery makes much in favour of his opinion.

Small as this spot is, one can nevertheless trace two different characters among its inhabitants. The Kenramer or western end, is craggy and mountainous; the land in the vallies is rich and well cultivated, but the coast destitute of harbours. A single native is here known to fix his rope to a stake driven into the summit of a precipice, and from thence, alone, and unassisted, to swing down the face of a rock in quest of the nests of sea fowl. From thence, activity, bodily strength, and self-dependence, are eminent among the Kenramer men. Want of intercourse with strangers has preserved many peculiarities, and their native Irish continues to be the universal language.

The Ushet end, on the contrary, is barren in its soil, but more open, and well supplied with little harbours; hence, its inhabitants are become fishermen, and are accustomed to make short voyages and. to barter. Intercourse with strangers has rubbed off many of their peculiarities, and the English language is well understood, and generally spoken among them.

This distinction I fear may seem foolishly speculative, considering the diminutive object of it, and yet I assure you it is a matter of fact; and the inhabitants themselves are so well aware of it, that in perilous situations, different offices and stations are appointed to each, according as he is an Ushet or Kenramer man."

Dr. Hamilton published a volume of his letters and several other literary works, but was killed in the early part of the '98 rebellion.

Robert Gage may have been activated by the literary doctor's comments on the roads for while High Sheriff of County Antrim in 1787, he managed to persuade the Grand Jury, who in those days performed most of the functions of a County Council, to start to make the switchback road which leads from Church Bay out to the west; its surface still has an eighteenth century feel!

A touching proof of the islanders' regard for Robert and his family came at the time of the 1798 Rebellion. Thomas Russell (who is said to have been later executed for his part) pretended to be a student of geology and visited the island as a guest at the Manor House, but spent his time in trying to raise support for the rising. A meeting took place in Bracken's cave with the co-operation of "Black Ned" McMullan, the Parish Priest, and a few of the islanders agreed to take part, probably rather reluctantly, for they made it clear that they would only do so if they would not in any way have to interfere with Mr. Gage and his family. In the event, the signal, the firing of an old schooner, the Amy, in Ballycastle dock, was never given. The unfortunate "Black Ned" was arrested and banished. The islanders luckily for themselves did not take any part in the '98 which was started with high ideals as an interdenominational liberation movement but only resulted in the death of some thirty thousand people.

Smuggler's Heyday

When Robert died in 1801, his son, another Robert, was still a minor and the island was administered by an agent who carried on an extensive smuggling trade which made him a fortune but did the island no good. Lace was one of the principal commodities; tobacco, rum and brandy, also whiskey and poteen would be collected in boats from passing clippers and hidden in caves or in specially built double gables in houses, for sending over to the mainland when the coast was clear. The Blue Eyed Maid was a famous smuggling vessel of the period; she was kept as smartly as any man o' war and so heavily armed that her captain boasted he could "thrash any cruiser of his own size and land a cargo six hours afterwards". When such a vessel arrived the agent would arrange for a fleet of boats to meet her, each carrying stones equivalent in weight to the contraband to be collected. These were transhipped into the smuggler who was thus kept in perfect trim for swift flight at any moment. Stress of weather was a risk these vessels always faced and the Maid in 1815 watched her consort, the Jane founder in a gale off Donegal.[2]

An island story which dates from this period tells of a small smuggling craft lying at anchor off the east shore when a revenue cutter was sighted rounding Torr Head. The smugglers had been asleep but dashing up on deck in their shirts, got under way, and were pursued three times clockwise round the island. When capture seemed inevitable they ran their vessel behind a rock about 20 feet high on the north side, known as Fargan Lack, behind which their hull was hidden. There was just room to lie in the 30 foot wide sound between the islet and the cliffs and the mystified preventive men were unable to find them.

Strategic Importance

The great international upheaval of the Napoleonic Wars and the naval activity of the twenty-year period do not appear to have had any direct relation to Rathlin, but in 1808 the island was mentioned in a military memoir on the defence of Ireland, which was drawn up by a General Charles Dumouriez, a distinguished French diplomat and soldier. He had refused to serve under Napoleon and come over to the British side where his opinion was much sought after on account of his experience. His report started by stating "*The fate of the British Empire depends on that of Ireland. That island is open to invasion in more than thirty deep bays on all its coasts*".

---

[2] Maxwell, "Wild Sports of the West."

After describing every section of the Irish coast, he gets on to the bit from Larne northwards. *"The coast which follows, turning to the north of Ballycastle, is not open to attack.*

RATHLIN or RAUGHLIN

This island has a bay which possesses a good anchorage. A squadron based on the island in summer could cover the whole coast of the north between Lough Swilly and Belfast. The tide in the narrows between this island and Sheep Island is very strong but the squadron could shelter in south west winds in the roadstead of Ballycastle which is very safe. In winds from west to east through north, the squadron is safe in the roadstead of Christ Church on the same island".

The gallant General must have had scanty knowledge of maritime affairs to suggest that Ballycastle is a good anchorage, for it has been looked on throughout the ages by seamen as notoriously unreliable. Nevertheless, if the British fleet could blockade Brest and Toulon, as it did month after month, winter and summer, it could undoubtedly have maintained a squadron in Rathlin Sound.

This section of the report finishes off in flamboyant style:

"But the great safeguard for Ireland which will prevent or defeat all landings, is the establishment arranged and planned in advance of four military cum naval stations,

(1   **Cork,** *which is already established.*

(2) **Valentia,** *which covers the whole west of Ireland, and whose squadron is able, without difficulty, to put the enemies fleet to windward and to follow all its movements to north and to south.*

(3) **Rathlin,** *which presents the same advantage to the north against all attacks setting out from the northern ports and from the Baltic.*

(4) **Dublin,** *which holds the safety of the whole channel.*

These four naval stations defend Ireland on all sides".

Like many another War Office report before and since, this one was pigeonholed, certainly in so far as the Rathlin recommendations are concerned. No naval squadron was stationed there.

The Pleasures of Yachting

Yachting in these waters was beginning to be discovered as a sport for gentlemen. In August 1816, some close relations of the Gage family set off from Strabragy Bay, near Malin Head, on a pleasure cruise to Iona. The skipper was Robert Harvey and his boat was called the Rambler. Possibly he had borrowed her from the Gages for many of their boats bore that name but little is known of her history before or after this one trip of which a manuscript log is preserved. Robert, a gay blade who had danced on his own dining table a year before to celebrate the news of Waterloo, was married to one of the Gage girls. On a voyage of a month's duration, much longer than intended, they reached Iona and visited Staffa, but were held up by south-west winds at Islay on the way back. One of the more amusing points in the log is the frequency of references to the purchase of high quality "potatoes" in Oban and elsewhere. They bought these with such regularity and they were delivered each time by good-looking fishermen's daughters, that it sounds as if a good time was had by all the bachelors on board as a result.

On the return passage after long delays at Port Ellen on Islay, the Ramblers found their way to Campbeltown and eventually reached Ireland via Rathlin, where Robert in presence of his in-laws bought no potatoes. They had previously sent word of their whereabouts with one "Dan'lbane of Rathlin" who was weather-bound beside the Rambler waiting with twenty other sailing craft for a fair wind to Ireland. It was an indication of the amount of traffic across the North Channel in those days, a traffic which was almost entirely to disappear with the coming of steam power in the next century.

G. J. A. C.

CHAPTER 15

A CENTURY OF ISLAND PEACE
1820-1914 A.D.

"May Ireland be your hinder end"—Rathlin Curse.

Ireland in the nineteenth century was anything but peaceful. In its early years the overseas demand for Irish grain and linen, built up in the last quarter of the previous century, was boosted by the long Napoleonic Wars. The high prices which shortages of these commodities created brought prosperity to much of the country, but it was based on an artificial situation which could not last. It did last long enough to foster an increase in population to an extent which the country had not the real resources to support. This was followed by the inevitable consequence of famines following any failure in crops.

Throughout the century on the Irish mainland, the long fight for agrarian reform and Home Rule was conducted with bitterness.

Rathlin had had its own population explosion some fifty years earlier and seems to have reached a ceiling of about 1,200 by the year 1784, above which it climbed little, if anything, while the population of Ireland continued to double and even treble.

The island was by-passed by the turbulent stream of events in Ireland for three reasons—its situation surrounded by the sea, the fact that its links of trade, kin and friendship lay with Scotland as much or more than Ireland, and lastly its system of government —Rathlin enjoyed throughout the century the despotic rule of a benevolent landlord—an arrangement which world experience seems to indicate is far superior to democracy.

In 1820 the Rector, Mr. Moore, was after forty years on the island becoming more of an encumbrance than an incumbent. He had scattered the bishop's library. The Protestant congregation dwindled rapidly, but he can hardly be blamed for this since the same thing was happening all over Ireland. In 1820 Robert Gage the second, aged thirty, was appointed Curate and four years later Rector of the island. This inaugurated a period of sustained activity.

To suppress the smuggling Robert Gage arranged that in 1821 coastguards should be placed on the island. One officer and six men lived in the range of houses which are still inhabited on the south shore of Church Bay. A pier, still the principal one today, was built for them in front of their quarters. This was one of the eight stations in the Ballycastle district. To make boat traffic easier to supervise for contraband Ushet port was deliberately blocked up with boulders. This decision, reached after discussions between the coast guard officer and Robert Gage, seems harshly restrictive today but it does indicate the acute nature of the problem.

In 1816 the Proprietor, as Robert was called, sold a barn to the Roman Catholic community for conversion, mainly with timber from shipwrecked vessels, into their first Church. The penal laws inhibiting the practice of their religion had in the main been repealed by 1790, but full emancipation was to come in 1829.

Shortly before being appointed curate, Robert had obtained money from the Diocese for the construction of a new church, the old one having fallen into very bad repair in less than a hundred years. This building, still the Parish church today, was completed in 1822. It occupies a unique position so close below the hill that from the terraced road you could almost toss a penny down into the top of the small tower, and yet so near the water that the salt spray washes its walls. I cannot think of a church elsewhere set so near the open sea. The graveyard is still used by all denominations. Some of the headstones date back to the sixteenth century and the ground is used many times over for the same sad purpose. A few years ago scenes reminiscent of the finding of Yorick in Hamlet used to take place when the bones of some not so long dead ancestor would be dug up and admired at a new interment.

At the beginning of the age of universal education the new Proprietor succeeded in getting a school built and a resident schoolmaster reinstated, for this service had apparently been discontinued at some time subsequent to the building of the original school a hundred years earlier. In the interim the only education had come from itinerant or "hedge" schoolmasters there for a few weeks in the summer. A girls' school near the present Rectory was added in 1826, and in 1834 another school in Ballygill at the west end.

In 1832 the first 6 inch Ordnance Survey Map of the island was published. A study of it today is not particularly illuminating except for the indication of numerous quarries and of a flagstaff on the highest point. This was used for signalling to the mainland or to passing ships. Robert built with tireless energy. He enlarged the Manor House and made and stocked a large walled orchard and garden just above the upper road in Church Bay. The trees, plum, apple and greengage, flourished up until a few years ago but have now all been cut down. A workshop and sawpit was constructed on the sea side of the road at the north east of the bay. His rent book shows the "Duty fowl" which were paid as well as a cash rent by each householder and in 1814 payments for eleven trips to the mainland, and one to Scotland.

Lewis's Topographical Dictionary, published in 1837, includes the following details: —

Population 1,039 inhabitants.

Area—3,398¾ *statute acres, including* 30½ *acres under water· About three fourths consist of rocks and stony pasture, and the remainder of arable land of medium quality. The western side is rocky and mountainous and the appearance of the coast strikingly magnificent; brown rocks and still darker masses of basaltic pillars in some places contrast with chalk cliffs. On the northern side the precipices towards the sea rise to the height of* 450 *feet without any projecting base. The soil is a light mould intermixed with fragments of basalt and limestone. The valleys are rich and well cultivated and arable land, meadows and a variety of rocky pastures are scattered over the whole island. The sub stratum of nearly the whole island is basalt and limestone. On the eastern side especially it forms beautiful ranges of columns differing from those of the Giants Causeway only in the dimensions, and in a greater variety of their arrangement being found in the same place perpendicular, horizontal and curved· Considerable beds of hard chalk extend for some distance along the southern shore, and in some places, as near Church Bay, where they are intersected by basaltic dikes the hard chalk or limestone is found to possess phosphoric qualities. Beds of puzzolana are also found there and on the shore a substance resembling pumice.*

Barley of excellent quality and cattle are sent off from this place. The former is chiefly purchased by Scottish merchants; there is a mill for grinding oats; there is neither any town or regular village; dwellings of the inhabitants are irregularly scattered throughout the island· The Proprietor, the Rev. R. Gage, is constantly resident and acts as magistrate. The Roman Catholic chapel is a plain building, but a hundred and eighty children are taught in three public schools. Near the black rock on the south side of Church Bay are four remarkable caverns which have calcareous stalactites[1] descending from the roof which by their continual dropping have deposited an incrustation about an inch in thickness on the floor beneath".

The Rev. Robert Gage is described in the Parliamentary Gazetteer of 1844 as "completely Lord of the island who banishes his subject to the continent of Ireland for misconduct or repeated offences against the law". He had a liveried boat crew in blue and white striped jerseys for transport to the mainland. They would set out to the softly spoken Gaelic prayer "Hack En A Mach Angram Yeach". "We go in the name of God."

Another account of this period is by Dr. J. D. Marshall. He found in 1834 a public house offering accommodation and a shop with some medical supplies but commented on the hardship caused to islanders by the absence of a resident doctor. Asthma and eye diseases were commoner than on the mainland due, he thought, to the sulphurous smoky atmosphere in peat fired houses with only a hole in the roof for a chimney. In a peat shortage people burned scraws which are scarcely combustible. Smoky interiors still accompany peat fires even with good chimneys. I have been driven coughing into the street from island cottages, while the natives, with a resistance derived from years of exposure, sat in comfort laughing at my plight.

Irish was the normal language of the islanders throughout the last century and was still spoken on the island up until the 1930s. According to a survey in 1934 the older people spoke Gaelic, the next generation understood it but did not use it while the children did neither.

The Famine

When the potato crop failed in 1847, Robert Gage, like many landlords on the mainland, was tireless in his efforts to help the islanders. All rents due to him were cancelled and he personally contributed generously towards supplies of food for Ireland. Through his good offices money was asked for from the Lord Lieutenant and a Rathlin Island Relief Committee was formed. One illuminating subscription came from a firm of London underwriters who sent £10 to help the islanders "in consequence of their honesty at shipwrecks".

Islanders in general did not suffer so badly in this period as those on the mainland, being able to rely on the fisheries and seabirds but these were hard to catch in winter, and with a

[1] These were all broken off and taken away by a group of visitors a few years ago.

population of 1,000 Rathlin must have been very crowded. Then in addition there were eels as another source of food—the tiny elvers work their way incredibly up streams trickling over the 200 foot cliffs to reach the ponds and sheughs at the top. Through Robert Gage's efforts there was not one death due to starvation, although there was no doubt a good deal of hardship and considerable emigration. Clogh-na-screeve, the "writing stone" in Claggan townland, records the names of some of the islanders who left for "Ameriky" at about that time. The population dropped from 1,110 in 1813 to 1,010 by 1841, and then sharply to 453 by 1861.

In 1849 Robert Gage's wife had the pleasure of laying the foundation stone of the first lighthouse to be built on the island. Hook Head at the entrance to Waterford harbour had had a light maintained by the monks as early as the sixth century. Howth Head, off Dublin, was first lit in 1750. Rathlin, in spite of the fact that it lies in such a dangerous position on a principal shipping route, was relatively late in being marked by a lighthouse. The Ballast Board, the predecessors of the Commissioners of Irish Lights, bought an area of ground at the north east corner of the island and there the light was first lit in 1856. It had at first two stationary lights, 295 ft. and 215 ft. above sea level, for this was before the days of the invention of revolving lights with characteristic flashes. The lights were so placed that a sailing ship trying to work the eddy and make way against the tide by keeping close along the north side of the island, could stand in, in safety, until it was obscured. Originally there were three cannons for use during fogs; these were used until 1920 when electric firing jibs were substituted by which two shots are fired every five minutes.

Today the light of 227,000 candlepower, 245 feet above sea level, stands magnificently at the apex of a right angled bend of the sheer cliffs, with heather growing close up to the white walls which surround its base. It gives four flashes every twenty seconds and is visible for twenty two miles. In thick weather each explosion is followed by a brilliant flash which can often be detected through fog thick enough to obscure the light itself.

Wrecks

The lighthouse did not, however, put an end to losses on the island for in 1884, the barque Girvan 182 feet long of 718 tons left the Clyde outward bound for Australia with a cargo of whiskey and was given a tow down as far as the Mull of Kintyre. The tow was slipped and the tug disappeared, but the Girvan failed to get under way and on a fine calm day drifted ashore on the west end of Rathlin. A good deal of her cargo was "liberated", and some is still said to be buried about the island in hiding places now long forgotten.

Only a tiny fraction of the wrecks which have taken place on the island are recorded; the islanders say that there are forty in one place alone off the reef known as the Clachen Bo, which extends west just south of the Bull Light. A catalogue of wrecks is not in itself of great interest except where occasionally one can glean a few details.   They averaged one a year on the island during the first part of the century. Sometimes nothing was seen or heard of the actual disaster—only broken timbers and mangled bodies found later told of the tragedy.   In Tony McCuaig's pub are preserved the nameboards of a few—The Girvan, the Arriero, a barquentine of 167 tons lost in Church Bay in March 1876, the Cambria, the Saracen lost east of the Bull Point, and a finely gilded one from Her Majesty, a paddle steamer with auxiliary sail, said to be an ex-Royal Yacht, lost in a fog on the north side.   Mr. McCuaig has an interesting plate with an illustration of this ship.

Other wrecks faintly remembered are the *Night Scarf* wrecked at Couraghy, and at the same place the *Bouncer,* a tug, said to have fought on the Nile during the campaign for the relief of General Gordon. She was trying to salvage parts of the *Night Scarf* when she herself got on the rocks.

Mrs. Gage died in 1852 having produced four sons and eight daughters, not to mention an illustrated manuscript history of the island; it is beautifully written, and she even made separate copies for several of the children. She must have been as talented and energetic as her husband.

The bold McDonnells never seem to have come back to the island in any strength after the massacre of '42. There are none shown in a roll of 1766; in 1832 there was one family in Ballinoe House but by 1862 the name disappears again. Perhaps the drowning in the McDonnell Bush or eddy off the East Light accounts for the disappearance. Two brothers who worked the water-powered corn mill in Portawillin were lost when their boat laden with grain for Scotland foundered, watched by their father from the cliff top, but the date of this incident is far from certain. Connections of the McDonnells and their associated clans are on the island, and also strung in a thin tartan line along the coast of Antrim. Politically many of those on the mainland have never really accepted Partition and the existence of a government in Belfast since 1921. Yet they have little or no connection with Dublin, so if time changes the present arrangement, one wonders whether they would much fancy being governed from there either.

ROBERT THE THIRD

Robert Gage died in 1862, having been rector for thirty eight years. He was succeeded as Proprietor by his son, Robert Gage, M.A., J.P., a bachelor who lived on the island and continued the close interest the family have always taken in the welfare of the

THE MANOR HOUSE, RATHLIN, ABOUT 1840, BY MRS. ROBERT GAGE. *Visitors are shown arriving at the old pier and being assisted ashore by the uniformed boats crew. Boat close to the pier is sprit rigged, the one lying off a lugger. The small boat at the bottom is a curragh propelled with a spade-like oar over the bow.*

By kind permission of Captain George Harvey.

islanders. He kept a stock of coal for their use, erected a limekiln and assisted in the introduction of boat-building and in the improvement of the piers and quays of which there have been a total of seven on the island, none of them entirely satisfactory. Four are in Church Bay, (inner one ruined) one now ruined at Killeany, another at Couraghy, one in Portawillin on the east side (see some details in Appendix 5).

The diaries of Robert the third for several years around 1880 have been preserved. He first records the weather in detail, an indication of how greatly it affected every activity. Next come the boats. Their names are evocative. His own were the *Gannet*, the *Ajax* and the *Rambler*. Others were the *Widgeon*, *Queen*, *Fox*, *Fame* and *Duck;* a contrast to today's favourites such as *Golden Dawn*, *Mystical Rose*, or none at all. Repairs to them occupied much attention and one May Day he was expansive enough to describe the *Ajax*, green outside and white within, and black on the gunwhale. "She looks uncommonly well." The larger boats were gaff rigged and lay on chain moorings in the bay for most of the summer, boarded by dinghy. Robert personally slaughtered and gralloched the highland cattle when meat was required. The finding of a huge seal 8 feet long by 5 feet 5 inches girth dead at Altachuile is recorded on 19th June 1879; it was brought round by a boat to the east side and then on a donkey cart to be flensed for the oil. Weighing of kelp and purchases of timber, grain and beans are frequently recorded, and on the 18th August 1879 the arrival of the small steamer *Ada* with coal from Newport, loading up with kelp for the return voyage. Most days Robert spent several hours in the workshop; one entry records how he fed some visitors there as they smelt too strong to bring into the house! Each passage to Ballycastle brings an entry with the duration and the weather conditions; sometimes on a calm day in the winter as many as seven island boats would go over; usually they sailed but sometimes had to row the whole way in a calm. In Ballycastle he attended Magistrate's Courts, Poor Law meetings and did banking and shopping. Occasionally there was a visit to Belfast, but he seemed unhappy away from the island and never stayed away for more than a night unless held up by the weather on a return journey. As well as being Magistrate he acted as doctor, effective enough no doubt, but very basic. His medicine chest which was preserved until recently, contained bottles with labels no fancier than "good for the heart", "good for the fever", or simply "good for the pains". A portrait of Robert shows a fine-looking man with a long, humorous face, clad in white canvas trousers, fisherman's guernsey and red knitted cap.

The life portrayed is very similar to that of an Irish country gentleman in more remote parts inland if for the interest in boats one substitutes horses.

Birds

With Robert lived his sister Catherine who produced a finely illustrated record of the island's bords and plants. The birds number almost all the common Irish ones and include such rarities for Ireland as the Twite, which has nested on the island, the Chough, Yellow and Snow Buntings, the Nightjar and the Quail. The White Tailed Eagle was once common but extinct by 1849. The Iceland Falcon and the Marsh Harrier are occasionally seen. Grey Lag, White Front, Barnacle and Brent as well as the rare Bean Goose have all been recorded on the island.

Of the sea birds all the common ones have, of course, been recorded; rarities include the Pomatorhine, Buffon and Richardson's Skua, the Roseate Tern and the Glaucous Gull. The Slavonian Grebe has also been seen and the little Grebe is common on the many loughs on the island. Fork-tailed and Stormy Petrels are seen regularly around the shores but have not been proved to nest. The Buzzard is now common on the island, four or five pairs regularly breeding. The Golden Eagle is, unfortunately, a rarity, but a pair managed to breed once or twice in recent years at Murlough and I have seen one once on the island.[1]

However, Robert and Catherine had more than birds to think about in 1864 for that year their youngest sister Dorothea went to take the waters at Baden-Baden. She was twenty-nine, dark, tall and so pretty that she caught the fancy of a German prince. The family quickly snatched her away from this frightful continental, and hoped that that was the end of the affair. However, a month or two later a rakish looking yacht anchored in Church Bay and out stepped His Serene Highness of Pyrmont and Walbeck, twirling his moustaches and dressed to kill. There was a ball on board and later Prince Albrecht wooed Dorothea so passionately in the sunken garden beside St. Columba's seat that she agreed to marry him.

German princes were quite fashionable at the time and Queen Victoria made Dorothea a Countess when she heard of the engagement. The couple were married in the Chapel Royal in Dublin Castle on 2nd June 1868, and later had three sons and two daughters. The prince returned from time to time to visit the island with his wife, and in 1868 his valet died and was buried there, but in time Albrecht developed a taste for other lady friends at which Robert no doubt said to his sister, "Miss Gage, I told you so."

---

[1] A count in 1960 showed 175 species, 79 of them breeding. J. Deane, Ulster Museum.

In 1865 the present Roman Catholic church, known as the Church of the Immaculate Conception, was finished. A beautiful little building of island basalt with freestone trim, it lies at the head of a very steep road up a break in the cliffs just west of Church Bay, and was dedicated with great ceremony and a large attendance of leading people from the mainland, by Dr. Dorrian, then Bishop of the Diocese, on the 22nd August that year.

The island in the nineteenth century was largely self-supporting. Clothes were made from fabrics spun and hand-woven on the islands. There were shoemakers and tailors as well as a blacksmith. Fish oil from "glashans," readily caught off the rocks, was used for lamps. Island corn was milled for bread. Timber came from shipwrecks and seaweed was there for manuring the land. Island beef and mutton with fish for variety, and a wild duck or a hare if you could get one, provided a fine enough diet for anyone. Poteen (illicit whiskey made from barley) was available for a party, or to warm the bones, mulled with sugar on a cold winter's night. Dulse, a red edible seaweed, made an aperitif. Sugar and tea were among the few things which had to be imported. Fuel was also scarce as there is little peat on the island, and "baughrans," or dried cow dung, was sometimes used for this purpose.

One of the principal exports was kelp, made by burning seaweed. This industry began as early as 1774, and ten years later a hundred tons were exported from Rathlin, but by 1830 this figure was down to 30. The Gages accumulated the kelp in a store against a credit to their tenants and periodically arranged for a ship to collect it. All the larger types of seaweed were used; women and children went out on the rocks, cut it with knives and spread it out to dry. When it was dry enough to be burned it was placed in a pit lined with stones called a kiln and once a fire was started the dried weeds were fed steadily in.   The alkali and anything not dissipated by the heat accumulated at the bottom where it had to be kept well stirred with an iron rod. When dried it formed a hard bluish mass. This in the early days was used at about a price of £5 a ton for the bleaching of linen. It also produced iodine and up until the 1930s material for a photographic film.

A few years ago people would wait eagerly for the "May Fleece," the storm which ripped the wrack from the rocks and threw it up on the shore, and on any fine day in summer the coast would be marked by the "reeks" of smoke from dozens of kilns. The girls engaged in this manufacture used to find that the smoke greatly darkened their complexions. The resort to cure this before going to the Lammas Fair at Ballycastle in August was to go into one of the sweat houses on the island; these were shaped like a beehive of rough stones and in the old days were in regular use as a cure for rheumatism and other ailments, as well as beauty salons. A peat fire was placed in the house until the whole of the walls became very hot and then the fire was drawn out and the clients, up to four in number, put inside and the door blocked up. A small air hole was opened or closed to control the temperature. When the sweating was completed the patient was removed and either wrapped up in warm clothing or immersed in cold water. The best preserved sweat house is at Knockans and may be in part a survival of a beehive hut of great antiquity. The base of another lies S.W. of the gate of the east light beside a tiny lough.

Most of the islanders worked extremely hard for a living but if some tended to take life too easily, sure it was not laziness, but the warm Atlantic air sapping their natural energy.

> "Do as little as ever ye can
> Is the properest way for a Raghery man"

was a jingle which summed up their attitude.

Princesses and Fairies

Superstitions used to abound on the island as they did in most country districts, in proportion to their isolation. Most of these fantasies were harmless, and something which we miss in this dull age which pays too little attention to the influence of luck in our lives and to the unseen world around us of which we still know so little. The Groga was a wee fairy man on Rathlin who guarded the Master's house and once woke the family to warn them of a fire started by a careless guest. A male form of banshee, he used to be heard sobbing when any of the family died. The same name (which means "the long haired one") is given to a creature, in form somewhere between the human race and the wee folk, on Colonsay and in other parts of Argyll.

There was Sack Bahn who had the peculiar habit of rolling along the roads at night in a sack and frightening those whom he met. This is very much a Rathlin story but shared with many isles is the seal maiden or mermaid who married a fisherman and stayed with him until she discovered her coghill or tail hidden in the rafters, slipped it on and was away to sea again.

Canan Dhu, an enchanted prince, lived in the form of a magnificent black horse in Loch An Canan near the west end. He had a golden spear protruding from his chest and impaled many victims, until one night he ran into a wall at Kilpatrick, the spear was driven into his own heart and he died.

The fairies danced, feasted and sang, but if you were unlucky enough to annoy them they might blight your cattle or even steal your child. There were tricks to ward off the dangers, like an ass's harness hung by the window to keep off the evil eye. Life was more exciting in that way, even if many of the east end islanders never travelled to the west in the whole of their lives, let alone faced the unknown perils of a visit to the mainland. East enders called themselves "cuddins", a name for small fish, while the west enders were "foorins", or wild fowl.

Great princesses lived on Rathlin in the old days—one was so beautiful that two lovers fought over her to the death. The loser with his last breath whispered to his servant, Tol Dhu by name, to avenge him by dancing with the maiden and whirling her over the cliffs. That's just what Tol Dhu did, not a word of a lie —the luckless princess was washed up east of Ballycastle and from her long blonde hair Fair Head was named. Two other princesses from Islay were turned into stone while trying to escape; these stand for ever off Kenramer cliffs—Marie Isla and Katrine Isla Rocks.[2]

"Sea Wrack", by Mrs. Campbell, written in 1951 from notes taken many years earlier, catches the dialect and outlook of an older generation of islanders in a way that could not now be repeated. Mrs. Campbell's mother was a Rathlin Gage and she spent much of her early life on the island. She has kindly allowed me to quote the following passages:

The rain spluttered into the black throat of the chimney, and the wind bundled up and down inside it.

"What's that, Agrah?" croaked the old woman, blinking smoke-reddened eyes, "Is't the legends? Deed ay! there's a good few o' them in Rathlin. But I'm not just mindin' them, an' they're sayin' they was gibberidge with little truth in them. Och! mebbe they was, and mebbe they was not! Sure the half of the lies isn't true. Dear ay! I knowed them wee tales well enough in the days that's long by; but the dirty cobbles of work an' nonsense has put them far from me, clean out o' me head.

"Lusten! They's a yarn o' a girl was trailed away by them fairies. Och, ay! it was a good time she'd been away in't. Well her father he sairched an' he sairched, an' not a trace of herself could he get! So this night he seen the 'Wee folk' pullin' docken-rods to turn intil horses. It was a terrible wet night, teemin' an' blowin' an' bitter dark. He seen a light racin' over the bogs before him, an' he follered it an' it went away an' away on him here an' there, through all the wind an' the rain, till it rested be a mountain-side. An' there he seen the way down intil the 'weefolks' palace, inside of the mountain. He followed the steps into a gran' lighted palace: ab' ogh! ogh! he said, fine an' bewtiful wasn't in't at all. The 'wee folk' was pairsuadin' him to remain with them (whenever

---

[2] The top of one of these stacks was pushed off by a daring islander some years ago with his feet.

*it was so coarse outside) an' they were for givin' him food an'
dhrink, an' all to the size o' that. Shegh! what did he see when
he turned an' looked, but his own daughter (just like one o' their-
selves), sittin' at the fire an' rockin' a wee cradle. She was singin'
a song, an' every now an' agen she'd be puttin' in an odd word
in the Gaelic, an' then on with the singin'. So he like fixed them
Gaelic words together and made out she was tellin' him for to
not eat, nor dhrink, no, nor remain with them. An' he minded
every word she said, an' he would not eat nor dhrink, nor would
he remain, so he wouldn't! Tut! Tut! I dishremember now how
it was he got her back afther that; but he did get her, och ay, he
did!"*

*She stoops over the fire, stirring the ashes till the piled-up
whins on top crackle and blaze, and a shower of sparks dance up
the wide chimney. The wind whistles softly, calling to her
through chinks in the door, as though to remind her of tales she
might have forgotten.*

*"There's many a crock o' gold to be found on this island. Ould
Jemmy was down the roddin' years back, an' the sheep on some
sort of a brew o' the hill, skelpin an' scuddin' round. They
loosened the brew with their feet, an' the gold was pourin' over
the rocks; ye'd hear the chink of it as it joined to fall.*

*"They've as big a crock as ye'd wish to see in the bottom
o' Kleggan Lough, ten fadom down. There's the two stones on
top o' the hills, one on either side, an' the crock'll be found in the
Lough, half ways between the two.*

*"An' there's one they say buried in under a hill beyont, but
it'll do no good to them that will find it."*

But the fairies no longer show themselves in Rathlin. *"One
day a rattlin' of stones was heerd an' the peoples had this placed
for the fairies leavin' Raghrey. But why they left it I could not
rightly say."* It is a duller place without them, but we must leave
Mrs. Campbell's delightful stories too, and return to more prosaic
history.

Marconi

In 1898 another form of magic was spun on the island, an
experiment that comprised an important step in one of the greatest
technical advances in world history. A Lloyds Signal Station
had been established a few years earlier near Altacarry light, for
reporting shipping freshly arrived from sea. This information was
of great importance to owners and insurers of ships and cargo in
days when a voyage from New York might vary in length by as
much as four or five weeks. Lloyds found Rathlin a much better
observation point than Torr Head but there was delay in getting
messages back from there so they requested a young Irish-Italian

called Marconi to try setting up his new-fangled wireless telegraphy system to link the island to the mainland. Marconi sent his assistant, Kemp, to Ballycastle in June, 1898. There were a number of setbacks but Kemp persevered and by the end of August ships were being reported by radio from Altacarry to a receiver at White Lodge, Ballycastle. Marconi himself arrived and visited the island on September 1st. He and Kemp must have felt elated at the success of almost the first commercial application. However, the equipment had to be dismantled a few days later as the Post Office authorities objected to this breach of their monopoly. They installed their own radio on a different system not long afterwards but it does not appear to have worked very well, for in 1905 the Marconi Company, now well established, was asked to run the service. So Marconi and Kemp reaped the fruits of their labour. The only evidence of it on the island now are a few concrete blocks in the grass east of the east wall of the lighthouse enclosure. Later when radio in ships became almost universal the importance of Lloyds Signal Stations diminished and the Rathlin one, along with many others was closed down.

What sort of ships did Marconi's men sight? The records of the Coastguard Station on the mainland at Ballycastle for the years 1880-85,[3] tell us and make an interesting contrast when compared with the different type of craft which is seen in these waters today.

SHIPS PASSING THROUGH RATHLIN SOUND

July to December, 1886	*January to June,* 1970
244 Steamers Large	40 "Cargo"—Large Coasters
226 Steamers Small	78 Tankers
354 After Dark	882 Coasters (under 1,200 tons)
19 Steam Tugs	
7 Steam Yachts	17 Small Coasters (Puffers)
6 Sailing Yachts	
4 Ships	132 Trawlers
10 Barques	164 Motor Fishing Vessels
41 Brigantines	15 Submarines
6 Brigs	14 R.A.F. Launches
198 Schooners	62 R.A.F. Aircraft
16 Yawls or Dandies	47 Helicopters
33 Sloop Smacks	28 Warships
22 Luggers	3 Weather Ships
1 Warship	
1 French Man o' War, Barque rig	
1188	1482

[3] Public Records Office, Belfast (McGildowney papers).

The record for a single day compares as follows:

August, 1885	March, 1970
1 Brig.	13 Coasters
3 Schooners	1 Tanker
2 Smacks	1 Cargo Vessel
1 Lugger	3 Trawlers
1 Steam Yacht at anchor in Church Bay	5 Motor Fishing Vessels
1 Smack driven ashore when at anchor in Church Bay, in tow by steamer	1 R.A.F. Launch
	2 R.A.F. Aircraft
	2 Helicopters
1 Cutter Yacht	

The total number of vessels in 1970 is considerably larger, and had it been at a later period in the year a number of yachts would have appeared. Most large vessels pass north of the island and are not sighted, but this must have been even more true of the unhandy square riggers still common in 1886. With the closing in 1970 of the only British naval base in Ireland, H.M.S. Sea Eagle in Derry, the number of warships, submarines and R.A.F. craft has declined.

Aesthetically the observer in 1885 had so much more. The dreamy sight of slow moving topsails protruding out of a morning mist, the splendour of a full-rigged ship, deep laden with American cotton for Liverpool, running past the white cliffs before a fresh gale, the taut twin luffs and raking masts of a fishing lugger standing out to fish off Inistrahull . . . these we shall not see again. Today we can only instead enjoy the much greater contrasts in the types of users of the Sound and the technical ingenuity which lies behind them.

The site of the Coastguard Station itself on the mainland close to the old castle of Donananie seems somewhat curious as its view is much restricted by the island. When it was rebuilt a few years ago the question of a new site on Fair Head was carefully gone into, but the road alone to give access would have cost some £5,000. The Coastguard Station, in its present situation, serves a most useful purpose, and in bad weather it is augmented by a lookout on the north side of the island, so that unless it is foggy, all passing ships are under friendly surveillance.

Robert Gage died unmarried in 1891 and was succeeded by his brother Major General Ezekiel Gage who had spent some 50 years in India. Because of advanced age he decided not to take up residence in Rathlin and lived in Ballycastle, whence he paid frequent visits to Rathlin. However, this allowed an interregnum when

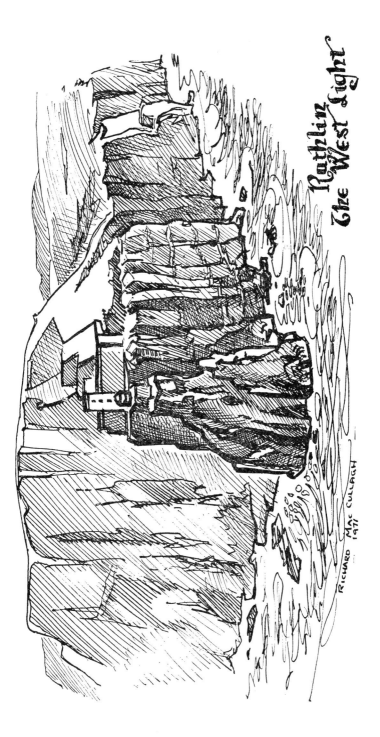

Rathlin
The West Light

RICHARD MAC CULLAGH
1971

the Manor House was empty for much of the time, and many articles of value and antiquities were lost. In 1902 the General persuaded his eldest surviving son, Captain Richard Gage, on return from the Boer War, to retire from the Army, take up residence in the Manor House, and manage the Rathlin Estate.

General Gage died in 1906 and, following some litigation to clarify the terms of Rev. Robert Gage's will, it was ruled that the Rathlin Estate was to be divided between General Gage's four sons. Captain Gage was killed in the presence of his two young sons in a shooting accident near the East Lighthouse on 30th October, 1909, a tragedy which stunned the island. He was succeeded by his widow who occupied the Manor House for the next 38 years and spent much of the time in Rathlin.

In 1910, Scott, a well known engineer, was given the job of constructing a light at the west end of Rathlin where the cliff top is 400 feet high. Lighthouses set high up tend to be obscured by fog more often than those lower down so a position half way up the cliffs had to be found. Scott got over the problem by designing an enormous concrete glacis at an angle of 45 degrees on the face of the rock, with steps which allow the slope to be easily traversed. This creates a curious situation where to reach the top of the lighthouse you go downstairs instead of up. The Keeper's house is a six storey building at the bottom of the glacis; you enter his attic and descend through various storeys until you eventually find yourself in the lantern—this is why from the sea the lighthouse looks like a man whose hat has fallen off. Before the glacis could be constructed much blasting had to be done and a great cave beside the light was choked with debris from the operation. The work of construction was started in 1912 and the light first shown in 1916, but the job was not complete until 1919. The work cost £400,000, an enormous sum when one considers that wage rates were no more than 2s. 6d. per day. Rathlin West Light or the Bull, as it is generally called, is the only red light round the Irish coast apart from minor lights and buoys marking the entrance to harbours. The Bull is a most appropriate name for the roar of the horn in fog has a distinctly bovine note, but the origin of it dates back far before the days of lighthouses, to a field so called at the top of the cliff.

In 1914 war came again to the island and around it were enacted scenes of strife and bloodshed in a new element beneath the surface of the sea.

CHAPTER 16

TWO WORLD WARS

1914-1945 A.D.

"The North Channel net barrage had become so effective that it could be regarded as completely barring the passage of submarines."—Naval Operations. July, 1915.

In August, 1914, when Britain declared war on the Kaiser, it must have seemed most unlikely to those on the island that Rathlin would be in the war zone. Within a month or two, however, as the nights grew longer, Germany decided to mine the Clyde. The old 14,000-ton liner Berlin was converted and dispatched to try to penetrate the defences. After several narrow escapes on the outward voyage Captain Pfundheller reached the North Channel at dusk on October 22nd, but the lights on Rathlin and Kintyre had been extinguished by order of the Admiralty and he was unable to pilot his ship through the narrows in the dark. The Berlin gave up the attempt and instead "laid her eggs" seventy miles north east, off Tory Island, where they soon claimed the battleship Audacious.

U-boats, which at the start of the war were expected to have a range of not more than a couple of hundred miles, soon began to prove that they could encircle the British Isles and penetrate where surface ships could not operate. When a number of sinkings by U-boats took place in the Irish Sea and the Clyde, the Admiralty decided that barrages across the narrows were the best method of prevention, for other methods of anti-submarine warfare were in a primitive stage. At Dover, surface nets forced the U-boats to dive, and run the hazard of row upon row of mines laid near the bottom. In the North Channel the waters were too deep and the tide too strong for mining to be effective; instead, it was decided to establish a zone some thirty miles by twenty from the north of Rathlin to the Mull of Galloway where submarines would be forced to remain submerged. At either end of such a submerged passage the U-boats would have to surface for air and a charge for the batteries, and could then be attacked.

Rathlin became the hinge-pin of the north half of the system. All shipping was diverted south of the island and a light installed on Rue Point to guide them through. East and north east of the island, a force of forty drifters maintained a system of wire nets stretching practically from Kintyre to Fair Head. The nets were 96 feet in depth and 2,000 yards long, with a 12-foot mesh, clumsy things to handle in a swirling tideway. They were designed not so much to catch the submarines as to indicate their presence. Many types were tried. In the later ones, if a submarine struck a section of net would pull away, releasing phosphorus flares at the break, while other flares ignited in the tearaway portion, remaining attached to the submarine and marking its course under water. At such a signal the watching ships closed in with depth bombs to attack. From the island, coastguards kept a lookout, reinforced by naval patrols. Overhead, "blimps" or airships based in Luce Bay and Larne watched for the telltale furrow which would show if a U-boat put up its periscope to spot the positions of the drifters. On shore a hydrophone station was established at Torr Head to detect the passage of submarines passing under the nets by listening for the sound of their propellors. The U-boats, however, once they learned of its presence, were able to minimise this risk by using a fair tide and running their engines at such a slow speed that they could not be heard.

In bad weather it was extremely difficult to maintain the nets in position. Nine-knot drifters could not be expected to keep close up to a lee shore in a winter gale. On February 28th, 1915, Kapitän-Leutnant Wegener, a famous U-boat commander who had already sunk two British warships, came up to periscope depth close west of the island. He carefully surveyed the position of the drifters and perhaps was struck by the close resemblance of Rathlin to Heligoland, the island close off his home port in the Ems, which he had left three days earlier, but it was no time for nostalgia. He pulled down his periscope and prayed that his compass would not play too many tricks as he dived deep and glided close past the dark bases of the north cliffs. He got safely past undetected to sink the coaster Hartdale off County Down a day later. In March he got through again, sank the armed merchant cruiser Bayano off Stranraer and returned again under the barrage. The defences were once again stepped up and, during the summer and most of the next winter few, if any, submarines got through.

The brave Wegener himself was sunk in August off the south coast by a Q-ship.

The U-boats, even if they could not get through, continued to watch for shipping just outside the barrage and, in May, 1916, in spite of all the naval activity, one of them had the boldness to surface in sight of Rathlin in daylight and open fire on the Wheatear, a potato boat on passage east from Coleraine. The Wheatear's skipper refused the call to heave to. Instead, he replied with his own gun, made a smokescreen and headed for the coast. A lengthy exchange of shots ensued during which some of the U-boat's "overs" exploded in Port Ballintrae on the mainland and hundreds of people turned out to watch the war come to their doorstep. This action has passed into north Antrim folklore. In the end the Wheatear reached Portrush harbour in safety "and an aeroplane came and dropped a Union Jack on her deck". A few months later such an action would have brought a swarm of warships to the scene within minutes for, as the U-boat menace increased, so did the counter measures.

In July, 1917, Ireland became an independent sea command with forces much larger than at any period in her history. Thirty or forty destroyers and up to four hundred and fifty armed yachts, trawlers, drifters, sloops and motor-boats were assembled to protect shipping in Irish waters, all under the command of Admiral Sir Lewis Bayly, at Queenstown. Under his direction Larne became the base for the North Channel barrage and at the peak of activity one hundred and fifty drifters worked from there under Admiral Boyle, maintaining two lines of nets across the narrows. A few submarines got through, but the work repaid the tremendous effort and expense which went into it, for with the Straits of Dover as well as the North Channel barred, submarines had to waste time by taking the long passage right round the British Isles to reach their hunting grounds in the Western Approaches and the Irish Sea. Throughout the war, winter and summer, day and night, twenty or thirty drifters armed with puny guns and primitive depth charges worked in sight of Rathlin carrying out the monotonous job of keeping their nets stretched athwart the tide in one of the most exposed waterways in the world.

The end of the Drake

Sinkings, however, continued to increase, and in 1917 the British Isles were near starvation. Late that year the convoy system was started. This marked the turning point and from then on the rate of sinkings dropped dramatically. North west of Rathlin, merchant ships and their escorts formed up for the Atlantic crossing, and after the return trip dispersed into smaller coastal convoys. At dawn on October 17th that year, the British heavy cruiser Drake, a ship of the ocean escort force which had brought Convoy HH24 from Gibraltar to the approaches to the Clyde handed over her charge off the north of Rathlin. A few minutes later she fell a prey to the well-aimed torpedoes of U79. The Drake, 14,000 tons, had been built in 1901 as the nameship of a class mounting two 9.2 inch and sixteen 6-inch guns. Her sister ship, the Good Hope, had gone down at Coronel in the Pacific fighting at long odds with a German cruiser force three years earlier.   Twenty-nine men were killed by the explosion of the torpedoes which hit the Drake, but Captain Radcliffe, finding that his ship could still steam, decided to make for Rathlin Sound and called up the destroyer escort of the convoy from which he had just parted.   Another division also took in his signal and within an hour eight destroyers, with four sloops following them, had surrounded the Drake to form an anti-submarine screen. A dramatic sight they must have made and a memorable one, even in those days when ships of the Grand Fleet were common on the coast—the Drake listing heavily and on fire aft, marked by her four tall funnels as she rounded Rue Point, surrounded by a flotilla of twelve small ships weaving to and fro in circular formation. On board the ships, every lookout strained his eyes for a periscope, and other watchkeepers below decks listened on their hydrophones for the distinctive sound of an enemy propeller. Submarines often came back for a second shot.

As they entered the Sound there was an explosion. H.M.S. Brisk was seen to be down by the head, but there was relief when it was found to be a mine, not another torpedo. She was towed off to Lough Foyle by a trawler. At noon Captain Radcliffe anchored the Drake in Church Bay in the hope of carrying out repairs, but even if Francis Drake was "in his hammock and a thousand leagues away", the ship bearing his name was destined to lay her bones beside the island he had once raided. Shortly after anchoring the big warship began to increase her heel rapidly and had to be abandoned, her crew being taken off by the Martin and Delphinium. As the Drake capsized at anchor, her captain must have bitterly regretted that he did not go half a mile further up and drive her onto the beach at Church Bay where there would have been a much better chance of salvage. But the risk of the magazines exploding was in his mind when he refrained from getting too close to the island. A Court Martial held afterwards decided that the captain had been justified in proceeding alone after leaving the convoy, but that in future an escort for major war vessels like the Drake, must be provided. The strain on destroyers at that period was extremely severe for the whole of the force based at Buncrana in Lough Swilly, twenty destroyers and ten sloops, were employed protecting three outward and four homeward convoys on the day when the Drake struck.

One of the islanders, Mr. Albert Glass, recalls that he was working at the limestone cliff quarries as the big ship came in and he and the men with him took to their heels fearing an explosion. A few hours later the Lugano, a flour ship, was torpedoed west of the island and much of her cargo floated ashore with the centre of the bags still in usable condition.

The capsized Drake's bottom remained on the surface for some time, but later she sank 18 feet below the surface. The wreck is marked by a buoy, but in spite of this, at least three ships have since got into trouble by striking the sunken hull. By a curious coincidence the Rev. Alex Gage of the Rathlin family, had been chaplain aboard the Drake from 1907 to 1909.

In spite of all the watchfulness the U-boats still operated close round the island. At dusk on February 5th, 1918, the liner Tuscania was sunk with the loss of forty-four lives seven miles north of Kenramer by UB77, and a month later the Santa Maria, an American tanker, was torpedoed in the Sound. Her wreck is marked on the chart today close north of Fair Head. With the longer days came two U-boat sinkings to cheer the trawlermen turned naval ratings in their monotonous task. On April 17th islanders awoke to the sound of gunfire and the boom of depth charges. The drifter Pilot Me (Skipper Walker) sighted a periscope off Torr Head and by dropping depth charges forced the U-boat to the surface. The Young Fred came up to assist, the submarine was driven by gunfire to submerge again and finally finished off with more depth charges. This was the end of UB82, a big submarine 181 feet long, with a 4.1 inch gun, a machine gun and five torpedo tubes; with this armament and a speed of 13 knots she was far more than a match for any pair of trawlers if she had fought it out on the surface. A fortnight later the UB85 surrendered to the trawler Coreopsis in the same area within sight of the island. Her crew were so sick with gas poisoning after two days submerged dodging nets that there was no fight left in them.

There were stories of U-boats obtaining supplies of food and petrol on the island, but if they ever did land men for such reasons on the Irish coast which has never been proved, Rathlin, at the centre of so much naval activity, would have been the last place they would have picked.

Between the Wars

Peace returned at last and the Rathlin men who had served at sea came home. The barrage nets were sold for scrap and the trawlers dispersed. One remaining relic, and a useful one, is the light on Rue Point. The hydrophone station from Torr Head was moved to Ballycastle as a tennis pavilion. One occasionally sees one of the glass balls used to float the nets retained as a garden ornament.

Hard on the heels of the war came the "troubles" in Ireland. Those interested in ending British rule in Ireland pursued their object by guerilla war throughout the land. Once again men "on the run" found the island a useful refuge and fled there as not altogether welcome guests. A year or two later came the truce and the Treaty. Rathlin and the north eastern six counties remained united to Scotland and England while the rest of the country became independent.

The population of the island continued slowly to decline. In the last hundred and fifty years life on islands has become progressively more difficult. The technical devices of our so-called civilisation should have made it easier, but what reverses the good effects is the constant way in which the gap in "standard of living" grows wider between remote communities and the cities.

Far gone were the conditions of the eighteenth century when island farmers were the envy of their neighbours on the mainland. In those days when roads ashore were almost non-existent, and the small farmer might have to hump a bale of wool on his back ten miles to market, island farmers had easy transport to their customers by water. In the days before "bagstuff" fertilisers, island shores produced wrack for manuring the land. Islanders could do a good trade at times by meeting the fashionable demands for seabirds' feathers: the birds themselves and their eggs provided a ready food supply. Steam trawlers had not invaded the inshore banks, and fish were easier to catch. There was always the chance of sudden wealth from a shipwreck. In the middle of the last century there were a hundred a year round the Irish coasts and islands got more than their share.

There was in those days for islanders a comforting feeling of belonging to a community, of self reliance, and, apart from the massacres which were almost confined among Irish islands to Rathlin alone, a sense of protection in the surrounding sea. Elsewhere in remoteness, it seemed to an islander, some less fortunate mortals struggled for existence in the great unknown of the mainland. I have met people with that cosy outlook within the last year or two. To its own people Rathlin is not just their world, it is the world.

Now the mass media of communication, newspapers, radio and television bring this other world into jarring and inevitable proximity. The specious delights of the dance hall, the coffee bar, the picture house, the apparent ease of changing jobs, of finding a marriage partner, of earning big money, of "living", act as almost irresistible inducement to emigration from islands. On Rathlin there are not good enough harbours to take advantage of easier fishing in large boats. Almost the only positive amenities that civilisation has brought to its people as an island community are the radio telephone for summoning help in illness or keeping in touch with friends ashore, and the marine engine to take much of the back-breaking labour out of boating, to which one might now add the helicopter for evacuating the seriously ill. Tractors for agriculture are a two edged benefit for they mean less jobs on the farm.

With these facts beginning to become apparent even fifty years ago it is not hard to see why the population of Rathlin has steadily declined. By 1922 it had dropped in eighty years from a peak of 1,200, an uneconomically high figure, to about 300.

In 1922, a Mr. Johnston who had obtained a lease of the mineral rights until 1959, opened a limestone quarry at Killeany, employing about a dozen island men to supply Glasgow City. Having made plans for further developments he purchased a share in the Estate from Captain Gage's brothers. However, soon afterwards he got into financial difficulties, and the quarry closed.

In 1930, most of the tenanted farms were acquired by the Government and were sold to the tenants, many of whom are still paying the land purchase annuity, under the terms of the Land Purchase Act. The Gage Estate was thus reduced to the Manor House and surrounding grounds, a number of dwellings and plots of land not forming part of a farm, most of the Loughs, and various easements and rights including all sporting rights.

In 1966, Brigadier Gage purchased all of Mr. Johnston's interests, and consequently what remains of the original Rathlin Estate is again in the hands of the Gage family.

In 1930 on the 1st March, the Rathlin life saving company were summoned just at dusk to help the steam trawler Shackleton ashore near Greenan Point on the north of the island, in dense fog. Unable to see more than 50 yards and so guided only by the shouts of the sailors, they succeeded at the seventh shot in firing a rocket so that the line fell directly across the ship. Then by means of a breeches buoy and a whole night's work the crew of 14 were hauled first to the shore then up the cliffs. This was recognised as the finest piece of life saving work of the year in the British Isles and an award made to the Rathlin team. A brass tablet on the door of the rocket store in Church Bay commemorates the event, and a marble one in the Hall records the names of all those who took part in the rescue.

The Second World War

During the Second World War, unlike many of the Scottish islands further north, Rathlin did not have servicemen stationed on it. Islanders did good work by manning an auxiliary lookout station on the north side, where in bad weather watch is still maintained today. The lighthouses were once again extinguished by order of the Admiralty and only switched on for a few minutes at a time to guide in a particular ship or convoy. Throughout the war, however, according to Sean O'Callaghan in "The Jackboot in Ireland", a man on the island kept an illicit radio transmitter going and reported the movements of shipping. It seems in retrospect impossible that he could have avoided detection for long once British control systems were built up. People who were on the island during the war consider the story to be bunkum.[1] There was no net barrage for submarines were too powerful for this to be effective while other anti-submarine devices had improved. The convoy system was introduced from the very beginning of the war and once again the long grey rows of ships formed up between Rathlin and Islay. There were again stories of U-boats calling. One islander even saw a midget submarine surfaced on the east coast and Hunnish crewmen drawing water from the well in Brackens Cave, but nothing was ever proved.

Sorley's bones, which had lain undisturbed in the vault of Bonamargy Abbey for 350 years, were upset by robbers in about 1940, looking for treasure or just lead. They were replaced in a new casket but this in turn was rifled in the 1960s. I dug him in the ribs the other day, for his great bones could be seen through a rent in the coffin.

A bucketful of seabirds' eggs has traditionally been a good "finisher" for cattle on the island; it puts a bit of a gloss on their coats and compensates for the rough handling they inevitably get being hog tied and lowered into a boat sometimes by the tail, for transport to the mainland. This is not due to any lack of consideration for the animals by island farmers; with the absence of adequate piers there is no other method. Seabirds' eggs in normal times are not much used on the island for human consumption but during the war, there was of course an insatiable demand from the mainland and many thousands were shipped to Ballycastle. In days gone by every family had rights to sections of the cliffs, marked sometimes by stakes set at the top. Every ledge and cranny had its name, now rapidly being forgotten. The island climbers had tremendous skill and confidence—I can speak from

---

[1] A possible explanation of this story and similar references in "Spies in Ireland" (Stephan) is that "Rathlin" was a code word for a station situated elsewhere.

a little experience having been over the cliffs to look for shear-waters' eggs many years ago. With Frank Craig at the top in control of the rope, I felt safer than in a city street. The feats of some of the cragsmen of olden days are still remembered—Paddy the climber reached the top of Stack an Fir Lea where today in summer 6,000 nesting guillemots and shearwaters can be counted from the platform by the west light. On the other side is Stack An Ooskey known to the climbers for the well near its top. A shepherd boy in the last century climbed Marie Isla Stack on the north side.

Rathlin tides helped Britain's war effort in an unexpected way, for early on it was found that British magnetic mines were detonating spontaneously and it was suspected that this was due to the effect on the electrical field of sudden reversals of the direction of the stream. I met a retired sailor a few years ago, who was ordered in 1941 when captain of a weapons research ship, to anchor in the strongest and most quickly changing stream he could find, to test out better forms of firing mechanism. Rathlin Sound was ideal and he anchored between Fair Head and the Rue for several days, but was embarrassed when island boat-men, coming out to offer assistance, urged him to move to a less crazy anchorage; he could not of course say why he was there, but was able to buy eggs from them—a considerable luxury in those days, for his crew.

Great were the pickings for bold boatmen during the war—barrels full of rum worth £70 a piece came ashore at one time, at others "ye could have walked across the Sound on the timber washed into it". A Dutch ship dragged her anchors and was wrecked near the Bull in 1940. The boats of the troop ship, Lock Garry, landed in rough weather and darkness near Doon Point in January, 1942, with the loss of twenty-nine lives. They were succoured at considerable personal risk and sacrifice by Rathlin men.

Just at the end of the war an investigation was made as to the cost and feasibility of a good sea link. The Brodie Report recommended a harbour in Church Bay based on the rock of the Bo, and improvements to Ballycastle, at a then cost of about £150,000, but doubts were expressed as to the durability of the recommended structures. For one reason or another nothing was done, and while the world proceeded rapidly to improve standards of living, Rathlin was left to face the post-war period still without an all weather harbour.

Circular Foundation of Sweat House, Rathlin Diameter = 2½ M.

Cattle ready for a passage to Ballycastle.

The south pier, Church Bay. A boat being heaved off the sand with levers as passengers wait. The Manor House in background.

CHAPTER 17

WANTED A HARBOUR

RATHLIN TODAY

*"To understand Rathlin, you have to be a dreamy ethereal
sort of person and stay there until Ireland becomes just a blur on
the horizon, and you forget all about the mainland and the rest of
the world."*—Mary Campbell, 1960

Not many people are lucky enough to be able to stay on
Rathlin for as long periods as Mrs. Campbell, the author of "Sea
Wrack," during her lengthy eventful life.

Once you are there, however, that feeling of nothing else in
the world mattering arrives remarkably promptly. To understand
the island, however, takes a good deal longer, and even understanding is not enough for Rathlin today; what the island needs now
is a fair share of the facilities nowadays available to communities
on the mainland, even isolated ones.

One of the things which helps towards an appreciation of the
island is to visit it in the winter. Cross the sound in an open boat
with the spray breaking over everyone on board for the full hour
of the passage, while your face becomes numb in a keen north wind
and the taste of salt freshens your lips. You begin to understand
how the island is surrounded and dominated by

*"The dragon-green, the luminous, the dark, the serpent-haunted
sea,*
*The snow besprinkled wine of earth, the blue and white flower
foaming sea."*[1]

Lights visible from Rathlin

Watch a fiery dawn come up over Torr Head, see it tinge
pink the huge cumulus clouds on the opposite side of the island
over Islay, and tip one hillock after another with gold. Stand on
a high point by night and watch the ten lighthouses that can be
seen from there in clear weather—Orsay (one flash every five
seconds) to the north west, Inistrahull (one flash every 20 seconds)
to the west, the smaller ones of Shrove at the entrance to the Foyle,
the Otter Rock lightship off Islay, and Sanda by the Clyde, high
Kintyre to the east (two flashes every 30 seconds) and The
Maidens to the south (three flashes every 20 seconds). In the
middle of the constellation is the island's own three sets of flashes.
You realise how centrally Rathlin is situated betwixt Scotland and
Ireland.

---

[1] Flecker.

Mr. James McCurdy and Mr. Paddy McQuilkin, two island boatmen, returning from Ballycastle, with Knocklayd Mountain in the background.

Photo Northern Ireland Tourist Board.

Stand on the pier the day you had meant to go home and see great grey-bearded seas, that no boat could face, racing down the Sound and feel the frustration of imprisonment. You have to experience a few strong emotions in a place to know it. In a fog when one of the island boats is overdue there is an almost tangible tension, near to fear, in the atmosphere. At the same time the fantasies of Gaelic mythology become understandable as the mist wraiths distort and enlarge familiar objects.

If fog or storm keep you a day or two extra on the island, it will also give you time to look for signs of what will happen to it next.

In the twenty-five years since the end of the war the population has continued to decline. In 1970 it stood at 109. This is a density of only 20 people per square mile as against 130 for the rural areas of Northern Ireland as a whole, so it is clearly very low. But Rathlin, its heathery rocky ridges interspersed with meadows, valleys and rushy lakes, is akin to a mountain area ashore. A hundred people is an adequate crew if other things are right. Today a high proportion of those remaining are elderly and in 1970 only nine children were attending school. The demand of the day for secondary education has been added to the other factors mentioned in the last chapter which have tended to depopulate all islands in this century.

Nevertheless Rathlin today is a self-confident community. Its people are sound observers of and shrewd commentators on events ashore and in the rest of the world. They know the advantages as well as the disadvantages of island life but are free from that constant expectation of change and "improvement" which is the mark of this generation ashore. By and large they like things to go on being the same. That makes them restful companions, and I know them for staunch friends.

The Gages are still in occupation of the Manor House. Captain Gage's widow, Mrs. Gage, died in 1947 and was succeeded by her surviving son, Brigadier Gage, who retired from the Army a year later and now resides on the island during the summer months.

A few events of recent years are worth chronicling. In 1950 the Ministry of Agriculture started a forestry scheme and during the next four years a hundred and twenty acres were planted. Spruce, chestnut, some pines and willow made some progress but the salt-laden winds proved too strong for growth to be at an economic rate, and further work has been suspended.

1955 saw the first car arrive, in a snowstorm perilously perched across the thwarts of a 30-foot open boat, for the use of the District Nurse. Now there are a couple of dozen on the island as well as many tractors and motor bikes. The first traffic accident has yet

to happen but although the roads are now given regular maintenance with the help of a stonebreaker supplied seven years ago by
the County Council, tyres have a shortish life for there is still no
tarmac. The stonebreaker, all seven tons of it, had to be trans-
ported by dredger from the Foyle, an indication of transport difficulties.

Rathlin Sound was swum for the first time when on the 11th
June, 1957, Jack McClelland succeeded in making his way across
the channel. The major part of the feat consisted in surviving the
cold water for I have always found Rathlin to be one of the coldest
places in the whole of Ireland for bathing. The water is never at
rest, and one of the few things the island lacks is shelving beaches
where it might warm a little.

In 1957, too, Lord Wakehurst, Governor of Northern Ireland,
visited the island; he must have noted the relative bareness of
Raghery compared to his native Colonsay.

Bruce came back, at least his front teeth did, in 1968, dang-
ling on the end of a string held by his descendant, the present Lord
Bruce. With the teeth (and what teeth!) came Bruce's huge two-
handed sword of hammered steel, the leather hilt as good as the
day he wielded it at Bannockburn.

In 1960 Rathlin ceased to be a separate parish in the Church
of Ireland when it was united with Ballintoy. Since then, after
having had a rector resident for more than two hundred and thirty
years, the island only has a Protestant clergyman on it for a month
or two in the summer. It is advertised as a holiday job for the
months from June to September and there is usually a waiting
list to get it.   In winter services are held once a month.   The
Roman Catholic Church maintains, however, a curate in charge,
resident there still.

Rathlin still claims its toll of wrecks. In 1949 the lifesaving
team won the national award for the second time. This was early
in the morning of February 28th, when the trawler Pintail ran on
the rocks just below the Bull Light. In complete darkness and a
fierce gale the lifesaving crew, under Mr. Daniel McQuilkin,
descended the cliff which would have been a difficult thing to do
even in daylight, and once again by means of a breeches buoy
rescued all eleven members of the ship's crew. They were brought
to Portrush later that day by the lifeboat which had stood by in
terrific seas during the rescue. Dan McQuilkin was awarded the
British Empire Medal for his services.

In 1962 the trawler, Ella Hewitt, sank after colliding with the
sunken Drake while coming in to anchor in the bay. She was outward bound and her fuel tanks full so the wreck is marked even
eight years later by a thin slick of oil. A Royal Naval submarine
also grounded on the wreck while hiding on a N.A.T.O. exercise

and had to be towed off by a destroyer which herself damaged her propellers during the operation. The submarine commander missed his promotion as a result and afterwards when passing the wreck used to "pipe the side" in mock salute remarking that his brass hat was hanging on the Drake.

In April, 1968, the brand new twenty seven foot fishery patrol boat, "Impetus," bound for Lough Neagh, was wrecked on the east side and the crew saved themselves by swimming ashore. This was a curious incident as it was a very fine night with, as one of the islanders told me, slack water "and just a wee swing of wind from the east." One of the crew claimed that it was his third shipwreck on Rathlin for he had been on the Pintail and the Shackleton, too. In February, 1971, a Dutch ship spent twenty-one hours on the rocks near the Rue.

The Drake, which has been slowly oozing cordite for the last fifty years is to be raised for scrap. A salvage firm has undertaken the job and so the conger eels who have laired secure in her gun barrels and disported themselves in the captain's day cabin will be in for a shock, and the islanders who have been exercising their talent for improvision by using cordite-sticks as firelighters will have to use paraffin instead.

Rathlin has had a radio telephone for about twenty years. In 1970 a 24-hour S.T.D. telephone was installed, mainly through the efforts of Henry Clark who was at that time M.P. for the area. The equipment came on a Western Isles car ferry which now operates between Red Bay in Antrim and Campbelltown in Scotland and just managed to scrape into Church Bay.

The National Playing Fields Association in 1966 provided money for posts and equipment to help the island football team. In 1971 the Army surveyed a site for an airstrip with a view to providing one as an amenity. Lord Grey of Naunton, Governor of Northern Ireland, visited the island in July of that year.

Rathlin's Neighbours

Those who like comparing one isle with another might ponder on the fact that Islay, sixteen miles away, has seven distilleries and earns more dollars per head than any other community in the British Isles.

Gigha, one of my favourite islands, is about the same size as Rathlin from which it lies thirty miles north-north-east. Its soil is similar but less elevated above sea level, and sheltered to some extent from the prevailing winds by a ridge of high ground along the west shore. It has a thriving milk and cheese industry, and at Achamore House owned by Sir James Horlick, one of the finest gardens in the British Isles, where tender shrubs thrive in the shelter of the trees he has laboriously grown with loving care over the last thirty years.

Milk and cheese manufacture have the advantage of giving much more employment than does the raising of beef. Gigha has a positive policy by which all the farmers stick to dairy farming for this reason. They improve their technique regularly and now collect the milk in tankers.

Jura, the next nearest neighbour, has good salmon fishing and on its mountains live thousands of head of deer, including some of the heaviest stags and finest heads in Scotland.

As compared to Islay and Jura, Rathlin has no rivers big enough for salmon or to produce water for distilling. It is too small for deer, except fenced in a park, but the poorest land would do, for deer can flourish on bare hillsides where cows would go blind looking for grass. Stags on the island skyline would look magnificent and add much to the attractions of a visit for there is nowhere in the north of Ireland at present where they can be seen to advantage.

As compared to Gigha, Rathlin's climate appears to be much colder, possibly because the North Atlantic Drift, the extension of the Gulf Stream which reaches the west of the British Isles, is deflected away from the north of Ireland towards the Scottish coast. So it is doubtful if it could ever produce a famous garden but it could turn out good milk and cheese. However, the pedigree beasts required for high milk yields would be too valuable to be hogtied and thrown into the bottom of an open boat, so they cannot be got to the island. Rathlin has to rely on beef, mutton and fishing for its livelihood, and wild flowers for its charms. Scenically it has far more grandeur than any of the other three.

The most important difference between Rathlin and the others is that each Scottish island has a steamer pier and several visits a week from a comfortable mail boat with good freight and passenger accommodation.[2]

---

[2] In answer to a Parliamentary question by Mr. Henry Clark, M.P. for North Antrim, designed to draw attention to Rathlin's problems in 1966, the Secretary of State for Scotland gave the following answer:

"Expenditure by central and local government on the provision and improvement of piers and harbours during the financial years 1955-56 and 1965-66 was as follows:

Tiree	...	£104,320
Coll	...	£108,068
Colonsay	...	£156,772
Islay	...	£41,958

These figures do not include the cost of repair and maintenance work which is met entirely by the local authority."

SCOTTISH OFFICE.

Expenditure on Rathlin in the same period was minimal.

Rathlin, however, has the advantage not enjoyed by the others of having an important town only five miles away on the mainland. To take advantage of this, and help towards efficient farming, what is needed is a good harbour at both ends of the crossing including a permanent berth safe in all weathers for a boat with covered accommodation. At present the Ballycastle end is more often the bugbear than the landing at Rathlin or the seas in the Sound. Often and often you could leave the island safely and make the crossing on days when Ballycastle pier is under white water and it is impossible to land there. Island communities need help, and piers and similar facilities are much better than unemployment pay, or a blind eye to unpaid rates. In the long run a hovercraft, which can be docked on dry land, may provide the answer, but at the present stage maintenance is too costly and intricate for one of these devices to be practical. Rathlin today is unspoiled or under-developed, depending on one's point of view. It is presumptuous for any outsider who has never lived on the island or owned any of it to say what should happen to it. That is up to those who live there today and who have played their part in making it the delightful place it is. Among them there are of course many shades of opinion. Even in terms of its future Rathlin remains a disputed isle. It does seem important, however, that whatever ferry service is developed a large share of the employment therefrom and the profit, if any, should remain with the islanders themselves.

"A shuttle boat service and hordes of visitors would wreck the island," say some, but others that it is unfair to expect Rathlin to be kept on in isolation as a piece of life of fifty years ago just to amuse a few dozen visitors a year. With proper connections to the mainland so that visitors could be sure of arriving and leaving in time during a season of say from April to October, there could be a good living on the island for a population far above the 1970 one.

In this rapidly overcrowding age when Northern Ireland has the fastest growth rate of population of any part of the British Isles, Rathlin, as its only major sea island, could become a tourist attraction of a high order. At present the island has no hotel and although the islanders are justly famed for their hospitality it is difficult for a stranger to arrange accommodation in advance. I can think of few pleasanter holidays than a week or a weekend in a rented cottage on the island. For a holiday it is just the right size—from a central point you can reach any part of it in the course of a leisurely morning's walk. It is big enough always to leave scope for further exploration, but sufficiently small for a visitor to retain in his memory the impression of an entity, not just a series of places visited.

An electric power supply would be useful to provide the amenities which holiday-makers demand. There is plenty of private but no public electricity on Rathlin at the moment but there has been talk at times, started by Irish Lights, of laying a power cable either under water or overhead from Fair Head to the island, and this would not be all that expensive a project. To put it in perspective, think of a village of one hundred or so inhabitants in the mountains of Mourne, a hundred miles away. Money would be provided with little question to build a road to it and for a cable for electricity to service it at anything up to £200,000, but although people romanticise about islands, administrators have for them a different standard.

Rathlin today, if you manage to get there, is a delightful place to visit whether you land on the white half circle of Church Bay, or by the old granary at Ushet, whether you walk up past the heather to the east lighthouse or get a lift out to the west to see the birds, or just wander round and talk to the people. If you want to hear a bit of "crack" and indulge in the ancient Irish pastime of talking and drinking there is no finer place in the world to do so than Tony McCuaig's public house.

Whatever happens to Rathlin in the future, short of a nuclear war, it will remain a place of beauty, of dramatic cliffs and of terraced roads, of brilliant light, and most important of all, of people who have more time to think about the real issues of life than those of us who have to live in the hurly-burly of the mainland: people whose views are worth listening to and whose friendship is something to be prized.

One hopes that all the island's wars are over. At least there is enough philosophy in the rugged smile with which she greets visitors to forget the bloodshed and remember the tenacity and courage of the hundred generations of warriors who have ruled her, each in its turn loving their island home as they grew familiar with every creek and cranny of her shoreline. To those who have visited Rathlin even once it is a place to want to go back to, a place of fresh air, of movement and light linked to the silences of huge headlands. The south face is a flash of winter sun illuminating white cliffs, the Ruecallan on the north is the soaring of a buzzard. Altandivan, beside it, is the deep croak of a raven, the vast amphitheatre of Altachuile the stoop of a peregrine, Kenramer the curling descent of a rock pigeon on half closed wings homing to its cave-hidden nest. Skerriagh is a huge sphinx seen through a curtain of seagulls. The frowning cliffs of Altacarry where the lighthouse peeps down from the top of the precipice, recall the hover of a kestrel. Bruce's Cave below with pink interior set in black cliffs is the mouth of a negress. On the east Doon Point is a psychedelic rearrangement of the Giants Causeway, the fretted shoreline beside it the zig-zag flight of a snipe.

As the visitor returns he crosses a Sound that has parted to the lifting bows of the Irish curraghs, Viking longships, Norman carracks, English frigates, Scottish galleys and pirate cutters, who have in turn made landfalls on this disputed isle.

Air view of the north side; in the bottom right hand corner is Doonigiall, the port which served the old fort Dunmore.

Photo by J. K. St. Joseph, Cambridge University, Collection.

APPENDIX I

A RAID ON RATHLIN IN ABOUT 200 B.C.

This account is based on the version in "The Martial Deeds of Congal Clarineach", published by the Irish Texts Society, and a translation of unknown authorship quoted by Hill in "McDonnells of Antrim". The original Irish tract is of seventeenth-century origin, but shows signs of very early sources. There are a number of circumstantial details which make it virtually certain that the storyteller knew Rathlin and is recording an attack which really took place there about two thousand years ago. Congal is listed in the Annals as having ruled Ireland in the second century B.C.

In reading the story one should have a picture of Dunmore (in Irish "The Great Fort"). As it stands today, it is a circular cake-shaped hill some 70 feet high and 250 feet in diameter at the base, rising out of flat ground. Outcrops of rock appear round the rim at the top, making a sheer edge in places and there are traces of the perimeter walls which originally crowned it, and of a long building inside them. It is a position of enormous natural strength and stands about a quarter of a mile back from the northern shore in one of the glens which traverse the island. The murmuring of the sea from the north seems to be echoed up the glen even on a calm day, and can easily be heard from the top of the fort. The walls of the fort may well have been constructed of limestone and this would conform with the description of the ships sighting "a lofty white palace" as they approached from the north. The situation is a commanding one, overlooking on the north the approach to Doonigiall, the only port on the outer side of the island, and on the south through a narrow defile, the axe factory at Brockley. On three sides the approach to the fort is guarded by bogs which may have been deeper and more treacherous in ancient times than they are today. On the east side are traces of a wall guarding the only dry land approach to the base of the castle.

About a quarter of a mile west of Dunmore is another fort, known as Dunbeg, "the small fort". On the south side of the island about half a mile away and a little to the east, but not visible from Dunmore, is a third fortified hill, of which the name has not been preserved. One of these seems to be the smaller "palace" which King Donn set aside for Congal on his arrival on Rathlin.

Just west of Doonigiall port is a point which is still called Greenan (a sunny place), which identifies with the spot where the messengers first saw Taise. The hill itself is bare, but there was probably a wooden bower where the ladies sat in the better clime of those ancient days enjoying the magnificent view of the cliffs on the north coast and the mountains of Scotland across the sea.

It seems likely that Nabghodon, son of Ioruadh, is an allegorical name, an Irish version of Nebuchadnezzer, son of Herod, and simply signifies in the story a powerful king coming over the sea from the north. For Huardha "the cold place", we need not look on the modern map, and its identification with Norway by some translators is, to say the least of it, uncertain. The main thread of the story, however, is likely to have been based on a real attempted conquest of Rathlin in a fight over a woman. The grating of the keels on the ships could have been heard by Feargus as he sat in the fort, and the short way down which the beaten forces of Nabghodon were pursued is the glen leading down to Doonigiall, the current name for the port on the north.

It must have been around the base of the fort on the flat ground that the fighting took place.

THE BATTLES OF CONGAL CLARINEACH

A king ruled Huardha whose name was Nabghodon, son of Ioruadh. He had a good wife named Bebid, but she became sick and died. Nabghodon fell into a deep decline through sorrow, and neither engaged in conflict or made arrangements of any kind for a whole year. Meanwhile, neighbouring states were harassing his kingdom most grievously. At the end of that period the people of Huardha assembled and came in a body before the king. "Nabghodon," said they, "your kingdom is being destroyed around you; tell us what disorder has been afflicting you that we may have it cured". "I do not wish to tell it," responded he. "If it be grief for the loss of your wife that troubles you, we will make a search throughout every country and race of people, and if we find a suitable match for you, in any part of the world, we will bring her to you either of her free will or by force". "There is certainly such a girl to be found," said Nabghodon. "What country is she to be found in?" asked they. "There is an island at the western extremity of Europe," said he, "and it is called Innis Fuineadh; its beautiful; and if any wife befitting me can be found in the world it is there." Thereupon the nobility of Huardha appointed thirty champions to proceed to Ireland; and a great galley was accordingly fitted out and they hoisted their speckled sails and sped over the foam-crested waves on their voyage to Ireland. They sighted the island of ships which is called Rachrin on the coast of Dalriada[1] and saw at a distance the lofty royal city, with its elegant white houses, its greenans of glass, and its wide palaces. "That is certainly a noble city,"[2] said Nabghodon's messengers; "and it may be as well for us to put in there and refresh ourselves since we have arrived on the coast of Ireland." As soon as they landed, they beheld the most youthful and fairest of the children of Adam, having clear blue eyes, and curling tresses and a melodious voice. She and her band of female attendants sat sewing in a sunny bower. Nabghodon's people stared at the symmetry and ornate dress of the girl while their eyes were fixed on her figure. "Our journey has been prosperous," said they, "for if we searched the whole world we should not find a finer woman, and we will bring her to Nabghodon". They inquired of the people who was the chief of this island? "King Donn, son of Iomchada, son of Miodhna, son of Caischlothach a descendent of Cearmad Milbheoll, son of Dagdha, of the prime line of the Tuatha De Danaan race, is king," replied they. "Who is the beautiful young lady who is head over yonder female band?" asked the messengers. "Ye must have been bred in some remote isle in the sea" said the islanders, "if ye have not heard of Taise Taobhgheal, daughter of King Donn." They thereupon brought them food and ale; and King Donn himself came to inquire of whence they came? "We are the people of Nabghodon," said they, "and we came to seek as a wife for him your daughter Taise". You shall have an answer from me without further deliberation; for, even though my daughter should not have been betrothed to another man, I would not give her to him, because the assistance of such a son-in-law would be too remote from me," replied King Donn. "She is the possession of Congal Clarineach, son of Rudhraidh, King of Ireland". "Then," said they, "you are not aware what trouble is in store for you, King Donn; for Nabghodon will come hither and kill all the inhabitants of your city, and all Ireland will be devastated, and you yourself will be slain, and your daughter carried away." "Only that I would not be guilty of an act of treachery towards any person," said King Donn, "a single man of you who would have said such things would never escape from me alive to tell your tidings."

---

1 That is to distinguish it from the two other Rathlins off the Irish coast.

2 The Irish word would be Caithir indicating a fortified settlement—City is the nearest English word.

They rose betimes the next morning, and having steered away over the same expanse of ocean, arrived in due time at their home port whence they proceeded to Nabghodon. Nabghodon asked them their news. "We have," said they, "found a wife really befitting you; and we have never seen an individual, either man or woman, of any race on earth display such beauty as she, and if you had heard of her before you would have put to death your former wife to marry her". When the king heard the account of the young lady, he became deeply enamoured of her, jumped out of his bed with great vigour and enquired who was her father and what was the reason they had not brought her along with them. "King Donn is her father," said they; "and we were not sufficiently numerous to give him battle. In fact, had not we been enjoying his hospitality, he would have put us all to death for asking his daughter." "Where does this man live?" inquired Nabghodon. "In an island on the coast of Ireland, where he owns a lofty, splendid city, and has a body of troops armed with keen-pointed javelins always prepared for battle," responded they. Nabghodon thereupon mustered his forces, and invited all the nobles of Huardha to attend.

King Donn learned that this great fleet was on its way against him, but his people advised him that he should not meet the forces of Huardha on his own since druidism could afford him no protection. "Well, then," said he, "it is better for me to go to Congal, since he himself will protect his wife against them, for I am unable to muster sufficient forces to meet them in battle, while your druidical mists are no protection unless Congal shall assist us." He accordingly set out from the island. It happened that Congal was repairing his ships and gathering his men, when he discerned a single curragh bounding over the waves of the ocean towards him; it contained only one noble-looking man. He continued to observe it for some time until he said, "I know that man in the curragh; he is King Donn, son of Iomchadha, and coming to me to know if I am ready to wed his daughter." King Donn steered his curragh towards the fleet of Congal, and saluted him. "Where is this fleet bound for?" inquired King Donn. "To your house," responded Congal. "That is good," said King Donn, "since a larger fleet than yours is on its way to invade us." "Whose fleet is it?" asked Congal. "That of Nabghodon son of Ioruadh, who sent to demand your wife from me," responded King Donn, "but I did not give her to him, and he is now on his way with a very formidable fleet to force her from me—come then and protect her from them." "O, King Donn, proceed before me, and prepare for the reception of those chieftains belonging to me, and tell Taise that I will myself encounter Nabghodon; for if he shall come to claim her as his prize, he shall fall by my hand."

King Donn, thereupon, departed and proceeded before them to his own city and Congal, with his whole strength of his forces followed, and they there received the refreshment of the bath and heroes' portions of food and ale in a palace outside his fortress which King Donn had prepared for them. They all afterwards came into the great fortress and King Donn said to Fraoch, "Tell us, druid, how shall this place fare tonight?" "This is the fortress which I foretold would be assaulted," said Fraoch, "and you will have to defend it well." "We shall do so," said they, "for though the forces of Nabghodon coming against us are numerous, nevertheless we shall be victorious." Congal then came into the hall and sat on his regal seat. "Feargus," said Congal, "in what part of this house will you be tonight," "I shall be in the northern porch," responded Feargus; "for should Nabghodon arrive he would make for the northern part." And Feargus went and placed his warlike weapons above his head in the open porch, and Muireadhach Meirgeach, son of the King of Alba, came to occupy the other open porch to support Feargus.

[There follows a description of the seating in the hall and of the banquet by all the warriors and Taise and her maidens.]

Nabghodon steered directly to Rachruinn, and saw the light of burning lamps while he was still out at sea. "Pilot," said Nabghodon, "what place is that where the great light is?" "It is King Donn's palace, and there is the woman we are seeking, and the man she was betrothed to—the son of the monarch of Ireland is there tonight celebrating his nuptials." "I hope he is there," said Nabghodon. "Let the crews of three ships proceed to explore the island." As to Feargus, he was listening to the murmuring of the sea on the northern side when he heard the grating of large ships being beached on the island. He armed himself and set out. When Muireadhach Meirgeach, son of the king of Alba, saw that, he followed Feargus out, and hastened to assist him in guarding the harbour. Feargus grasped the prow of the first ship with his powerful hands, and shook it so that its planks started asunder, its binding bolts flew out, as well as all its other fastenings, and its timbers separated, and the crew fell through the yawning wreck on the strand . . . And Muireadhach Meirgeach, began to slaughter the warriors, while Feargus boarded the next ship, and commenced to kill the crew. Muireadhach Meirgeach followed him into each ship and they succeeded in slaying, without giving quarter, every man. They then returned to the hall, and having hung their weapons above their heads, each of them sat in his own place; yet they made no boast at all of the achievements they performed. Nabghodon, accompanied by the full fleet, then came after his people, and found them dead, mangled and bleeding and their ships complete wrecks. "Let us march to the fortress," said Nabghodon, "and avenge the murder of our people upon all the Irishmen within it. Fetch rocks and stones from the harbour with you, that we may shatter the hall with them." Thus they came against the fortress armed with heavy loads of stones from the strand. And when they reached it they made a furious assault so that the shields, javelins, and swords that were hung up fell upon the heads of the men, and only the upright columns of stone that supported the roof prevented it from falling in upon them. Thereupon Feargus, starting up, rushed out, and Muireadhach Meirgeach followed him; they took a speedy circuit around the fortress and made a courageous attack on the besiegers, and one hundred warriors of them were slain. They returned into the hall after that, once again hung their bloody weapons above their heads and refreshed themselves. All the foreigners in a body returned to the fortress, and made an assault upon all the gates around it. When Anadhal Eachtach, son of the King of the Connicati, and his three hundred men saw what they had done, they rushed out and made great slaughter, and they routed and pursued them until they reached the place where Nabghodon was. After that they returned to the hall and quenched their thirst.

Nabghodon then said, "Let us proceed again to the fortress and burn it and all that are in it." A strong force of the noble youths of Huardha proceeded to attack and shot fiery arrows at the walls. The three companions of Congal, Merne, Semhne, and Lathairne, rushed out by the southern gate, and quenched the fire and the firebrands and having slain the party of incendiaries did not stop until they entered by the same gate. So the army of the fortress succeeded in dispersing the enemy.

They passed the night in watchfulness until day came with its lustrous lights of morning. When it grew light Congal said, "Arise, my watchful sentries, assume your arms, and make a sortie from the gates." It was then they took their shields from the pins on which they were suspended, and their javelins from their rests, so that the whole hall shook terribly with the noise made by the four companies, for there was no other fortress like that fortress. Then Congal went forth with his companies in array and his splendid banners raised above their heads against the foreigners. When the King of Huardha observed this he arranged his men so as to form a shield ring round him. The kings recognised each other and their companies engaged in a furious conflict, and thinned the ranks of each other. Feargus then made his way forward, and carved the passage of a hero through the ranks of the foreigners. It was on that occasion that the first anger ever known to have seized Feargus was observed. Anadhal, son of the king of the Connicati, with his three hundred Connicatians, joined in the conflict, and they blew their fiery breathing upon the enemy's forces, making a gap of one hundred men in the battle, and dispersing and putting to flight the array. Then the valour and fury of Nabghodon was aroused, and he made a vigorous attack upon Congal, who had not before entered into personal conflict with him. Knowing that no help was at hand he did not much care if he died, provided that his fame should be preserved. So the champions engaged in single combat and they displayed the courage of two lions, the ferocity of two bears, and the strength of two oxen during their conflict. They suffered no person to approach within a distance of thirty feet of them on either side, in consequence of the fury of their combat. They fought from the dawn of early morning until the close of the day. The anger and animosity of Nabghodon against Congal increased at that time, when all the poets, musicians, women, and children of the city were near them looking on the fight. Bricne was likewise there, and seeing Congal on the point of being vanquished, Bricne roared so loud that he attracted the attention of all the Ultonians in the city upon him, and he said: "Upon thee, O Congal, be they cowardice. Feargus, son of Lede, has banished you from Ulster for your weakness; Nabghodon will cut off your head and carry away your wife." It was then Congal assumed his real strength and power, and he made a furious blow at Nabghodon by which he cleft his shield completely; he made a second blow at him by which he severed his head from his body, and having taken up the head in his hand exhibited it before the whole army of Huardha, which smote them with so much terror that they were easily vanquished. They had a very short way to flee to the sea; and though the carnage on the field of battle was great, it was still much greater on the shore, when the victorious warriors reached the ships. So was all the army of Huardha slain by Congal and his people. Their heads were piled into cairns and their clothes burned into ashes in that place, while the spoil was given to Congal. Hearing that Congal himself was severely hurt, King Donn and Taise came to visit him, and Taise placed her arm around his neck and looked at his wounds and scars. Then she examined the head of Nabghodon, "It is a royal countenance indeed," said she.

The victors retired to the city after that, and were placed in well glazed greenans, and in white well furnished houses; physicians were employed to heal their wounds, and they remained a fortnight over a month in the residence of King Donn. . . . .

When they were able to travel they enjoyed a great banquet, and the marriage feast of Congal and Taise. But they did not live happily ever after. Congal, according to the next episode in the saga, did not tarry long with Taise but made a long distance raid on Loughlan, the name sometimes given to Denmark, to seek another bride and had many adventures in Huardha itself as a result. He became high king after killing Lugaigh in a hand to hand battle as fierce as the one with Nabghodon.

APPENDIX 2

THE PLACE-NAME "RATHLIN"

By Dr. A. B. TAYLOR, C.B.E., F.R.S.E.

Rathlin is a very old island name, and its history is somewhat complicated.

An older generation called it *Raghry* or *Rachra*. The first of these names survives as *Raghery*, which is the name still used by many of the islanders and fishermen on the coast. The form *Rathlin*, which appears as early as 1213, is from Irish *Reachlainn*; *Reachlainn* is from Irish *Reachrainn*, which was the genitive case of *Reachra*.

The common form *Raghery* is also old, occurring in 1278. It sounds very like a Norse pronunciation of the Irish, for "ey" is Old Norse for "island".

Our Rathlin is not the only island with this name. It is shared with Rathlin O'Byrne off Donegal; and Rechra, now Lambay, just north of Dublin. There is another Rathlin, a peninsula with a narrow neck on the south side of Lough Neagh.

We learn the Old Irish form of the name from Adomnan's *Life of Saint Columba*, written in the seventh century. Adomnan was an Irishman, and spelled the name *Rechru*. This appears to be the earliest mention of the name in this form. In the Irish Annals, written somewhat later, it usually appears in the genitive, as for example *Rechrainne* in the Annals of Ulster.

The genitive form also occurs in the earliest European map to contain the island. This is a chart of Western European coasts by Angellino de Dalorto of Florence, drawn in 1325. His spelling is *Ragrin*.

But the name is still older than Adomnan. For it is to be found in some of the Latin and Greek geographers. The earliest of these is Pliny, whose *Natural History*, written in Rome about 77 A.D., gives *Riginea* after *Mona* and *Monapia* (i.e. Anglesea and the Isle of Man) as being "between Hibernia and Britannia." This suggests that he meant Rathlin. Next there is Ptolemy, the Greek geographer of Alexandria, writing about 150 A.D., who names *Rhikina* among other islands off the west of Scotland. At the end of the seventh century, an anonymous geographer of Ravenna in Italy spells the name *Regaina*. The letter "n" in these three forms suggests that they all derive from an Irish genitive like that quoted from the Annals of Ulster.

(It may be added that it is not quite certain that Ptolemy and the Ravenna geographer were definitely referring to Rathlin, although they are clearly using the old name that was applied to it.)

There are other occurrences of the name in early records in both the nominative and genitive cases, but these do not add substantially to the information given above. What we have discovered is that the name has its origin in Early Celtic before the time of Christ. In 1949, Professor Ifor Williams suggested in a note in *Archaelogia*, vol. 93, that *Rechru* had a Celtic root now represented by two Welsh words: *rhygnu*, "to scrape" or "to saw", and *rhygn-bran*, "a tally", which suggest a root-word *rhygn*, "a notch". This, he says, might suit a rugged island. And with this possible explanation it would seem wise to be content.

This discussion of the name Rathlin is based largely upon the following: P. W. Joyce, **Irish Names of Places**, Dublin 1887, vol. 1, pp. 111-112; J. H. Todd, **War of the Gaidhil with the Gaill**, London 1867, p. xxxiii; A. O. Anderson, **Adomnan's Life of St. Columba**, London 1961; I. A. Richmond and O. G. S. Crawford, "The British Section of the Ravenna Geographer," **Archaelogia**, London 1949, vol. 93, p. 44; Pliny, **Natural History**, Loeb Classics, London, Book IV, section xvi. List of Early forms of Rathlin in Dinnseanchas, Dublin, vol. II (1966), No. 1, 22-25.

APPENDIX 3

OTHER RATHLIN PLACE NAMES

Most Irish place names are much better untranslated e.g. the Clocka-doos sounds much more interesting than the Black Rocks, but sometimes bits of history are retained in the original version, so here is a list.

Ballycarry, baile carrac, the crooked townland.
Ballyconaghan, baile cuineocan, the townland of Coonaghan.
Ballygill, baile garol, the townland of seabirds.
Ballynagard, townland of the tinsmiths.

Carravinally, the quarterland of the swans.
Carrick-a-gile, rock of the sea birds.
Carrick-na-garrowna, the bream rock.
Carrowvindoon, the quarterland of the fort.
Cooraghy, a place of curraghs or boats.
Crockanagh, Cnoc-na-n-eac, the hill of the steeds. Eac was the general Irish word for horse in Rathlin.
Crockascridlin, Croc-a-Scriolm. Hill of screaming or of Scriolm (the heroine of a famous contest between two chiefs.)
Crockboy, Yellow Hill.
Crocknooey, Croc (cnoc)-na-h-uaime, the hill of the cave.

Illancarragh, the crooked rock (island).
Inancooan, Inan, an easy place for getting down to the shore in a cliff district. Cuan, a narrow inlet.
Inandrian, Inan of the sloe bushes.

Kebble, a burying-ground.
Killbrida, St. Brigid's Church.
Kinramer, thick or broad head.

Lacknakilly, the flagstone of the church. (There is a great stretch of flat rock on the shore near the church).
Loughaltacaille, the lake of the glen of the swans.

Maddygalla, white dogs (rocks).
Magherantarrive, the field of the bull. (Near Bull Point).
Mullindress. Place of Briars.
Owendoo, black cave.

Owennagolmen, pigeon cave.

Portantonish, the lucky port.
Portawillin, port of the mill.
Portcruin, round port.
Portnaminnawn, the port of the kids.

Roonavoolin, a very obvious personal name.
Ruecuit, cat point.
Ruenarone, the point of the seals.
Ruenascarrive, cormorant point.

Shandragh, old ruin.
Slieveanaille, mountain of the swan.
Sloaknacailly, the pit of the hags, the place where the women were thrown into the sea.
Soerneog, Sornog, a kiln.
Stackabirragh, pointed stack.
Stronderg, red point, from the colour of the rock.

APPENDIX 4

REPORT BY ESSEX TO THE QUEEN ON RATHLIN RAID
OF JULY, 1575

May it please your most Excellent Majesty. When I had taken order for the breaking up of the camp, which I was forced to do by want of victuals, as I have by my last letters advertised your highness, I thought good, notwithstanding, to lose no opportunity that might serve to the annoying of the Scot, against whom only I have now to make war; and finding it a thing very necessary to leave a good garrison at Carrickfergus for that purpose, I appointed 300 footmen and 80 horsemen to reside there under the rule of Captain John Norreys, to whom I gave a secret charge, that having at Carrickfergus the three frigates, and wind and weather serving, to confer with the captains of them, and on the sudden to set out for the taking of the island of the Raghlins, with care in their absence to leave a sufficient guard for the keeping of the town of Carrickfergus; and when I had given this direction, to make the Scots less suspicious of any such matter pretended, I withdrew myself towards the Pale, and Captain Norreys with his company to Carrickfergus, with my letters of direction unto the captains of the three frigates, which he found there ready for any service.

Captain Norreys, according to the instructions given him, upon his arrival called unto him the sea captains, and delivered unto them my letters and further declaring unto them my pleasure, spent some time in conference together about this enterprise, which they all found a matter so likely, as using the present time, and wind and weather well for their purpose, they concluded to take the matter in hand, and with all speed embarked their men. So on the 20th of the present July, taking with them all the small boats belonging to the town of Carrickfergus, they set out altogether, and being at seaboard they found the winds very variable, which made some division of their fleet; notwithstanding, they all so well guided themselves, as they met at the landing place of the Raghlins the 22nd day in the morning at one instant, where they found they were discovered by the island men, who had put themselves in readiness with all their force to make resistence; which the captains and soldiers nothing regarding, did with valiant minds leap to land, and charged them so hotly, as they drave them to retire with speed, chasing them to a castle which they had of very great strength; and at the first charge was slain only one soldier. The Scots, being thus put into their fort, were presently environed with your Majesty's force; and thereupon the captains landed two pieces of great ordnance, which they brought with them for that purpose, and approached them to the castle, which they battered right upon the gate, where they made a breach; which being made, they assaulted the 25th day in the afternoon; but it was so reinforced within as after they had passed the bridge, the gate and part of the entry, and not able to enter any farther without better provision, which they did foresee, they were compelled to retire for that time; where were slain at that assault but two soldiers, and eight were hurt; and within were slain, by good hap and the soldiers' stout service, the captain of the island and three of his soldiers, and six were hurt. After which small retire of our men, they set upon it again, and fired certain ramparts which the Scots had made of timber, against the determining another assault by the next break of day; but the slaughter of their chieftain, and the continual hurt that was done unto them so abated their pride, as before they called for a parle, which Captain Norreys, wisely considering the danger that might light upon his company, and willing to avoid the killing of the soldiers, which in such cases doth often happen, although he saw the place likely enough to be taken with some loss of men, was content to accept the parle, and to hear their offers, so as the constable would come himself in person out unto him without delay to make his demands. And yet not agreeing that he should safely return to the castle, but only upon his word to stand to his hap; upon which he came out and made large requests, as their lives, their goods, and to be put into Scotland, which requests Captain Norreys refused, offering them as slenderly as they did largely require; viz., to the aforesaid constable his life only, and his wife's and his child's the place and goods to be delivered at Captain Norrey's disposition, the constable to be prisoner one month, the lives of all within to stand upon the courtesy of the soldiers. The constable, knowing his estate and safety to be very doubtful, accepted this composition, and came out with all his company. The soldiers being moved and much stirred with the loss of their fellows that were slain, and desirous of revenge, made request, or rather pressed, to have the killing of them, which they did all saving the persons to whom life was promised; and a pledge, which was prisoner in the castle, was also saved, who is son to Alexander Oge Macalister Harry, who pretendeth to be a chief of the Glinnes, which prisoner Sorley boy held pledge for his father's better obedience unto him. There were slain that came out of the castle of all sorts 200; and presently news is brought me out of Tyrone that they be occupied still in killing, and have slain that they have found hidden in caves and in the cliffs of the sea, to the number of 300 or 400 more. They had within the island 300 kine, 3,000 sheep and 100 stud mares, and of bear corn upon the ground there is sufficient to find 200 men for a whole year.

When this was ended, Captain Norreys, taking the advice of the rest of the captains, finding the place both strong and fit to be kept for the service of your Majesty, which no doubt will greatly annoy the Scots, besides the keeping them out of this your highness's realm, hath appointed to leave a ward there of 80 soldiers, until he shall have farther directions from me, which I have thought good to allow of until I shall understand your Majesty's farther pleasure for the same, which, how necessary the keeping of it is, your highness may please to take knowledge of those of your Council that have served here, and best can judge of it, and accordingly to do your best liking. In my opinion, 100 men kept there, whereof 60 to remain on the island, and 40 to be employed to the sea, shall do your Majesty more service, both against the Scots and Irish, than 300 can do in any place within the north parts; that is my opinion, which I do not utter unto your Majesty as any persuasion for any further matter than shall be to your highness' liking, for that I know your determination for that enter-prize I took in hand, but only in discharge of my duty, to declare my knowledge, referring all things to your highness's own good pleasure, which I am ready to obey.

The taking of this island upon the neck of the late service done upon the Scot, doth no doubt put him to his wit's end. There hath been also burned by your Majesty's frigates lately eleven Scottish galleys, so as by sea and by land they have as little left as I can give them.

Now I am to recommend unto your Majesty's good favour all your highness' captains and soldiers serving under me, who do so generally deserve well in all their actions, as I am bound generally to say, that for those who have served here some good time, and those that came over with me, be such as I do assure your highness no prince of Christendom can overmatch for so small a company; for neither travail, misery, adventure of life, nor any pain that can reasonably be laid on them for your Majesty's service, is by them refused at any time; but with as willing minds as any men can do, they think themselves happy when they may have any occasion offered them that is to do your highness acceptable service; and as I have had sundry proofs of them, and lately in the service done gainst the Scots in the fastness, and this now done in the Raghlins, so do I find them full willing to follow it until they shall have ended what your Majesty intendeth to have done.

Thus most humbly desiring your Majesty's resolution, I beseech Almighty God to send your highness a long and happy life, and victory on all your enemies. From the Newry, this last of July, 1575.

APPENDIX 5

IRISH CRUISING CLUB YACHT SAILING DIRECTIONS
FOR ISLAND OF RATHLIN

RATHLIN ISLAND. Chart 2798 H.W. 2 hours before Dover springs 4¼ hours before Dover Neaps Rise 3 feet springs and neaps. There is a lighthouse at each of the three corners of the island as follows:

Rue Point: (U) Gp. Fl. (2) every 5 secs.; elev. 52 ft. from White Tower with 2 black bands, 35 ft. high. Vis. 12 miles.

Rathlin West (The Bull): R. Fl. every 5 secs.; elev. 204 ft. from Grey Tower, 60 ft. high situated half-way down the cliff. Vis. 20 miles. Fog: Diaphone 4 blasts every min. Ht. 350 ft. The lantern is beside the base of the tower.

Rathlin East (Altacarry Head): Gp. Fl. (4) every 20 secs.; elev. 243 ft. from White Tower with black band 88 ft. high. Vis. 22 miles. Fog: Explosive 2 reports every 5 seconds. The small light tower now disused at the base of the main one, was originally designed to assist sailing vessels standing close to work the eddy along the N. shore of the island. It was safe to stand in until the lower light became obscured by the cliff.

GENERAL. Population about 100. Telephone, P.O., a small general shop and public house. Water from the spring beside the Manor House in Church Bay; private stocks of petrol only; Mail Boat about twice weekly to Ballycastle.

ANCHORAGES

1. CHURCH BAY (See Plan) which has three small piers and provides shelter between N.W. and S.S.E. through E. The inner part of the bay and piers are enclosed by a semi-circular reef of weed-covered rock known as the Bo, which has about 3 ft. L.W.S. and 3½ ft. in the gap which lies exactly in line with a lane leading down to the bay from the east. In very settled weather anchor between the two inner piers in 6 to 7 ft. L.W.S. sand, or tie up along the inside of the north pier. If doubtful of the weather the best anchorage is about 200 yards W. of the church 50 to 100 yards off shore in 3 fms. good holding.

CAUTION. A heavy swell locally known as a "Shore" is liable to get up throughout Rathlin Sound during the E.-going tide. It is at its worst during the first 3 hours of that tide, greater at springs than neaps and subsides when the tide turns W. It is only likely to occur (a) if there is a swell running out in the North Channel and (b) if there is a fresh strong N.W. or N. wind blowing to bring it in. It breaks heavily on the Bo and in these circumstances the best landing is at Sheep House pier, 100 yards west of the church.

WRECK. The wreck of H.M.S. Drake lies in Church Bay about ¼-mile N.N.W. of a green wreck-marking buoy. To clear it, approaching from the south, keep Rue Point open until Altacarry light disappears behind the high ground to the W. of it. Then steer in keeping Altacarry light hidden. The buoy itself is not much use as it is too far away. There is normally 18 ft. over the wreck but an odd plate may stick up at times. Two vessels have struck it in recent years.

2. USHET PORT is a small disused port to the south of a ruined stone storehouse ½ mile up the eastern shore from Rue Point. This provides emergency shelter for shallow draft boats in W. winds, but should be approached with caution due to the presence of a shallow reef running out to sea immediately north of the port. The gut is almost

tideless and at its head there is a lot of rotting seaweed which is alleged to pollute the water to the extent of damaging the paint on boats lying there. Deeper draft yachts must anchor off the mouth of the gut, in 9 ft. sheltered from winds between S.W. and N. through W. It is generally necessary to put out two anchors if staying for any length of time to avoid swinging out into the tide, which runs strongly just outside the point. There are no dwellings or facilities nearby.

3. ILLANCARRAGH BAY, the small bay just N. of Doon Point, is a better place and provides shelter from the south in addition, well clear of the stream. It has 6 to 9 ft. close up to the rocks all round.

PIERS

The depths at H.W. at the piers in Church Bay are as follows: —

Sheephouse pier   11 ft.
North pier   6 ft.
South pier   4 ft.

There is a pier now disused, originally built for lighthouse stores at Couraghy, a disused pier at Killeany and a small one built within the last two years on the E. side by the Irish Lights Commissioners.

APPENDIX 6

POPULATIONS

YEAR	POPULATION
1675	75
1721	490
1784	1200
1813	1148
1841	1010
1851	753
1871	413
1881	361
1891	365
1901	368
1911	351
1926	299
1937	245
1951	196
1961	159
1966	118
1968	111

APPENDIX 7

HOW TO GET THERE

Ballycastle is the base for boat trips to Rathlin. It may be reached by bus from Belfast in about three hours. The boat service to the island is frequent in summer but not sufficiently regular to be tabulated. A telephone call a day in advance to Mr. Jack Coyles, Ballycastle 386 or Mr. James McCurdy, Rathlin 216, will produce information. There is no hotel, but accommodation on the island can sometimes be arranged privately on local enquiry.

The journey takes about 50 minutes and sailing may be cancelled for the bad weather, but this is infrequent in summer.

Those wishing to sail there themselves will find a leaflet entitled 'The Tides of Ballycastle Bay and Rathlin Sound' which I published two years ago, proceeds in aid of the Churches of Rathlin, price 2/6, to be of assistance.

BIBLIOGRAPHY

Calendar of State Papers, Ireland.   (C.S.P.)
Calendar of State Papers, Carew.
History of Ireland.   Curtis.
Life of Francis Drake.   Mason.
Colonsay and Oronsay.   Loder.
The History of the English Speaking Peoples.   Churchill.
History of Ulster.   Colles.
Irish Folk Ways.   Evans.
Ancient Ireland.   Macalister.
Elizabethan Ulster.   Lord Ernest Hamilton.
The McDonnells of Antrim.   Hill.
Ecclesiastical Antiquities.   Reeves.
The Course of Irish History.   Moody and Martin.
A History of the Vikings.   Kendrick.
British Coracles and Irish Curraghs.   Hornell.
Adomnan, Life of Columba.   Anderson.
Diocese of Down and Connor.   O'Laverty.
Rathlin Island.   Boyd.
Rathlin Island.   Marshall.
Sea Wrack.   Mary Campbell.
History of Rathlin.   Gage (Manuscript).
Rathlin Island and Parish.   Law.
Elizabeth's Irish Wars.   Falls.
Birds of the Grey Wind.   Armstrong.
English Seamen in the Sixteenth Century.   Froude.
The Irish Sword.   Journal of the Military History Society of Ireland.
Proceedings of the Royal Irish Academy (P.R.I.A.).
Proceedings of the Royal Society of Antiquities of Ireland (P.R.S.A.I.).
Ulster Journal of Archaeology (U.J.A.).
Rathlin, a hitherto omitted chapter in its history, Coleraine Chronicle.
      Rev. George Hill.
The Vikings.   Brondsted.
Highways and Byways in the West Highlands.   Gordon.
Highways and Byways in Antrim and Donegal.   Gwynn.
Letters from Antrim.   Hamilton.
The Glens of Antrim.   Garrett.
The Story of Burnt Njal.   Dasent.
The Islands of Ireland.   Mason.
The Earls of Essex.   W. B. Devereux.
History of Carrickfergus.   Miskimmin.
Scots Mercenary Forces in Ireland.   Hayes McCoy.
Inishowen.   "Maghtohair".
Four Thousand Years Ago.   Bibby.
Ireland Under The Tudors.   Bagwell.
The Golden Age of the Celtic Church.   Chadwick.
Naval Operations.   Newbolt and Corbett.
Danger Zone.   Keble Chatterton.
The Auxiliary Patrol.   Keble Chatterton.
Aran.   O'Siochain.
History of Isle of Man.   Moore.
The Sudreys in Early Viking Times.   Marshall.
History of The Western Isles.   Gregory.
Survey of Rathlin Island, 1968.   St. Gabriel's Youth Centre.
Ulster Naturalists Journal Vol. X, 1952.   (Geology of Island).
The Irish Lights Service.   T. G. Wilson.
Geology of the Country around Ballycastle.   H.M.S.O.
The Irish Stone Age.   Movius.

INDEX

Abbots, 52, 56, 57
Argyll, 3rd Earl, 72, 74, 83
　　　 7th Earl, 113
　　　 8th Earl, 116
Aran (Co. Galway), 33, 34, 48
Armada, 106
Arran (Clyde), 33, 60, 70, 79
Aura, 81
Axes, 29—32

Bagenal, family, 105
　　　 Sir Henry, 102—104
　　　 Sir Ralph, 76, 77
　　　 Ralph, 104
Bangor, 48, 114
Bede, Venerable, 38
Birds, 18, 25, 26, 73, 140, 156, 157
Bonemargy, 102, 120, 156
Brecain, 39, 41, 43, 47
Bruce, Robert, 68, 70, 163
Bruce's Castle, 45, 64, 65, 76, **93**, 90—97
Bull, The, 25, 137, **147**, 148
Bysset, Sir Hugh, 68—70
　　　 John and Walter, 67
　　　 Margery, 70, 111, 112, 123

Campbell, Lady Agnes, 74, 83, 84, 85, 100, 106
Canan Dhu, 142
Carrickavaan, 15
Carrickfergus, 63, 66, 76, 77, 88, 89, 90, 95, 97, 98, 104, 176
Churches, St. Thomas', 16, 119, 133
　　　 Immaculate Conception, 133, 141
Clark, Henry, M.P., 164, 165
Coastguard, 133, 145, 146, 150
Colonsay, 31, 34, 35, 163, 165
Curry, William, (Find of coins), 117
Corryvreckan, 41, 43
Coyles, Jack, 23, 181
Crawford, Capt., 100, 112
Crawford of Lisnorris, 109—114
Crofts, Sir James, 76, 99
Cuchalain, 36, 37

Dalriada, 13, 47, 51, 54, 66, 110
Dan Na Doon, 59—60
D'Athy, John, 70
De Burgo, Richard, 66, 67
De Courcy, John, 62—66, 89, 123
De Lacy, 65, 66
Deirdre, 20, 35
Derry, Seige of, 118
Devorgilla, 36, 37
Donananie, 63, 64, 75, 80, 102, 107, 110, 146
Drake, Francis, 89—93, 98, 164
Drake, H.M.S., **150**, 151—153, 164, 178
Drumceat, 110, 111
Dumouriez, General, 129, 130
Dunluce, Description, 63, 72, 74, 75, 78, 80
　　　 Capt. by Shane, 82
　　　 Capt. by Perrot, 101
　　　 Recaptured by Scots, 106, 110
Dunmore, 34, 35, 111, 170—173
Dunseverick, 46, 47, 54, 56, 63, 75, 82

Essex, Walter Devereux, Earl of, 78, 85—87, 97, 99, 176, 177

Famine, 132, 134
Fairies, 142—144
Firbolg, 27, 32, 33, 35, 37
Fomorians, 3, 27, 33—35, 37
Forestry, 162

Gage, 5, 16, 17, 26
　　　 Rev. John, 122—125
　　　 Robert the First, 125—129
　　　 Rev. Robert 129—137
　　　 Robert the Third, 137—140, 146, 153
　　　 Brigadier Rex, 162
Galleys, Scots, **71**, 78, 83
Galloway, Earls of, 66, 111
Gerona, 106
Gigha, 51, 79, 108, 123, 164, 165

Gray, Justiciar, 69
Grey, Lord, 164
Groga, 142

Hamilton, Rev. William, 126—128
Heligoland, 150
Holiday facilities, 166, 178, 181

Ineenduv, 84
Inishbofin, 40
Inishkea, 40
Inishmurray, 52
Inistrahull, 51, 109, 146, 160
Iona, 28, 47, 48, 50 56, 114, 131
Irish Language, 119, 135
Islay 19, 51, 72, 78, 79, 108, 114,
   117, 118, 131, 143, 156, 164, 165
Italy, 72, 174

Jura, 19, 42, 43, 165

Kenbane, 15, 21, 71, 74, 75, 80

Lambay, 42, 45, 58, 174
Land Purchase Act, 26, 155
Larne, 42, 60, 70, 81, 85, 150, 151
Leicester, Earl of, 87, 99
Lighthouses, 125, 136, **147,** 148, 150,
   153, 156, 167 Characteristics, 160,
   178
Lir, Children of, 20
Lord of the Isles, 70, 71, 74, 75, 82

Man, Isle of, 62, 63, 110
Manannan McLir, 21
Marconi, 144, 145
Massacres, 56, 60, 67, 79, 93, 116—
   118
         Ethics of, 79, 97
McCuaig, Tony, 16, 118, 137, 167
McCurdy, 97, 118
         James, 23, 161, **161,** 181
McQuilkin, Johnny, 17
McDonnells, 22, 62, 68—72, 74
   Victory at Aura 81, 114, 118, Last
      on Rathlin, 137
         Angus Og., 84, 106, 112
         Colla, 74, 75, 77, 80, 82

McDonnells (continued)
   Coll Kittagh, 108, 118
   James of Islay, 72, 76, 77, 79,
      80, Builds mansion 81,
      Death 82, Widow 83, Son
      84, Estate 112
   Randal, Defends Dunluce,
      100; Knighted, 108; Law-
      suit, 109—114; Earldom,
      116
   Sorley Boy. Captured, 76;
      Ransomed, Raids Carrick-
      fergus, 77; Captain of
      Route, 80; Capt. by Shane,
      82; at wedding, 83; Kintyre,
      85; Fight near Coleraine,
      88; during Essex massacre,
      94, 96; Raids Carrick, 98;
      Defends Rathlin, 104;
      Small boat, 106; Remarries,
      106; Death, 107; Tomb,
      120, Bones, 156

North Channel Barrage, 149—151

O'Donnell, Red Hugh, 84
O'Neill, Conn Bacagh, 80
   Hugh, 107, 109, 114, 116
   Shane, 80—83

Perrot, Sir John, 100—105, 109
Piracy, 72, 100, 108, 119, 125
Pliny, 42
Population, 17, 119, 126, 132, 136,
   154, 155, 180
Ptolemy, 42, 112, 175

Rathlin:
   Appearance, **13,** 19, 23, 25, 167
   Area, 134
   Axe Trade, 29—32
   Doctor, Diseases, 127, 135
   Dowry, 70
   How To Get There, 178, 181
   In Irish Coast Pilot, 15
   North Side, 23
   Passage to, 18, 125, 126, 139,
      159

Rathlin (continued)
    Piers, 139, 179
    Place Names, 175
    Plans for Plantation, 85
    Sale of, 122, 155
    Size, 15, 23
Rebellion, '98, 128
Romans, 13, 45, 46
Rooke, Capt., 118

Saint Columba, 45, 47, 49, 101, 111
Saint Comgall, 47, 48
Saint Patrick, 27, 40, 46, 47

Schools, 119, 134, 162

Scillies, 33
Sidney, Sir Henry, 79, 82, 85, 98, 100
Sigurd the Stout, 60
Slough Na More, 22, 23, 26, 41, 125
Smuggling, 129, 133
Snakes, 27, 110, 114
Somerled, 62

Stanley, Sir William, 102—104
Stewart, Archibald, 119
Sweathouses, 142, **158**

Taise, Taobgeal, 36, 176, 177
Thornton, Capt., Career, 100, 104,
    105
Tides, 14, 15, 18, 22, Strength, 23,
    136, 157, 181
Tonns, 21
Tory Island 34, 51, 54, 149
U-boats, 149, 150, 156
        UB 77; UB 85; 153
        U 79; 152
        UB 82; 153

Viking, Saga, 58—59

Wakehurst, Lord, 163
Walsyngham, 96, 100
Wheatear, 151
Wrecks, 18, 22, 76, 79, 135, 136,
    137, 155, 163, 164